Paul Ansel Chadbourne

Lectures on Natural Theology

Or, Nature and the Bible

Paul Ansel Chadbourne

Lectures on Natural Theology
Or, Nature and the Bible

ISBN/EAN: 9783337099701

Printed in Europe, USA, Canada, Australia, Japan

Cover: Foto ©Lupo / pixelio.de

More available books at **www.hansebooks.com**

LECTURES

ON

NATURAL THEOLOGY;

OR,

NATURE AND THE BIBLE FROM THE SAME AUTHOR.

DELIVERED BEFORE THE

LOWELL INSTITUTE, BOSTON.

BY

P. A. CHADBOURNE, A.M., M.D.,

Professor of Natural History in Williams College; Author of Lectures on the "Relations of Natural History," etc.

NEW YORK:
G. P. PUTNAM & SON, 661 BROADWAY.
1869.

Entered according to Act of Congress, in the year 1867, by

G. P. PUTNAM & SON,

In the Clerk's Office of the District Court of the United States, for the Southern District of New York.

THE NEW YORK PRINTING COMPANY,
81, 83, *and* 85 *Centre Street*,
NEW YORK.

To

REV. MARK HOPKINS, DD., LL.D.,
PRESIDENT OF WILLIAMS COLLEGE.

Sir—It is not as a mere formality, nor from a desire to connect my name with one so distinguished in the higher departments of Philosophy, that I inscribe these Lectures to you. It is especially fitting that I should now acknowledge my indebtedness to you for that kindness which is the most pleasant remembrance of my student life, and which has remained unchanged through all the relations of fifteen years of official labor. It was at your suggestion, that I first commenced a distinct work on Natural Theology. It has taken its present form in the moments snatched from the varied duties that have daily demanded my time and strength. And whatever may now be its value depends much upon the counsel and encouragement which you have given me during the whole course of its preparation.

With great respect and esteem,
I am most truly yours,
P. A. CHADBOURNE.

ADVERTISEMENT.

———o———

THE Lectures are published in the form and order in which they were originally delivered. Nothing would be gained for the general reader by dividing them into chapters. For the convenience of students and teachers a very full Table of Contents has been prepared, which will materially aid the teacher in recitation, and render frequent reviews easy for the student. It is hoped that while the Lectures present the great outlines of Natural Theology in a form easily understood by all, they will also awaken in the student a love for the study of Nature, and lead him on to independent observation in this most profitable field of human thought.

CONTENTS.

---o---

LECTURE I.

INTRODUCTORY.

PAGE

Man's Origin and Destiny.—Questions presented for study.—Effect of superstition—Religious nature.—The great questions in reference to man.—Man naturally seeks to know if there is a God.—Sufficiency of the proof of His existence.—Theory of our case.—Answers that have been given from nature. The Bible.—It must stand the tests of science.—Natural Religion defined.—Design of the Lowell Lectures.—Our situation in this world like that of children in a palace.—Knowledge of Religion which men can obtain from nature alone.—Difficulty of deciding the question.—All that Natural Religion has done.—Man without the Bible unprovided for.—Civilization without it self-destructive.—Religion implies relationship to a Higher Being.—Topics presented.—Amount of science required for the study.—Conditions necessary for fair discussion 17

LECTURE II.

PRINCIPLES OF BELIEF.—ADAPTATION OF OUR BODIES TO OUR WANTS AND TO THE WORLD.

Perfect provision for organic beings.—No provision in material world for man's highest nature.—Claims of the Bible.—A natural provision for man.—Principles of belief.—Theories of creation.—First cause.—Matter might be eternal. —Beginning of life.—Antagonism of physical forces and vitality.—Apparent harmony between them.—Man an effect.—His creation to be accounted for. The germ as wonderful as the developed being.—Bible account of creation. —What we should expect to find in such a creation.—Nature an unchangeable record.—Questions that would arise without the Bible.—Aid of Geology. —The existence of beings, and not their mode of origin, proof of skill and power.—Adaptation of our bodies to our use and to the world.—Relations to the world established through the senses—Distinctive use of each sense.—Conditions necessary for sight.—Relation of light to the atmosphere.—Form of objects and effects of surface.—Structure of the eye.—Sense of hearing gives knowledge of objects beyond the range of vision.—Mechanism of the ear.—Taste and smell.—No special mechanism.—Design shown by the use. —Touch.—Kinds of knowledge given by it.—All the senses connected with the nervous system.—Vegetative life.—Relation of the body to the world considered.—The atmosphere.—Structure of the lung.—Nutrition.—Sleep. —Animals fitted for particular zones.—Man for all.—No special sciences needed to show our adaptation to the world.—Personality of the Creator inferred from the provision for our personality.—Antagonism in nature...... 46

LECTURE III.

ADAPTATION OF ANIMALS TO THE WORLD BY STRUCTURE, FUNCTION, AND INSTINCT.

PAGE

Adaptation of Animals to the World.—Special adaptations.—Chance excluded. —Man as a physical being differs only in degree.—His sources of enjoyment complex.—In animals nothing but adaptations to this world.—Whole classes to be treated of.—Water Animals—Microscopic.—Coral Animals.—Jellyfishes—Starfishes.—Mollusks.—Perfect provision for each form.—The Pinna. —Saxicavas.—Nautilus.—Worms.—Crustaceans.—Insects.—Fishes.—Reptiles.—Birds.—Fitted for change of season.—Hibernation.—Relation to length of year.—Instinct.—Supplements structure and function.—Gives higher type of life—Defined—Intelligence in Animals.—Vegetative life in Animals.—Relation of instinct to specific structure.—The Natica.—Instinct often blind in its action.—The Cicada.—Tent moth.—Migration of fishes.— Conscious parental relation in birds.—Uniformity of action resulting from instinct.—Wide range of instinct in Mammals.—The Muskrat.—Instinct of the young supplemented by that of the parent.—The body and mind fitted for each other.. 78

LECTURE IV.

SPECIAL CONTRIVANCES—PRESERVATION OF SPECIES.

Special adaptations.—Functions.—Cases mentioned by Paley.—Ball and socket joint.—Cuttle-fish.—Terebratulas.—Leech.—Gnats.—Bees.—Spiders.—Variation of substance according to their instinct.—Silk-worm.—Lobsters and Crabs.—Rattlesnake.—Birds.—Fitted for fight.—Oil gland.—Structure of birds of prey.—Water birds.—Form of bills.—Grebe and Loon.—Waders.— Woodpeckers—Development from use considered.—Homologous structure. —Limbs of animals.—Teeth.—Whales and Rays.—Crop of birds.—Preservation of species.—Definition of.—Multiplicity of germs.—Distribution of seeds—Springs, balloons, hooks, barbs.—Same end secured by diverse means—Vitality of seeds.—Fertilization of flowers.—Growth of plants supplementing instinct.—Carnivorous animals limited in number.—Destruction of animals provided for.—Suffering and death.—Goodness of Deity to be vindicated.—Man's enjoyment and suffering on different grounds.—Present discussion confined to lower animals.—Suffering never inflicted for its own sake.—Enjoyment in excess of suffering.—Death secures parental relation.— Sum of enjoyment increased by succession of animals—Introduction of carnivorous animals increases the sum of enjoyment.—Disease.—Provision for its alleviation.—Design may show cruelty.—Apparent cruelty often real benevolence.—Creator Infinite in His attributes........................... 103

LECTURE V.

ADAPTATION OF PLANTS TO THE WORLD.

Design in plants seen only in organization.—Natural selection.—Provision made by plants compared with instinct.—Wisdom manifested by instinct referred to the Creator.—Relation of plants to earth and air.—Polarity.— Structure of leaves.—Fall of leaf—Structure of wide-leaved trees.—Of evergreens.—Position of buds.—Mathematical order.—Symmetry and welfare of tree secured.—Variety of habit—Fitted for soil—Climate and place in the solar system.—Power of the bud.—Young fruits.—Structure of buds.—Food stored up.—The potato.—Beet and Parsnip.—Century plant.—Orchis.—Solomon's-seal.—Structure of seed.—Perfection and variety of machinery.—Relation of plants and animals.—Effect of each on the air.—Vegetable kingdom subservient to the animal.—Its support.—Oak galls.—Plants respond to the insect's instinct.—Fertilization of plants by insects.—Squashes.—Forget-me-nots.—Orchids.—Results.................................. 126

LECTURE VI.

PRODUCTION OF VARIETIES AND THEIR FINAL CAUSE.

Origin of species.—May be varied for a wise purpose.—Living and fossil forms, parts of one whole.—Four plans of structure.—The rocks the true record.—May be mistranslated, but not changed.—Unity of plan in the Divine mind.—Changes that favor development theory.—Quotation from Darwin.—Variation considered historically.—For a definite purpose—Adapts species to wide geographical range.—To man.—Definition of varieties.—Cause not known.—Quotation from Gray.—Final cause.—Reference to man.—Beauty of crystal.—Difference in kingdom of life.—Organs of plants.—Anthers.—Petals.—Double flowers.—Propagation of double plants.—Fleshy fruits.—Idea of beauty in some plants.—Of fruit in others.—Two series according to lines of development.—Corn.—Sugar-cane.—Potato.—Tomato.—Indications in wild plants.—Exceptions.—Some plants for a double purpose.—Vegetable kingdom for the animal.—Appears primarily for itself.—Multitude of germs.—Grains of wheat represent food and plant life.—Use of soft fruits—Plants and animals constructed for man as an intellectual being.—Increase of beauty not for the plant.—Varieties offer condition of continual progress.—Development theory not Atheistic.—Incurable scepticism.—Geology must explain origin of species.—Law of variation, evidence of design and wisdom........ 148

LECTURE VII.

CHEMICAL ELEMENTS AND THEIR MUTUAL RELATION.

Argument for design may rest on collocation alone.—Character of Creator learned from the very proofs of His existence.—Number of elements known.—Results secured by their nature and relative quantity.—Fixed laws of combination.—Neither matter nor force lost.—Pillars of organic life.—Evidence of design in the constitution of matter.—Equilibrium, how restored in the four elements—Balanced affinity.—Nature of their compounds.—Oxygen specially considered.—Its compounds.—The air.—Original condition of matter.—Oxygen in the air a residual substance.—Essential to animals.—Helps form the tissues and secures activity.—Produces artificial light and heat.—Common and active state.—Ozone.—Affinity of oxygen varied by temperature.—Hydrogen.—Basis of flame—Its inflammable compounds.—Combination of properties fitting it for a light-producer.—Combines with carbon to produce light.—Summation of properties.—Its fitness for organic structures.—Constant change in animal bodies.—Relation of hydrogen to nitrogen.—Nitrogen adds to weight of atmosphere.—Moderates the action of hydrogen.—Negative properties.—Nature of its compounds.—Carbon.—Different forms.—Supplements hydrogen in combustion.—As an element, always solid.—Coal.—Indestructible at common temperature.—Carbonic acid...... 177

LECTURE VIII.

PROVISION FOR THE INTELLECT OF MAN IN THE STRUCTURE OF MINERALS AND LAWS OF CHEMICAL COMBINATION.

                                                                                                               PAGE

Preservation of man requires preservation of other beings.—The whole plan to be grasped.—Field of mind.—Animals remain the same.—Man's physical nature conditional for his higher.—Provision for our personality to be expected.—Personality of the Creator.—Mind seeks for the laws of nature.—Physical good never sought for by the great leaders in science.—Search for thought among ancient inscriptions.—Physical and intellectual appetite compared.—Mind of man and the order of nature from the same Creator.—Nature the great teacher.—Her models perfect.—Proofs of the provision for mind.—Minerals.—Mind must be taxed.—Language of Minerals.—Our work is to translate it.—Perfectly adapted to the human mind.—Crystalline forms.—Progress of mind in unfolding them.—Fundamental forms.—Effect of crystalline force in the crust of the earth.—Beauty of crystals for man.—Taylor's description of the Russian jewels.—Bible language.—Chemical relation of the elements.—Power of the chemist.—Condition of progress.—Beyond the reach of development theories.—Man has increased in knowledge, but not in mental power.—Answers which nature gives 210

LECTURE IX.

PROVISION FOR MAN'S INTELLECT IN THE RELATIONS OF ORGANIC BEINGS AND IN THE CRUST OF THE EARTH.

Kingdom of life.—Mathematical law continued.—Orders of plants.—Animals.—Fossils.—All form one picture.—Science discovered.—Manifestation of thought in nature.—Astronomy.—Enthusiasm of Naturalist.—Geology.—Present changes.—Its key.—Provisions for man's physical wants presuppose his intellectual nature.—Crust of the Earth shows design.—Man multiplies his powers.—Properties of metals.—Gold and Silver.—Platinum, Mercury, Iron.—Loadstone.—Metals essential to man's progress.—Fuel for man alone—Power which Chemistry gives him.—Plants and Animals made to minister to his physical wants through his intellectual power...................... 231

LECTURE X.

PROVISION FOR THE EMOTIONAL NATURE AND THE VARIED INTELLECTUAL TASTES AND POWERS OF MEN.

Love of the beautiful.—Provision for it in nature.—Taste.—Fine Arts founded upon nature.—Poetry.—Bible language.—Painting and sculpture.—Music.—Conditions necessary for it.—Beauty of outline and color.—Clouds.—Crystals.—Plants.—Increase of beauty in leaf and flower.—Double flowers.—Microscopic animals.—Corals.—Jelly-fishes.—Shells.—Their beauty not for themselves.—Insects.—Distribution of their color.—Vertebrates.—Beauty of fossils.—Grandeur and sublimity.—Emotional nature perfect in man ages ago.—Different intellectual tastes provided for.—Advance in science and art thus secured.—Sciences yet to be unfolded 251

LECTURE XI.

THE MORAL NATURE OF MAN AND THE BIBLE AS A NATURAL PROVISION FOR HIM.

PAGE

Decisions of the moral nature.—Chief characteristic of man.—Conscience.—Implies accountability.—The existence of a moral governor.—Approval of conscience.—Public opinion.—Others suffer from our acts.—Malevolent feelings produce unhappiness.—Appetites.—Physical suffering from sin.—Labor tends to virtue.—The world as it is best for us.—This world not enough for man's powers.—His immortality inferred.—Questions which we need to have answered.—The Bible a natural provision.—Adapted to meet the wants of man's moral nature.—Answers questions which nature cannot answer.—Forgiveness of sin.—Immortality brought to light —With the Bible, man completely provided for.. 277

LECTURE XII.

THE MOSAIC AND GEOLOGIC RECORDS.

Natural religion not sufficient —Supposed origin of the Bible.—Correspondence to the works of nature.—Seeming disagreement.—First chapter of Genesis.—Testimony of Humboldt.—Purpose of the Bible demands some account of the creation.—The position taken in the argument.—Chemistry our guide before the sedimentary rocks.—Progress in creation.—First condition of matter. — Gravitation. — Effect of bringing particles together. — Light. — Nott and Gliddon.—Geologic day.—Hugh Miller's view.—Firmament —Office of the atmosphere   Dry land. Introduction of life. Plants created first.—Sun and Moon.—Water animals and birds.—Land animals.—Man.—Picture of creation as presented to an intelligent being.—Seventh day.—Conclusion.. 296

PREFACE.

―――o―――

THE following lectures are the natural outgrowth of professional study and instruction in College. Portions of them have already appeared in Reviews and in my published addresses. In fact, several of them are but the unfolding of the fourth lecture on "THE RELATIONS OF NATURAL HISTORY," delivered at the Smithsonian Institution in 1859.

When I received the invitation to lecture before the Lowell Institute, the press of other duties left no time to do more than to arrange the materials already on hand. In the text, I have endeavored to indicate the authors from whom special aid was derived. All who have studied any subject for years, without thought of publication, know how difficult a task it is to tell all the sources of their knowledge. Much of Natural Theology, instead of commencing with Paley, or with Nieuwentyt, to whom Paley was probably much indebted, has so long been the common inheritance of thinking men that, like some of the fruits and grains, it is impossible to trace it back to its original source. Much of it, indeed, is so apparent to every student of Nature, that it is like the sunlight, seen by all without aid from others.

To the leading idea in these lectures, exceptions will be taken by some at the outset; especially by those who, following the lead of Compte, regard all inquiries respecting efficient and final causes as unphilosophical and useless.

The world is here represented as having been made for man. To him as an intelligent and moral being, all nature is subservient. Where he has to yield, it is not evidence, that man is disregarded in the mechanism of the universe, nor is he overcome as inferior to inanimate nature; but it is simply the individual suffering under the operation of some law made inflexible for the benefit of the race.

And when all had been done for man that it seems possible to do through an irrational creation, and his highest wants were still unprovided for, the Bible was given to complete the provision.

In the highest sense, the final cause of all things is the glory of God. So far as the general structure of this world is concerned, the final cause of everything is ultimately found in the intellectual and moral nature of man. And it is in the provision for man, that the high character of a Personal Creator is especially manifested. But among the myriads of organic beings below man, there is such a constant series of adaptations and dependencies, that in presenting the argument for design, the doctrine of final causes is ever before us.

It may be objected to some of the lectures, that theories are introduced in respect to which we know nothing with certainty now, and perhaps never can know anything. The question of the validity of such theories will not affect the general argument. They are presented as theories only. It is impossible that the human mind should always stop with ascertained facts. When it has reached the limit of the known it will push on, as best it may, into the region of the unknown. No harm can be done, if the writer fairly states where he is, and relies upon facts alone for proof.

In treating of Chemistry and other Sciences, the common language and most familiar formulas and theories have been adopted. As the facts will always remain the same, no advantage would be gained by introducing into a work on Natural Theology discussions on the nature of force, and on the constitution of matter, or the language and formulas that have come into partial use in consequence of new theories.

The Theory of Development has not been attacked directly. In fact, those who hold to that theory present so many phases of belief, that it is difficult for one to refer to it at all, without being liable to the charge of unfairness. The learning and the labors of the men who hold to it, in some form, entitle it to respectful consideration. Its leading principles, grounds of proof, and theological tendencies, are evidently misunderstood by many who oppose it. It is believed, however, that the arguments from the final cause of varieties and from the chemical relation of the elements to each other and to the wants of man are strongly opposed to that theory as it is generally held.

Natural Theology, like the study of Nature in general, can never be exhausted. We have in these lectures been like a traveller passing through a continent from side to side, describing only the narrow territory that comes within his own range of vision. Other explorers will have new wonders to tell, and whole regions are ready to unfold yet other proof of the being and character of the Creator to those who, in the future, shall search for them.

WILLIAMS COLLEGE, January, 1867.

NATURAL THEOLOGY.

LECTURE I.

INTRODUCTORY.

Man's Origin and Destiny.—Questions presented for study.—Effect of superstition.—Religious nature.—The great questions in reference to man.—Man naturally seeks to know if there is a God.—Sufficiency of the proof of His existence.—Theory of our case.—Answers that have been given from nature.—The Bible.—It must stand the tests of science.—Natural Religion defined.—Design of the Lowell Lectures.—Our situation in this world like that of children in a palace.—Knowledge of Religion which men can obtain from nature alone.—Difficulty of deciding the question.—All that Natural Religion has done.—Man without the Bible unprovided for.—Civilization without it self-destructive.—Religion implies relationship to a Higher Being.—Topics presented.—Amount of science required for the study.—Conditions necessary for fair discussion.

WHAT is man's origin, and what is his destiny? These two questions will at some time engross the attention of every thinking man, in spite of all systems of Positive Philosophy. In seeking for the answers, every field of knowledge will be explored. All history and all science will be called upon to throw their light upon the past condition of the race, and upon its future destiny. It is not possible that man should measure the heavens and comprehend the dust of the earth, read its past history in the rocks and predict the coming changes in this physical universe, and yet so far ignore himself as to forget to ask how he came upon this earth, and for what purpose he is here. We see a vast chain of being stretching below us, but no race above us. Are we then the highest order of beings in the universe, or are there other orders to whom we sustain relations, and by whom we may be affected for good or for evil? We know that our course on earth will soon be run. Is this our only theatre of action; or is there another yet to come, independent of this, or having some relation to it? This is the great question that must force itself upon the thoughts of every civilized man. An attempt to give an answer involves the consideration of all those subjects, which give us the great outlines of Natural Theology and of Natural Religion. Among these subjects thus presented for our study, we find the being and character of God—the origin and final destiny of man—his relations to God and the duties growing out of those relations. All observation shows that before man becomes civilized, he is under the power of a superstition that takes the place of rational belief in reference to all these subjects. This superstition may retain its hold long upon the mind even in the midst of civilization, and may be joined with some of its highest manifestations in literature and art. The first bursting away from that superstition is often to infidelity and sometimes even to atheism. But neither atheism nor infidelity is the natural state of man. He has a religious nature. We may say that there is no foundation for it, nothing that corresponds to it out of himself. But no student of the human mind would deny the possession of this nature to the race, any more than he would deny man's social nature or his appreciation and love of the beautiful. This religious nature has ever proved too powerful to allow infidelity and atheism more than a passing triumph. They have sometimes, indeed, fallen like a disease upon whole masses of men; but generally they have appeared only here and there, as blindness and deafness are the misfortunes of but few. This religious nature, which no condition of the race has ever been able to eradicate or weaken, except under abnormal and temporary conditions, marshals the highest powers of the mind to seek by reason that certainty for its advanced life which superstitious belief gave to the race in the times of ignorance. It becomes a great moving power, that can no more be destroyed nor restrained from its legitimate action than any of the great forces of nature. Under its promptings, man will not believe that progress in knowledge is to shut the soul out from that enjoyment which ignorant belief gave it. The conviction of the great thinkers of the race has been that even the absurd superstitions and religious beliefs of ignorance are not entirely groundless—that they must rest on a basis of truth, because they meet so fully the desires of the soul. As the light of civilization advances, those desires are not weakened, but strengthened ; and therefore it follows that when superstition has lost its dominion over the mind, an attempt will always be made to satisfy by reason that want which the soul demands to have met. And thus it has come to pass that the history of the human mind includes a history of struggles with these questions. Am I a creature of chance? Am I like the brutes, except in degree? Am I the highest intelligence in the universe, or is this whole world the work of an intelligent personal Being, and does its Creator rule and govern it, so that I am now accountable to Him, and ever to remain so? In other words, am I a mortal being with power to close my existence at any moment, accountable while I live only to my fellow-men ; or am I immortal, and is my destiny in the hands of a Higher Power? It is necessary for the peace and true dignity of man that these questions should be settled. What peace can there be for him while he is in doubt whether death brings to him eternal oblivion, or opens the portal of another life related to the present? How can man rise to the dignity of an immortal in thought and action, while uncertain that there remains to him another hour of conscious existence? We do not wonder then that these questions have engrossed the great minds of all ages. They speak in a language so loud that they must be heard even above the roar of passion and the thousand tongues of this physical universe. All questions of mere physical science sink into insignificance compared with these.

Indeed the value of questions in physical science depends much upon how these higher questions are answered.

We assumed in the outset a religious nature in man—manifesting its existence by his religious impulses and desires. Man naturally seeks to know if there is a God, and what relations he sustains to that God. ·No one will deny this who is at all versed in the history of human belief. Men have in their untutored state received a belief in the existence of some higher power, either from tradition or as the outgrowth of their nature. In the highest forms of society, investigations have led most men to the same result. These investigations have been so uniform in producing a belief in God, that we have in this fact a strong presumptive evidence of the sufficiency of the proof of His existence, and of the power of the human mind to weigh that proof. As the childish credulity of an early age gave way before advancing knowledge, it was only the few who failed to find higher and surer ground of belief—to grasp proof fitted to satisfy the progressing mind. As more proof became necessary to produce conviction, more proof always presented itself; so that the great majority of men who have left in words or in acts a record of their thoughts and convictions, have believed in an invisible world, in a divine Personal Being, and in a future state of existence. So uniformly has this opinion prevailed that we are justified in assuming that there are some things in this universe that tend to show that it is the creation of a Personal Being, and that it has somewhere in its structure marks that may fairly be presumed to indicate the character of its Creator; that there is also some proof that man is an accountable being, and that there are some means by which he can establish such relations with his Creator as that accountability requires. This may not be true; but it has been held by so many of the best minds the world has seen, that we may be allowed to start with this theory of our case. Our theory then is, that man and all creatures in the universe are the work of a Personal Being. That Personal Being we wish to search for, to learn His character and our relations to Him. For such a result, no journey would be too long, no fatigue too great. In this investigation, we naturally look to see what those who have gone before us have to offer for our aid and guidance. We ask where they searched for an answer to these questions which seem to have been the common inheritance of the race? We ask them what answer they received, and in what language the oracle gave its response? And lo! all down the ages come the answers from those philosophers, who claim to have found their oracles speaking from the heavens, or from the foundations and adornings of this earth. Others have found, or fancied that they have found, the answer in the wondrous powers and relationships of their own being. Above all these sources of knowledge, we have a Book, claiming divine origin, claiming to be the written Word of the Being we are searching for, revealing His character and answering every question we need to propound respecting Him and our relations to Him. If this Book is all it claims to be, it is all we need in this investigation. But we have not yet learned even that there is such a Being ; or, granting His existence, that the Book is His work. We are not yet prepared to pronounce the Bible obsolete, a collection of old wives fables mingled here and there with flashes of a high philosophy; but we freely acknowledge that the Bible must stand the tests which science can fairly put it to. If, by fair interpretation, it is shown to conflict with the revelations of nature, it can no longer claim authority as the Word of God. But we find this Book boldly proclaiming its own Author to be the same that created the world and all it contains. We find it boldly referring to the world as evidence of the existence and attributes of this Being. The heavens, the sea, and dry land, the change of seasons and the history of nations, are all referred to as proof of the existence of this Creator and Governor of the universe. It makes no attempt to stand by itself; but claiming to be the Word of God, it claims also that the world was made by Him. Whether, therefore, we ignore the Bible in religion or desire to accept it, we are shut up in the first place to the study of nature. But if that Book is shown to be false, we are shut up to the study of nature alone for all knowledge of God and of a future life. Is there any evidence then in nature, not only of the existence of God, but that this Book with such wonderful claims is the word or work of Him who laid the foundations of the hills, and fashioned man with this curious body, and made him an intelligent being? That we may be able to answer this question, we will gather the wisdom of the past, we will ourselves dig for some marble not yet discovered, that we may read on it the name and works of the Great Builder. If we can from this accumulated evidence satisfy ourselves not only of the existence of a God, who has left His witness in the dust of the earth, in the varied forms of life, and in the golden stars that adorn the blue enamel of the sky, but can be sure that He has declared to us His counsel in a written Word, our work is done. No possible question can man ask for himself, either for his highest gratification or good, that is not answered in the Bible. Assure him that this Book is what it claims to be, and he can learn there, in language too plain to be misunderstood, both his duty and his destiny. Natural Religion, as generally defined, is what can be learned of God and our relations to Him without the Bible. But if the Bible is what it claims to be, Natural Religion will appear in its greatest perfection, not when standing (alone) like an incomplete shaft, as it certainly now is, and probably must of itself ever remain, but when surmounted by that gorgeous capital, the revealed Word, wrought by the same hand. They will thus both blend in a divine harmony of proportion and structure, each one the completion and explainer of the other. It was the desire to show not only that there is a Natural Religion, but that it either embraces the Bible as a part of its complete development, or at least that it so harmonizes with the Bible as to show their unity of origin, that led the generous founder of this Institute to direct lectures to be given on this subject. His design is best expressed in his own words, which we here give as our guide in limiting the range of this discussion: *"As the most certain and most important part of philosophy appears to me to be that which shows the connection between God's revelations and the knowledge of good and evil implanted by Him in our nature, I wish a course of lectures to be delivered on Natural Religion showing its conformity to that of our Saviour."* We have here the recognition of the great truth that there is but one religion, and that nature and the Bible are parts of the same divine revelation. If this is so, if the founder of this lectureship was not mistaken in what seemed to him the most certain as well as the most important part of philosophy, then nature and the Bible must be studied together; and those who would separate them, are like those who would study astronomy and ignore the sun; or, charmed with the glorious effulgence of the day, scorn to study the brilliant hosts that bestud the canopy of night.

We find ourselves in this world like children in a palace built and furnished by a royal father whom they have never seen. They admire its grandeur and beauty, and wonder at its marvellous adaptations to their wants. As they increase in age and their wants increase, new adaptations are constantly discovered to meet those wants. They see in one place evidence of power, in another of matchless skill and of exhaustless wealth, all so conspiring to their gratification that they cannot doubt it was intended for them. They may not be able to understand the use of all the parts, but the more they study them the more they discover adaptations intended for their good; so that love towards them, and care for them, are plainly apparent as controlling the entire plan. Certainly these conditions would awaken in them some desire to know the builder and owner. Gratitude would seek an occasion of manifesting itself; or if gratitude found no place in the heart, there would be the desire to know, if they were to continue tenants at their own pleasure, and enjoy such provisions for ever, without any accountability to the provider. While much might be learned from the building and its provisions of the character of the builder, it is evident many questions would arise for which no definite answer could be found in the structure itself. It might be doubtful how far the owner still cared for the building and those it contained, or what new relations they might yet sustain to him. If he still exercised watchful care over them, there might be doubt as to what use of these provisions would meet his approbation, or what return he might require to be made for the benefits bestowed. If now a writing were presented to them claiming to be indited by him, in which his character was fully set forth, for their more perfect instruction, we can well imagine what a treasure it would be regarded. With what eagerness would they examine the proof of its authenticity, when one set of witnesses appeared, assuring them that their father had spoken the words recorded to them, stamping the writings with his own royal signet, while bold declaimers were heard on every side declaring the book to be a forgery, or the work of men so deluded that they thought themselves recording the words of the king, when they were penning their own fanatical or mystical notions! Still more would this interest be increased, if it were shown that the gravest consequences depended upon deciding this question aright. If we were called upon to decide the question, what would be our method of investigation, and what would be to us ample proof that the palace and the book were the offspring of the same mind, that they were the work of the same master's hand? Plainly we should never expect fairly and successfully to settle the question by the examination of either alone; but making ourselves complete masters of both, we should institute between them the strictest comparison. Suppose we find in the book a (pretended) history of our palace, even to its foundation-stones, and, removing the rubbish of ages, we find the gigantic courses laid as they are described in the book, while beneath the corner-stones are found the historic memorials confirming the written record, though we know those who penned it never could have personally known of their existence. And the more we study the writing the more it agrees with what we have found out by observation and experience of the structure and its provisions, until it comes to be a grand epic giving in words what the solid stone and cunning ornaments of the palace both reveal. There is harmony, there is nothing to lead us to doubt ; there is on the other hand a net-work of proof to convince us that both book and palace are the product of the same royal intellect and skill. We are satisfied now that we understand the king's will ; we have the law that is to guide us, the assurance of his constant, watchful care, and of untold future blessings in store for us. None but the most sordid and guilty could fail to rejoice at such a result, or to look upon every beauty of his home with increased delight and affection, and to cherish the written words as the most precious gift, not only because of the blessings they promise, but because they were indited by a father's heart.

If we inquire now what knowledge of religion man can reach from the study of nature alone, the answer is most difficult. The trial has never been made under the best possible conditions. If we are to judge from what has already been done, we should say that in reference to the highest truths of religion, nature merely suggests probable results, simply creates the desire for religious knowledge without giving it. It prepares the moral system for its food, but the demand thus created must be supplied from a higher source. The ancients with minds equal, to say the least, to ours, were under the dominion of a false philosophy, and were mere children in their knowledge of nature compared to us. They had neither the background of history, nor the thousand means of physical research that we possess. They might be our masters in poetry and sculpture, and even in mental acumen and philosophic power, and yet not be able to grapple with this question of God in nature as we can, any more than they were able to unfold the wonders of the heavens as we do, armed as we are with our telescopes that multiply the eye's power a thousand times, and with our analysis that traces planets that even the telescope has not revealed. Socrates, that great master of ancient times, seemed to consider the movement of the stars as above the comprehension of men, and all study of the heavens a useless waste of time, an attempt to pry into what belonged to the gods alone to know. Burdened as they were by false philosophy, and beclouded by ignorance of physical science, we can only wonder at the judicious use they made of the materials at hand, and rejoice above all in the strength of the religious nature which impelled them to accept the great truths of religion, though sustained at that time only by sophistry or defective proof.

If we ask what progress has been made in modern times, even in the boldest attempts at establishing an absolute religion without the aid of revelation, we know not, the authors of such systems know not, how much of their light was first borrowed, and then reflected. Are the most brilliant and leading truths that shine in the firmament of their systems like the fixed stars that give their light constantly and certainly from their own bodies, or are they like the moon and primary planets, bodies that would have eluded all human power of discovery were they not gilded by a great central light? If our earth were lighted by the stars alone, we could with our present organs of sight guide ourselves in some places in safety. Probably we should infer from the amount of light received that more would be highly desirable, and that we were fitted to enjoy and profit by more. Perhaps we might argue from our need of it, and from our power to profit by it, that more would be given, if we were assured that what we already enjoyed was provided for us by a benevolent Being, the Creator of the eye and the Author of light. But all we should be certain of would be the desirableness of more. This is as far as Natural Religion has ever gone, that we can learn. It has established the proof of a God or Creator of all things. It has shown that while all the desires and capacities of the inferior animals have a perfect provision made for them, and that while the desires and capacities of man, as a physical being, have had full provision made for them, those desires which we call religious have never yet been satisfied by the study of nature alone. In fact, none of those great truths which relate to a future life have ever yet been substantiated except by a written Word. We simply indicate here as the result, what we hope to prove and illustrate. The assertion may be denied now; it may be denied in spite of any amount of proof to support it. But it must be overthrown by proof of what has been done, and not by the mere assertion of what may be done, as the grand fruiting of some specious or arrogant philosophy.

That some should claim that they have already found in Natural Religion all the light they need, is by no means strange. In such a world as I have supposed, lighted only by glimmering fixed stars, no doubt some would be found to declare the light sufficient. If they did so, it would not be proof that they enjoyed more light, or had better eyes than their neighbors, but rather that they did not fully appreciate the capacity of the eye, and had no conception of the advantages and glorious splendor of perfect day. And if the written Word is proved to be an imposition, then man stands an anomaly among the creatures of the globe, with capacities and desires for which no adequate provision has been made. For us, who have always lived in the light of the Bible, it is specially difficult to know what we should have been without it, or rather what it is possible for society to become without its influence.

Certainly, the highest civilizations that the race ever attained without it were marred by acknowledged principles of injustice, cruelty, and impurity. They contained within themselves the very principles of self-destruction or degradation. The brilliancy of such civilizations is no more to be compared with a civilization founded upon the righteous, self-preserving, and elevating principles of the Bible, than the flash of lightning is to be compared to the sunlight. But though the sun is the great source of light and life, it is not the only light that beams from the heavens. The stars are still worthy of our study and admiration. When the sun is down, they give light to the traveller. By them the mariner makes his way sure upon the pathless deep. They are like the sun itself, eternal sources of light, the same in kind, though to us offering faint and feeble rays compared with his. From the study of them, we arrive at a more perfect knowledge of the sun itself than ever could be obtained from the study of the sun alone. They are scattered over the whole concave, some blazing with the brilliant light of Sirius, others apparent only to the long-continued gaze of the best-trained eye, and whole firmaments are glittering with thousands beyond, that only telescopic power can reveal. They well represent the truths of Natural Religion.

Whatever ideas may have been connected with the word religion, it now involves the idea of relationship to a higher Being. The first condition, the very foundation of this idea, is belief in the existence of such a Being. If proof of this is impossible, then the word religion may remain, and it may come to mean something; but its present significance must be entirely lost. Nor is the mere existence of such a Being a sufficient basis for religion. It may be a grand theme for philosophic speculation; but to make religion possible, it must be shown that this Being sustains relations to us ; that we either now are, or in some future time shall be affected by Him. This would be sufficient to raise in the mind apprehension, and a desire to know more of what that relationship required of us, or at least what it would bring to us. So far as we might be able to determine the character of this Being, His relations to us, and the results that would flow to us from that relationship, would our religious knowledge be perfect ; and so far as we should act upon that knowledge, our religious practice would be perfect also.

We have, then, the following general topics presented for our consideration :

First.—The existence and attributes of God.

Second.—His relationship to us, and the results that will flow from that relationship. This involves a discussion of our religious capacities and of our immortality.

Third.—The necessary failure of nature to answer fully all questions demanded by our intellectual and religious desires.

Fourth.—Proof from the physical universe and the spiritual constitution of man that the Bible is the work of God, because it is an absolute necessity to man, completing in its provisions what his nature demands, and the light of nature fails to reveal— involving a discussion of the harmony of nature and the written word.

The first two of these general topics are essential to the presentation of Natural Religion as generally defined; the last two grow legitimately from the discussion of the others, and are needed to complete the scheme by which it is attempted to show that natural and revealed religion are parts of the same system of truth, and that nature and the Bible supplement each other in making the great provision for the religious nature of man.

We have here no array of subjects for brilliant declamation, but those great questions that ever have moved the soul of man to its profoundest depths, and ever will move it, as the silent moon lifts the tidal waves from the depths of the ocean, and ever shall lift them in eternal succession, while the earth revolves upon its axis. In a field so vast, we can only make a few excursions at random; but if in every exploration we find evidence of the same handiwork, we may well believe that the Great Master has left no place without evidence of His being. It need not deter us from the examination of so broad a field, that the cry is raised that sciences are so vast in their requirements that only a few men can speak on each with authority. This is true in regard to some questions connected with every science. Only a few stand upon the dividing line between the known and the unknown, peering out into the dark ocean for new discoveries. But when truths are discovered, they soon become the property of every educated mind. And every department of nature, so far as it is really needed for our purpose, is open to every man of ordinary scientific attainment. And we call upon those who can look so far beyond their fellows to bring out their discoveries and place them where they belong in science, and then others can judge as well as they of the simple question of the bearing of such discoveries upon the proof of the being and attributes of God, and upon the destiny of man. And the pretence that is sometimes made, that no one can judge of the bearings of a science upon these questions, who is not in a position to undertake original research in such sciences, is unsound in argument, to apply no harsher term to it. We simply say that there is enough within the reach of all to prove every point we wish to make, and we challenge those who have entered the very arcana of the sciences to bring opposing testimony.

We shall occupy the remainder of this lecture in a consideration of the conditions necessary for the fair discussion of this subject, and of the difficulties likely to be encountered in the presentation and judging of the proof.

It is a maxim of common law and of commonsense, that it is useless to try a case and present proof before one whose mind is already made up. To be fitted for a juror, one must be free from personal bias, and competent to weigh the proof. In all that relates to Natural Religion, we may have decided opinions now; but from the very nature of the proof—from the impossibility of our having examined and weighed it all, we can, if we choose, put ourselves into the condition of honest and competent jurors. All that we are called upon to grant in the outset is, that the theory of the case is a possible one ; that the case in its nature is one capable of proof. We do not ask you to grant that it can be proved with the means at our command, but simply that it is a supposable case that convincing proof might be produced. With this concession there is also need of a determination to give a careful and candid consideration to the facts and arguments presented as proof. The condition of the mind will not be favorable to a just consideration of the proof, if the result aimed at by the investigation is considered undesirable, or in any respect adverse to our interests. Our desires and our interests, real or fancied, insensibly affect our judgment of the validity of arguments. It requires not only honesty of purpose, but the highest sagacity in unravelling our mental processes, to guard against the vitiating element of our own interest in the decision of any case. So readily is this acknowledged by all, that it is taken as one of the plainest maxims in human action. In the question before us, our highest interests are involved. Answer it one way, and we are accountable to men alone. We can free ourselves from all accountability and from all troubles with the stiletto or with poison. Answer it another way, and it becomes as impossible for us to escape responsibility as it is for us to stop the earth in its course. We are all either in favor of, or opposed to the results which we shall attempt to reach in this investigation. Would it delight us to know

Difficulties. 37

that God not only created the world, but that He is the Author of the Bible; that we are now in His power, and must ever remain there? According as we honestly answer these questions, we find ourselves ready to accept or reject the great truths which are essential to religion, natural or revealed. But the fact that our decision will not change our relationships, and the infinite interests that are at stake if those relationships really do exist, will do much, if rightly appreciated, to make us honest. The hazard would seem to be too great for us to be willing to make the least mistake in our investigations. We ought to be willing to admit every new proof, and be ready to abandon, if need be, our long-cherished opinions.

The difficulties in the way of a proper presentation of the subject are various, and not easily remedied. We meet with one formidable at the very outset. The subject is thought to be hackneyed. For thousands of years it has been one of the staples of human thought, and in its investigation every field of knowledge has been explored by most successful observers. The Paleys and Bucklands will never be surpassed, and probably never equalled, in their peculiar style and line of argument. And if there is much that is false, and much that is worthless, yearly spoken and written on this subject, it only shows how familiar must be all its leading truths to the common mind. It has then no charm like that which new discoveries and new subjects of human thought possess for the moment.

We are to tread ground that has been worn like the great thoroughfares, where we have travelled so often that not only the great monuments along the wayside, but the humblest flowers even, have been seen, and every spot of beauty has lost the charm of novelty. If there is delight in store for us, it must be from deepened convictions and clearer views of truths already acknowledged, or perchance from some new truth which we may gather as gleaners find here and there a scattered ear after the harvest has been carefully garnered.

Still another difficulty which must always be taken into consideration is the impossibility of presenting the proof in its fulness. To do this, a naturalist must present the studies and observations of a lifetime. All he can do is to present the great outcrops of proof, while with the mental eye he can himself follow the strata deep beyond the reach of mere sight as surely as though they were open to every observer. One viewing the outcropping rocks upon a mountain-top for the first time, wonders that the geologist can tell what will be found by those who tunnel through its base; so there may reasonably be expected to be doubt when disconnected proof is presented for the first time, while that proof, if pondered on and seen in all its relations, would seem as firm as the hills upon their rocky thrones. When we have accepted the great truths of astronomy and other physical sciences because they have been proved to us, we are seldom aware how much our ready acceptance was due to the common belief of the world. The rejection of the same proof by minds of the highest order, and perfectly conversant with all the facts of the case, shows this. That proof which now seems to us like mathematical demonstration, was long years in overcoming the prejudices of the learned as well as of the vulgar, so as to have any weight at all. Tycho Brahe, with his eye almost continually fixed upon the heavens, would not believe the sun to be the centre of our system, although daily recording observations that would now be received by every intelligent man as proof of this accepted truth. We do not accept the proof because we have greater mental power or greater knowledge than Tycho Brahe. We accept the truth on the belief of the world, and then examine the proof of what we are ready and willing to believe on the testimony of others. The belief of men who have given long and patient investigation to any subject ought to have weight with us. The world would make slow progress were it not a principle in our nature to have faith in the knowledge of such men. They are sometimes mistaken, and their mistakes do mischief and prevent progress for a time. And for this reason, while their opinions are entitled to weight, we should hold ourselves ready to reject them at once when they are shown to be mistaken. The men who have gone before us are worthy of our respect, and are generally entitled to our confidence in the conclusions they have reached; but as they have differed on many points, they are not infallible, and therefore it is that every generation has need to tread the ground for itself.

Still another difficulty is the fact that objects in nature have so long been familiar that they fail to excite the emotions, or to convince the understanding as they ought, and they thus fail to impress us as proof of creative power. They appear in the ordinary course of nature; and this unchanging course, always referable in the first analysis to the acknowledged forces of the physical world, fails to impress us as the expression of a personal power. The harmony of nature becomes to us like the mysterious notes of the Æolian harp, as the light air touches its strings, and wakes the sweetest music. We have always seen the combinations and changes around us. Or if some new and wonderful combination is discovered, we are able to refer it at once to some force already well known. We content our minds with the word "natural." Whatever is common makes little impression on the senses, or rather the mind ceases to take cognizance of the impressions. Novelty, on the other hand, has a charm that rouses the mind to activity, and this activity is necessary to the full apprehension of the value of the facts and relations upon which we rely for producing conviction of the truth. Aristotle, in a fragment preserved by Cicero in his DE NATURA DEORUM, beautifully illustrates the effect of common things, if seen for the first time. "If," said he, "there were beings who lived in the depths of the earth in dwellings adorned with statues and paintings, and everything which is possessed in rich abundance by those whom we esteem fortunate; and if these beings could receive tidings of the power and might of the gods, and could then emerge from their hidden dwellings, through the open fissures of the earth, to the places which we inhabit—if they could suddenly behold the earth, and the sea, and the vault of heaven—could recognise the expanse of the cloudy firmament, and the might of the winds of heaven, and admire the sun in its majesty, beauty, and radiant effulgence; and lastly, when night had veiled the earth in darkness, they could behold the starry heavens, the changing moon, and the stars rising and setting in the unvarying course ordained from eternity, they would surely exclaim, 'There are gods, and such great things must be the work of their hands.'"

These wonderful works have been ever before us, so that it is hard for us to realize that there was a time when they were not—and harder still to feel the full force of the proof which their mechanism ought to be to us. And the humbler objects of natural history, not calculated to excite emotions of grandeur and sublimity, which we daily tread beneath our feet, according to the common laws of mind pass unnoticed, or when noticed, fail to convince us as they ought. There may be a wonderful arrangement of parts, all fitted to produce a certain result; but then we cannot see the hand of God tinting the flower and arranging each part for its appropriate work. The plant springs from the ground, and its kind has done so for thousands of generations. If we could but for a moment see the Divine Hand apply the rule, weigh the elements, and join the varied cells, how different the case would be! But from the work alone, the builder must be known to us. As we walk among the old ruins, it is hard to realize that the stones were hewn and raised and joined by men. When the American first visits Mount Vernon, how difficult for him to realize that here really is the home of the hero whose name he has revered. It is not strange, then, that this difficulty of realizing should in the case of natural objects sometimes end in doubt of a Personal God. It is not strange, at least, that it should result so to those who see no more than they saw when they were children—the merest fragments of the common forms that surround them. And though the wondrous works of design should be described, it is not he who studies them in books alone, but he whose eye has seen the living loop and hinge, that can understand their power to convince. What knows the man who has merely read of Mount Washington, of the sense of power he feels who climbs the Titan blocks which form that grand monument of nature's forces? What knows the man who has simply read of Niagara, of the emotions of him who looks up to the bending flood and is deafened by its thunder? It is the real thing, and not its description, that must be relied upon to convince. And if we wish to prove the strength of the argument from design, must we look to those who have only read books and looked upon the same unvarying surface all their lives, or to the naturalist, who has been walking within the great cabinets of nature all his life, each day opening some alcove filled with new beauties and adaptations? Shall we inquire respecting the landscape in the distance, of him who has always walked upon the plain at the base of the mountain, or of him who daily ascends that mountain and views that landscape from every possible point? The common observer is like Aristotle's fancied beings in the centre of the earth—remaining there for ever, hearing of the gods and their works, but seeing the whole array of nature only as delineated in pictures of landscapes and the orreries invented by men to represent the movements of the heavenly bodies. But the naturalist, with his trained senses for observing, is as it were raised from the centre to the surface to look off upon a new world.

And when the question is raised respecting the Bible, as to its claim to being a part of the great revelation, shall we accept the dicta of those men who are so ignorant of the Bible as hardly to know the Old Testament from the New? Any man who should pretend to give a scientific opinion with the same ignorance of nature that most of those men have of the Bible who undertake to decide upon its claims, would be driven from all intelligent society as charlatans and impostors. Theologians declaiming against the deductions of sciences of which they know nothing, and scientific men who have so much arrogance or so little philosophy as to ridicule the Bible of which they are often profoundly ignorant, it is to be hoped will soon be among the things of the past.

We are also met with the objection that we may not be right in our physical explanations. Old theories in science have been thrown aside as the dreams of children. Why may not ours ? Many of the theories now received may be modified or rejected. But the facts upon which we shall in the main rely never change. If we introduce theories at all, it will not be as an essential part of the argument. It may not be true that water contains an equal number of atoms of hydrogen and oxygen, according to the commonly accepted chemical theory. There may not be atoms at all ; but the fact still remains, and will be unchanged while the world stands, that one-ninth of water by weight is hydrogen, and eight-ninths oxygen, and that its greatest density is between seven and eight degrees above the freezing point.

And yet once more we have the unpopular side, because we attempt to sustain the old belief. It is more popular and more flattering to our pride to pull down and build anew with startling paradoxes, than to accept the old, although it may be the right. To tear down is a short and exciting work that seldom fails to attract a wondering crowd. Some minds can never be satisfied unless the thing presented is new. If new, its truth is little considered. We have no new and startling theories to present.

We reverently enter the temple of Nature, that we

may there read the character of the Builder. Its walls, we believe, were not piled by chance; its cunning adjustments are not the sporting of the elements. From foundation-stone to topmost turret, we hope to read our Father's wisdom, power, and love. We hope to open the ark of the testimony and find his own seal stamped upon his written Word. We hope to hear Him speaking with one voice from Nature and the Bible, declaring himself the Great First Cause, the Creator of the world, our Creator, our God, and our Father.

LECTURE II.

PRINCIPLES OF BELIEF.—ADAPTATION OF OUR BODIES TO OUR WANTS AND TO THE WORLD.

Perfect provision for organic beings.—No provision in material world for man's highest nature.—Claims of the Bible. —A natural provision for man.—Principles of belief.— Theories of creation.—First cause.—Matter might be eternal.—Beginning of life.—Antagonism of physical forces and vitality.—Apparent harmony between them.—Man an effect.—His creation to be accounted for.—The germ as wonderful as the developed being.—Bible account of creation. —What we should expect to find in such a creation.—Nature an unchangeable record.—Questions that would arise without the Bible.—Aid of geology.—The existence of beings, and not their mode of origin, proof of skill and power.— Adaptation of our bodies to our use and to the world.—Relations to the world established through the senses.—Distinctive use of each sense.—Conditions necessary for sight.— Relation of light to the atmosphere.—Form of objects and effects of surface.—Structure of the eye.—Sense of hearing gives knowledge of objects beyond the range of vision.—Mechanism of the ear.—Taste and smell.—No special mechanism.—Design shown by the use.—Touch.—Kinds of knowledge given by it.—All the senses connected with the nervous system.—Vegetative life.—Relation of the body to the world considered.—The atmosphere.—Structure of the lung.— Nutrition.—Sleep.—Animals fitted for particular zones.— Man for all.—No special sciences needed to show our adaptation to the world.—Personality of the Creator inferred from the provision for our personality. Antagonism in nature.

In the last lecture we indicated something of the object aimed at in this course, and the topics to be introduced for proof and illustration. We shall first attempt to show that provision has been made in the material world for every organic being on the globe, including man, considered merely as a physical being; and that this provision is of such a nature as to show the contrivance and oversight of a personal Creator. In the second place, we expect to show that no adequate provision is found in the material world for man's highest nature, so that a written Word is absolutely demanded to make as full provision for man as has been made to satisfy the capacities and desires of every other creature. And in the third place, the question will arise how far the Bible can claim to be from the Author of Nature, by providing the information which man's highest nature demands, and thus becoming just as natural a provision for man's higher needs, as the sunlight and atmosphere and fruits of the earth are for his physical wants.

Our first work then is to show the nature and perfection of the provision that has been made in the world for organic beings, commencing with man as the highest. But before proceeding to this examination, I ask your attention to the consideration of some principles of belief, which must be accepted in all such discussions, and to the Bible account, and possible scientific theories of creation. In the preceding lecture, we took it for granted that the nature of the cause may be inferred from its effect. The palace must have a builder, and something of the character of the designer and builder can be learned from his work. It is impossible for us to believe that anything has been produced without a cause—that anything can begin to exist of itself. Everything in the universe must either be self-existent or be an effect. If self-existent, it must have existed from all eternity; if an effect, it must have been mediately or immediately produced by that which is self-existent and eternal. We are driven by our analysis back from cause to cause till we come to a First Cause, necessarily self-existent and eternal. That cause could not spring from nothing, and therefore could not begin to be. This we are sure of, or nothing can be accepted as truth. As we trace back the chain of cause and effect, we come necessarily to believe in something which is not an effect, but the source of all effects. Not to believe in something eternal is simply absurd. And that something has produced all secondary causes and the results which we see in the universe. What was that something? Was it simply matter and the forces of matter? So far as we know, matter may have existed for ever. There seems to be perfect evidence of design in the very constitution of matter and in the relation of its forces; but still, if one chooses to regard simple matter as eternal, we see no absurdity in such a belief. But we then ask, if matter is self-existent, is it able to produce all the results which we witness? We know that it has not existed always in its present form upon our globe. But all the geologic changes, so far as mere matter and the physical changes were concerned, might have been produced by the action of these forces that we acknowledge to be the constant accompaniments, if not essential properties of matter. But there was a time when life was not here. This will be acknowledged by every geologist. Now, life is only manifested in connection with organization. Did the vital principle seize upon matter, and organize it? This would imply that it resides somewhere free from matter. Is vitality a force accidental in its manifestation, correlated to some other force, developed by the relationship of different kinds of matter; or was matter first organized by a creator, and then life joined to it? There are those who accept the second supposition and believe in spontaneous generation, the production of life from matter and physical forces, and the evolution of higher types by development from lower. We pass for the present the geologic argument, which we believe to be conclusive against this theory, and ask its supporters how it comes to pass that the physical forces tend to originate an organism, when the moment it is produced they tend to destroy it. And it is a remarkable fact, that some authors who have expressed their belief in the production of life through chemical forces, have also expressed their belief in the antagonism of life and those forces. We leave to them the task of harmonizing their own views. The organic being struggles for existence and lives only because the vital principle holds in abeyance the physical forces and makes them its servants. In a certain sense it is true that the physical forces build up all organic structures. But the moment vitality is gone, they tear down the structure which they have unwillingly labored to construct under its control, and they cease not their work until every particle has taken the inorganic form. In the perfectly adjusted steam-engine moving the ship against wind and tide, or weaving finest fabrics with iron fingers, it seems to the thoughtless observer that the steam is a willing servant, bending its energies to the work. But the mission of the steam is to shatter and destroy. It rushes into the cylinder not to move the machinery, but in very hatred of itself, and struggles to escape. It is the genius of man that controls the struggling monster by bands of iron too strong for him to break, till in his rage he lifts the piston and moves the swift machinery, as he darts howling into the air. Thus also does vitality control and use the adverse forces of the inorganic world. As well might we think that the steam which drives the piston originated the locomotive, or the locomotive the engineer that controls it, as to think that life is the offspring of electricity or any other physical force. It is latest born of all the forces, if it is proper to call it a force at all; and the time may come when it will vanish from our globe and leave the physical forces victors on the field. But while it is here, it holds its ground by warfare. It builds up only through the agency of physical forces. They build organized beings only under its control. We have had of late the announcement made that we must expunge from our text-books the assertion that the vital principle overrides or controls the chemical forces. We may **expunge** it from our text-books, but we might as well expunge the satellites of Jupiter or the planet Neptune from our astronomies.

But let us for the sake of the argument grant that matter may originate life. As it is impossible for us to accept anything as a cause, unless it is adequate to produce the effect, we look at once for the cause of man. We know with certainty that his body is produced. Physical man is therefore an effect. If matter and the physical forces produce life, they must also produce life with all the adjuncts which we find in physical man, or his creation is still to be accounted for. It is not enough to say that a germ was originated by matter, and that germ by development became man. To be satisfied with this statement is to deceive ourselves with words. That germ must have had in it from the beginning all the capacity of developing into man. It must have been sufficient to produce man. And no one can intelligently believe that matter could produce such a germ, unless he believes matter could produce a man in his highest possible physical and intellectual development. One result is just as wonderful as the other; one supposition is just as reasonable as the other. And any attempt to account for man upon this globe from a germ not as wonderful as man, and requiring as high creative power, is simply illogical and a deceiving of ourselves with sophistry. Like an attempt to produce force where no force exists, it is worthy of the wildest dreamers of perpetual motion. We have now in the Bible a simple account of creation. A Great First Cause is introduced.

We are not told that He created matter and ordained the manifestation of its forces; but we are certainly left to infer this, since He is represented as producing by His command those changes, the introduction of light and the gathering of the seas, that we know were produced by the operation of these forces. According to this account, up to a certain time there was simply matter, whether created or eternal, passive in the hand of God. When the appointed time had come, he joined life to matter. Man was first organized in full perfection, and then the breath of life was breathed into him. We may reject this account; but it is impossible to find among all the speculations with which the world has been favored another method of creation more simple or less wonderful, viewed simply from a scientific stand-point. Having shown that the Bible account of the introduction of man upon the earth requires no greater power than the production of this germ that should in the end produce man, we have the same ground *a priori*, for accepting the Bible account as any other. We are not called upon to ignore the Bible, but impartially to compare its teachings with those of nature, that we may accept or reject its claims.

And we may say, as the first result of the comparison, that the Bible account of the introduction of life upon the globe, and even of the creation of man, is as reasonable, when tested by the relations of cause and effect, as any theory of creation the most orthodox development theorists have ever been able to give us.

Man the Image of God. 53

If they ask us to grant the creation of a germ that in myriads of ages should develop into man, we answer that if we accept their method of creation, we require the same power to produce the result. If they ask us to believe that a germ of low type developed into higher types until in ages it came to be man, we answer that the very first principles of belief forbid it. It is asking us to believe in an effect produced without an adequate cause.

Among the assertions of the Bible, we find this in the very first chapter, that God created the heavens and the earth. If matter is eternal, certainly all its relations in constituting this world are here referred to His wisdom and power. Every order of creature was made by Him, and last of all man, fashioned in his own image. If this is true, and if God is such a being as He is set forth to be in the Bible, there are certain things that we should naturally expect to find in the universe. If we failed to find them, we should so far be led to doubt the truth of the record, unless the record itself gave notice of the defect and gave a satisfactory reason for its occurrence.

1. If man is the image of God, then he will be able in some measure to enter into His plans and comprehend His character.

2. If God is infinite in all His attributes, it would naturally be expected that some of His plans would be too vast for man to comprehend fully, embracing too much of space and requiring too much time for their completion.

3. We should expect that all things would show design—design of the same kind as the works of man would exhibit, and never falling below them in perfection.

4. Man being confessedly the highest type of creation on the earth, we should expect that the world would be, in a certain sense, created for him, or at least that it would have more important relations to him than to any other being—that he would be the central figure of creation.

5. We should expect provision to be made not only for the body, but for the mind ; or at least we should expect as full provision to be made for all the powers and faculties of man as has been made for the lower animals ; this would involve provision for his emotional nature and for unlimited improvement in all his faculties.

Finally, we should expect to find man and the world fitted for each other, and the same fitness running down through the whole order of nature ; every animal, and plant, and grain of dust, showing evidence of the work of a Being like man—above him indeed, but above him only in degree and condition of existence.

All this we should expect, if we had never given one thought to the study of nature, but were now coming to it for the first time to find proof in support of the Bible. If we found all these conditions fully met, we might well be satisfied with the proof. If we failed to find them, we should doubt the record ; because a book, though claiming to be from God,

Geology.

is written by man. But the everlasting hills were not raised by man. No man can roll back the stony tablets of the earth and blot out their record. No skill of man can adjust the nice mechanism of the living beings now upon earth; no power of his can sustain them for a moment when it is adjusted. If there is a God who created all things, we know that in nature we can find his handiwork, which all the wisdom and strength of men are as powerless to create or change as they are to bind the earth in its course, or to blot out the sun in the heavens.

On the other hand, suppose we had never seen or heard of a written Revelation, but were possessed of all the knowledge of nature we now have, what are some of the questions that would be suggested to us, and some of the inferences we should draw from the world as it is? How came man upon the earth?—would certainly be a question that could not fail to demand an answer. With our present knowledge, the argument of endless succession is folly, and its labored refutation by Paley and others, mere lumber. Such arguments were needed in the day when Paley could say that if asked how a stone came upon the heath, he might answer that, for aught he knew, it had lain there for ever. But in our day, when that stone can be traced back to the bed from which it was torn; when the forces that formed it, and those that tore it from its resting-place are well understood—we should expect a different line of argument. In fact, the whole science of geology has come in since Paley's day; a science not yet perfect, but entirely changing the field of argument for or against natural religion. By its light we can go back into the dark ages of the globe's history, when there was not only no man, but no living thing upon the earth. To this all men of science are agreed. This is certainly an important point, and makes an important difference in the argument. We can go back to the barren rocks and trace in the successive strata rising above them the introduction of all new forms of life. The only question is, how they were introduced, or how they began to be. There is no question about the fact of a beginning. As to the mode of their origin, two diverse views are held, one requiring the same creative power as the other, as we have already shown, so that an *a priori* argument cannot be made out conclusively in favor of either. We must rely entirely upon facts observed in nature. We are now leaving out of view the Bible account, relying solely upon nature to tell us of God. And if left entirely to nature, we could not see a particle of difference between the theory of distinct creations and the so-called development theory in proving the existence and perfections of God. For we have already shown that the creation of a germ that shall develop into a perfect being, involves the same creative power as the creation of the being itself. So the creation of a germ that should evolve all created beings in their geologic and living order, would require equal skill and power with the distinct creation of every specific form. If we look at an oak, we see in it evidence of design in every fibre of its wood, in its leaf, its flower, and fruit. But that monarch of the forest was once represented by a single cell, containing a power that was to determine the form of every fibre of that tree; that, by controlling the physical forces, was to originate every tissue in the exact order and proportion in which it was needed, to determine the outline of every leaf, and the form and flavor of the fruit. Surely, the evidence of skill and power was as great in the creation of that germ as it would be in the creation of the full-grown tree in the twinkling of an eye. And the creation of a germ that should give origin to trees of every kind, with all their adaptations to the world and to the animal kingdom, would certainly be as wonderful, and be proof of as great skill and power, as the creation of the germ of a single oak. The existence of such creatures as are found upon the globe is the proof of skill and power, and the manner of their origin does not in the least affect the question. We are to inquire what the creation of all the plants and animals now upon the globe, in a single moment, would prove in regard to their Creator. And whatever such an instantaneous creation would prove, the present creation proves, without regard to the time or manner that the species were introduced.

In our first lecture we stated our case to be like that of children, who, on coming to the years of understanding, find themselves in a palace perfectly furnished for their use, and set themselves to find from the provisions of the structure evidence of the character of the builder, and of his relationship to them. I propose now to apply the same line of argument to another purpose, the adaptation of our bodies to our use, as well as the adaptation of the world to them. It is evident that a castle would, if built by a wise designer, have reference to the locality in which it was placed. It could only meet the wants of its occupants, as its structure should have reference to the climate and other conditions of the country. In a land of snow and rain, we should expect carefully-formed roofs, and only there. We should expect windows where light could reach them, and in fact all the changes of day and night, and change of season to be provided for. We should find then certain contrivances which would be adapted to our wants in all places, and certain other provisions and contrivances having reference to the particular condition of the outward world in that place. In the same light we may view our own bodies, or the world in reference to our bodies. We are conscious of our own existence, and that we use our bodies. They are as distinct from us as the houses we inhabit. They were prepared for us. They are not only temples for us to dwell in, but it is by means of them alone that we establish relations with the external world. So far as the senses are wanting, so far the external world is a blank to us. As we know from geology that there was a time when there was no man on this earth, so we know from observation that each one of us must die, and that we must crumble back to dust. We know that there is nothing in our bodies that cannot be found in every spadeful of garden soil. If the Bible declares that the first man was made of the dust of the earth, science declares that all living men are fashioned of the same material. Having this knowledge, we are prepared to present certain considerations in regard to our bodies, showing their adaptation to the world in which we live. And for the present we shall regard man simply as a physical being, reserving for some future lecture the mutual adaptation of the world and the higher nature of man. And we care nothing now about geologic development theories. We take the fact of our own existence as it is, and inquire in regard to our present relations. Our physical good demands that we should have the power of comprehending the world in all the respects in which it is possible for matter or its forces to affect our bodies. The senses completely meet this want. And we wish now to consider the senses simply as a means of establishing relations with the external world. We are too apt to confine ourselves to the mere mechanism of the eye or ear, without considering how the senses supplement each other, and without considering the provision made in the world that it may be a fit place for the exercise of the senses. The eye would be useless without all the properties of light; the ear would have no power in a world without an atmosphere. Sight enables us to avoid danger, and seek distant needful objects. What a vast length of time and wearisome labor would it require for a blind man to learn what one glance of the eye may give to one blessed with sight! This sense also gives certain ideas which the blind could never acquire, as of color, transparency, and play of light. But of those properties and relations that could be learned by the sense of touch, the eye will take in more in the landscape in one moment than could be otherwise learned in a lifetime. A race of blind men could not exist on this globe.

The sense of sight alone, as a means of adapting us to the world, would strike us as wonderful in its results, and worthy of the conception of the highest intelligence in adapting means to ends, if we knew nothing of the adjustments by which sight is secured. We can conceive of the power of sight as direct perception, without the aid of light, or of a special organ corresponding to the eye. But constituted as we are, we see only through the agency of light; and we perceive light only by a special organ; and objects only in consequence of a peculiar structure of that organ. Of all of these relationships of light to objects, and of light to the eye, and of the parts of the eye to each other, not one of them is a necessary condition of matter. The arrangement of so many things by which this wonderful power of perceiving distant objects is secured, is the only one that will secure the end desired, out of an endless number of arrangements that can be conceived of. The first thing we notice is the relation of the light to the atmosphere, by which it bathes all objects, unless they are cut off from it by special obstructions. That is, every particle of the atmosphere seems to be a point from which light is reflected in all directions in right lines. And every object, either in consequence of its reflection or absorption of light at every point, forms an image at every possible position that can be taken, from which straight lines can be drawn to the object. And the rays, passing from a multitude of objects across each other, never interfere. Even when passing through an opening in the shutter, a thousand objects may be painted on the screen, and yet each one be as perfect as though that were the only object in the range of vision. The glowing threads that weave the gorgeous web of light never tangle, and never blend the pictures that they are ever forming. Whether we take the proof with the eye or with the photographic plate, we find these crossing lines tracing at the same moment in a thousand places the perfect picture of every object on the landscape. We cannot but admire the varied forms of objects, and the effect of surface in producing color, by which distinctness of every part is secured. The wisdom and skill of man might be challenged to conceive of means more perfect than light in its varied relations to matter, to secure distinctness of individual objects. No less worthy of admiration is the organ through which we are to perceive. Whoever contrived it, understood perfectly all the properties of light, and the wants of the being that was to use it. We might introduce here modifications of the eye in the lower animals suited to their special wants. But as we are considering the relations of man to the world, we need not pass beyond our subject to find arguments for design. The eye of man, though limited in its power to a certain range, gives all that the common wants of life demand. And if man needs greater range of vision, he has but to study the eye itself, and fashion instruments to increase its power ; as he is able when the proper time has come in his civilization, to increase by science and art the efficacy of nearly all his physical powers. For the ordinary purposes of life, neither telescopic nor microscopic adjustment of the eye is needed.

But the eye has not only the power of vision so necessary to man, but it is an instrument of power, an instrument made up of distinct parts, of solids and liquids, of transparent and opaque tissues, of curtains, and lenses, and screens. Its mechanism can be accurately examined and the use of each part as perfectly understood as any of the works of man. We examine every part of it as we would a microscope. We have first the solid case which is to hold all the machinery, and upon which are to be fastened the cords and pulleys of its skilful mounting. This covering, opaque, white, and glistening, like silver on the back and sides of the eye, in front, where the light must enter, suddenly becomes transparent as the clearest crystal. Within this is a second coating, that coming to the front changes just as suddenly into an opaque screen, through the tissues of which no ray of light can pass. That screen is self-adjusting, with a net-work that no art of man ever equalled. Whether expanding or contracting, its opening in the centre always remains a perfect circle, adapted in size to the intensity of light. How much light shall enter the eye it determines without aid from us. Next there must be connection with the brain, the seat of the being for whom the provision is made. These two coatings are pierced upon the back part of the eye, and a thread drawn out from the brain is passed through this opening and spread out within the eye as a delicate screen upon which all impressions are to be made. To fill the larger portion of the cavity, there is packed into it a clear jelly, and imbedded in this a lens, fashioned with a skill that no artist can equal, to refract the light and throw the image on the perceptive screen. In front of this lens is another humor, not like jelly as the other, because in this, that delicate fringe, the iris, is to float, and nothing but a watery fluid will answer its purpose. Here then we have a great variety of materials all brought together, of the exact quality and in the quantity needed, placed in the exact position which they ought to occupy, so perfectly adjusted that the most that man can do is to imitate the eye without ever hoping to equal it.

Nor is the curious structure of the eye itself all that is worthy of our attention. The instrument when finished must be mounted for use. A cavity is formed in solid bone, with grooves and perforations for all the required machinery. The eye, when placed, is packed with soft elastic cushions and fastened by strings and pulleys to give it variety and rapidity of motion. Its outer case is to cover it when not in use, and protect it when in danger. The delicate fringe upon its border never needs clipping ; and set like a well-arranged defence, its points all gracefully turn back, that no ray of light may be obstructed. Above the projecting brow is another defence to turn aside the acrid fluids from the forehead, while near the eye is placed a gland that bathes the whole organ with a clear, soothing fluid, to prevent all friction and keep its outward lens free from dust, and polished for constant use. When we consider all this, the perfect adaptation of the eye to our wants, the arrangement of every part of its structure on strict mechanical and optical principles, and all the provisions for its protection, we pronounce the instrument perfect, the work of a Being like man, but raised immeasurably above the most skilful human workman. What shall we say when we learn that this instrument was prepared in long anticipation of its use ; that there is a machinery within it to keep it in constant repair ; that the Maker not only adjusted the materials, but that he was the chemist who formed all these substances from the dust of the earth ? We may be told that the architect found this dust ready at hand, existing from all eternity. We may not be able to prove the contrary, nor do we need to for this argument. It is enough for our present purpose to know that the eyes with which we now see, these wonderfully complex and perfect instruments, were not long since common earth, dust upon which we perchance have trod.

We can understand the mechanism of the eye, we can comprehend the wisdom that devised it ; but the preparation of materials, and the adjustment of parts, speak of a power and skill to which man can never hope to attain. When he sees his most cunning workmanship surpassed both in plan and execution, shall he fail to recognise design ? Shall we fail to recognise a builder when we contemplate such a work ?

Hearing is the only other sense connected with special mechanical contrivance. It is as well adapted to its purpose as the sense of sight, although the ear in its mechanism may not be so wonderful as the eye, and the use of some of its parts more difficult of comprehension. Hearing gives us knowledge of objects far beyond the reach of vision, when thick walls, mountain ranges, and part of the convex earth divides them from us. It is perfect in darkness, when the eye is powerless. This sense is affected only by vibrations of the air, and the machinery connected with it is adapted to collect them and transmit the impression to the inner portion of the ear, where the auditory nerve like a watchful sentinel waits and watches to telegraph the signals to the brain. We are thus warned of danger in the distance ; we are invited to enjoyment ; we hold converse with friends ; and have poured in upon us, for our instruction, the mingled sounds of all animate and inanimate nature. The ear thus beautifully supplements the eye in revealing distant objects, and thus connecting us with the world in which we live.

The senses of taste and smell are more intimately connected with food; and the securing and selecting of this are of prime importance in our relations to the world. We can gain no knowledge of the taste of objects unless they are within our reach, and we need none. But odors may be to us a means of enjoying distant objects, or of avoiding poisons floating in the air. There is no special mechanism connected with either. There is simply a power. And hardly less wonderful is the power of a simple membrane to distinguish the numberless flavors and odors, than the most complex machinery, although design can only be shown in the use of these senses to man in multiplying and perfecting his relations to the world.

The sense of touch supplements sight, by giving us knowledge of solids as distinguished from surfaces, of hardness and temperature. So far as it is needed for our protection, it is diffused over the whole body; but for securing certain knowledge it is keenest in the finger-tips—in those organs best fitted to trace out varied surfaces and curious forms. When now we group the senses, what a marvellous combination! Impressions of objects come darting through space on the wings of light, crossing in ten thousand lines, yet never mingling. The ear is charmed with sounds. Odors and flavors delight us, and touch protects from danger, or thrills us with pleasure. What other knowledge could we desire to have of the world of matter which the senses do not give? What other is needed for our life or our enjoyment? We stand in bodies protected by the senses, like armies with picket-guards, through which nothing can enter without giving the countersign; and these guards telegraph to us all knowledge of the outer world.

We have seen some wonderful instruments that indicate the presence of electricity, or change of temperature. But how all human contrivances sink into insignificance when compared with the perceptive powers of these bodies, through the combined action of the senses! We recognise the body as but an instrument, but its relations to the world through the senses is a marvel. It is a tenement worthy to be the habitation of the being made in the image of God. In its relations to the world, there is a wisdom and skill manifested worthy of a God. We look up to the stars, take in the glories of the landscape, and drink in delicious music, without once considering the thousand strings that have been adjusted by the Master's hand that there may be this divine harmony of adaptation for the whole race from age to age.

The senses are connected with a nervous system, or, where no nerves can be detected, with a nervous power. Sensation is distinctive of animal life, and is the foundation of all the functions of relation. But there is in man a vegetative life, by which the body is built up and preserved. The functions of this lower life involve perhaps as perfect and striking correspondence between the organs of the body and the inanimate world, as has been seen in connection with the senses. It has long been the custom of natural theologians to trace out the mechanism of the organs of the body which certainly show design; but we propose to direct attention rather to the same sort of correspondence between the body and the world, which has already been shown when treating of the senses. So long as we confine our attention to the minute structure of the body, the Creator is represented rather as a cunning artificer. But when we consider the relations of the body to the world, we are impressed more with the wisdom and benevolence of the Great Architect, and we thus gain fuller revelations of His character. The investigation requires thought and patience, but in the scheme we have marked out we cannot omit it. It makes but little difference what relation of the body we consider first. For convenience, we will take one that is most constant. We must breathe. The oxygen of the air is the great chemical agent to aid in giving heat, and that constant change of material in the body by which strength and even life itself are secured. It is a constant want; and to make the world inhabitable, it must be everywhere. Water and food may be taken at stated intervals, but the air must be ever present. We walk in an ocean of it. In deepest caverns, on highest mountains, on every foot of the earth, we are sure to find air, and always of the same composition. Although there are two gases simply mixed together, their nature is such that the mixture is exactly the same in all parts of the world. No chemical analysis can detect a deficiency of either element. We may have occasion to point out other manifestations of design in the atmosphere, but for the present we notice its adaptation to the wants of man in the uniformity of its composition and its constant presence. But in man we find the lung for its reception. What a wonderful organ, ready when the first breath of the new-born child is to be taken! It has never been used before; but it is all ready, like the engine when the steam is first thrown into it. The opening is there for the air to enter; the thousand tubes wind through the substance till it becomes a mere mass of thinnest membrane. But all through these delicate linings the arteries weave their scarlet, gauzy web, to spread the blood to every part, and when the air has wrought its change, the thousand veins gather the vital fluid and send it back to do its appointed work. Every breath involves a combination of mechanical and chemical action compared with which the steam-engine is a rude machine. The pouring of the blood to the lung, and its passage to the heart, and all this complex machinery, was adjusted with reference to the air. Was it air, think you, that formed those channels to bring and carry the vital fluid? Had it any tendency to adjust them? What but the wisdom and skill of a High Intelligence could contrive so complex but perfect arrangements; as perfect before the circulation of the blood was known to man as it is now! He may learn how not to interfere with this work of nature, but no contrivance of his can supersede or even change it.

The body must be nourished. Made of the dust of the earth, it must have the power of gathering up that dust, and of moulding it into bone and sinew and nerve. This is the problem before us. To do this directly the body has no power. The vegetable kingdom is the channel through which the elements are made available for our use. The corn and the fruits are so much soil, or so much air moulded and flavored to delight us, while they pass into the very tissues of our bodies and become a part of them. We need not speak now of the complex machinery nor the mysterious chemistry by which the transformations are produced; but the course by which the nerve and muscle of the arm, or the delicate materials of the eye, came from the dark cold earth into their present living forms, we know as well as though we could with the eye trace each particle in its complete circuit. The sunlight and the showers bring up the precious fruits. The stomach of man is adapted to the fruits which the earth produces. They are adapted to give him life and enjoyment.

Other adaptations are of importance, though less marked. Sleep has an obvious relation to the revolution of the earth ; our strength to the attraction of the earth ; our power of endurance to its temperature. While other animals are fitted by their nature for the zone they are to inhabit, and by the process of moulting for the change of seasons, man, made to wander over the whole earth, to change his place rapidly, has no fixed provision for his protection. He is left to clothe himself, and thus to fit himself at any time for any place on this earth of which he is the lord and ruler.

We find our bodies then wonderfully adapted to our wants, to give us a knowledge of the world and minister to our pleasure. Things are fitted for their use. We want no chemistry and no anatomy to tell us this. It would be just as apparent to a reasonable being that the body of man is fitted for its work, adapted to the world and adapted to the intelligent being that inhabits the body, though he had never looked beneath the skin and knew nothing of the curious chemical changes in the body, as it would to the best anatomist and physiologist in the world. We know that our eyes are fitted for sight, our ears for hearing, our limbs for walking, our tongues for speech, and our hands for cunning work. If we can look upon a little child when first waking to consciousness of a new world, or upon a trained man in the fulness of his strength, and not feel that there is a perfect adaptation of means to ends to bring the person into proper relations to this world in which it is to dwell, then the scalpel may remain in its case, and the crucible of the chemist may remain cold. They can simply multiply proof, but they can never present any proof higher in kind than we have without them. It may be said that they show more special contrivance in the structure of the body, and that the principle of perfect adaptation is continued to the last analysis of every organ and every process ; and this is true. But if this adaptation is not seen and recognised as proof of an intelligent Creator at the outset, then it never will be seen. When you fairly come to the edge of the ocean, if your friend cannot see it, he never will, though he sail a thousand leagues upon it. If we see that man is fitted to this world, the question naturally arises, was he fitted to a world eternally existing, or was the earth made in reference to him ? The earth was before man, that is, before his body. His body was either fashioned to the existing world, or the world was all pre-arranged in reference to the being that should be placed upon it. Either of these suppositions implies design, and would be enough to establish the existence of a Personal Creator. There is a great deal of discussion as to what constitutes personality. But man is a person, and his wants have been fully understood and provided for. Grant, if you please, that we existed from all eternity, and that it is only in connection with the body that we become conscious ; still, we find ourselves with these bodies which we did not prepare. We know that we have no more direct power over the structure and growth of our own bodies, or of our offspring, than we have over the bodies of other persons. The body of the savage is as perfect in all its parts as the body of him who can number every bone and locate every nerve. The knowledge implied in the structure of our bodies, which fits them so perfectly to our wants, is the same in kind as we possess, but infinitely higher in degree. It is of the same kind, because we can understand the work and approve of it. It is higher, because we feel conscious that we never could have devised it.

We need not spend time in pointing out the exact adaptation of each part of the body, in form, to its function. Every part is so well adapted to its office, that no contrivance of man could improve it. He can discover no new principle in science that might have been introduced to better advantage. We do not suppose that the most ardent believer in human improvement expects the time will ever come when human science can suggest a single improvement in the mechanical structure or chemical laboratory of the human system. This wonderful machine is a model towards which he can always work, but which he can never equal. This he is ready to acknowledge, whatever may be his belief as to how it came into existence. The more we dissect and examine, the more every part meets our commendation. We would not dare to alter a single joint, nor add a nerve or tendon ; and when the chemical or vital process is beyond our ken, as it often is, the result worked out in the healthy body is the exact result which is needed for the perfection of the machine. We feel sure that the hidden machinery is wisely adjusted, although so minute as to be beyond the reach of our microscopes. We have first a framework of the best materials we could desire, every piece made on mathematical principles, all parts formed and joined so as to secure the greatest strength and motion where most needed ; so formed as to protect the most important organs, and to give attachment to the hundreds of cords that are to give it motion, perforated here and there for the nerves and arteries. Some of these nerves are taken from the control of the will, but only those which are necessary for carrying on the vital processes. These might become a burden to man, or he might abuse them. The heart asks no leave of us to beat. These bands of telegraphic wires are all bound into symmetrical wholes and covered to protect them from injury, and yet not so covered as to impede their action, or to shut off from the external world those that are needed to establish relations with it. The body, thus wonderfully arranged, is ever kept in order by its own machinery. From one central organ, the stomach, is carried to every part of the system, not only material enough to make all repairs, but, most marvellous of all, just the kind of material which is needed. If lime is wanted, lime is carried. If silica is the required substance, silica is never wanting. If iron, or carbon, or chlorine, or any other element is required, wonderful to tell, at the appointed time, without thought on our part, that element is selected and sent to its appointed place. Every worn piece is carefully removed, made, perhaps, to subserve some secondary use for a time, but finally it is thrown from the machine, while a new piece takes its place. The machine never wears out, but running a certain round, finishes the work for which it was made.

And this is the machine some would have us believe to be the work of chance, or a sort of accumulation of improvements like the steam-engine, with this important difference, that while the steam-engine is the result of all the mechanical skill the greatest men of the world have been able to bring to bear upon it, the human body, thousands of years ago just as perfect as it now is, has become what it is without a personal architect. If one can believe this, we have no controversy with him. We frankly acknowledge that we have no proof that we believe will satisfy him. We do not expect him to believe in a God, and of course not in a Bible. We say that his mind runs in such a channel, and his standard of proof is such, that we can have nothing in common in science, and nothing in religion. But if, on the other hand, when we know that there was an era in the history of this globe when man came to exist for the first time; when we consider all the adaptations of this body to our use, without any contrivance or thought on our part; when we find this machine kept in constant working order, doing its own repairs, completing a given round of labor, if the conditions only are observed; when we see all this, if compelled by the very law of our being to believe that these bodies are the contrivance of a personal Creator, then we have a starting-point. Then we are prepared to show the proof of the handiwork of the same Being in every department of nature—we are prepared for the possibility of a written Word, and of His constant government and control of His works. If we do not see in all this proof of the existence of such a Being, then further search in nature is useless. We must admit the existence of a Being before we can intelligently seek to understand His character and relations. Throwing aside all study of nature as useless, there may, indeed, be metaphysical speculations in regard to the existence of God; but all natural theology and natural religion, as these terms are now understood, vanish. The human mind, even, would not be absolute proof of the existence of such a Being; for it, according to the speculations of Plato, may have existed from all eternity. It is the body alone that we know began to be; and in its perfect adaptation to our personality, created or uncreated, must we find our first argument for a personal Creator, and in the provisions made for it, the first indications of His fatherly care. But the adaptation of the body to the world and its physical forces is not perfect. There is pain and premature death, an absolute struggle for existence. And this antagonism is plainly not necessary in the nature of things. We shall endeavor, in some future lectures, to show that the world, with all its antagonisms, is best for man as he is. His physical nature is rendered liable to suffer, by the very constitution of things, for the benefit of his moral nature, to which the physical is subservient. But why, we may still ask, was it necessary that there should be such an antagonism, that the higher nature could reach its fullest development only through the labor, and pain, and suffering, of the lower nature? We do not believe such an antagonism was necessary, although we must acknowledge that it does exist. It does not come within the scope of these lectures to discuss the theories of these antagonisms, how they were produced, nor their ultimate tendency. We are content to take man and the world as we find them, and attempt to show that this physical antagonism works out for man in his present imperfect state a higher good.

LECTURE III.

ADAPTATION OF ANIMALS TO THE WORLD BY STRUCTURE, FUNCTION, AND INSTINCT.

Adaptation of Animals to the World.—Special adaptations. —Chance excluded.—Man as a physical being differs only in degree.—His sources of enjoyment complex.—In animals nothing but adaptations to this world.—Whole classes to be treated of.—Water Animals.—Microscopic.—Coral Animals.—Jelly-fishes.—Starfishes.—Mollusks.—Perfect provision for each form.—The Pinna.—Saxicavas.—Nautilus. —Worms.— Crustaceans. — Insects.—Fishes.—Reptiles. — Birds.—Mammals.—Fitted for change of season.—Hibernation.—Relation to length of year.—Instinct.—Supplements structure and function.—Gives higher type of life. —Defined.—Intelligence in Animals.— Vegetative life in Animals.—Relation of instinct to specific structure.—The Natica.—Instinct often blind in its action.—The Cicada.— Tent moth. — Migration of fishes. — Conscious parental relation in birds.—Uniformity of action resulting from instinct.—Wide range of instinct in Mammals.—The Muskrat.—Instinct of the young supplemented by that of the parent.—The body and mind fitted for each other.

WE have thus far considered man merely as an animal; and, as such, we have seen the adaptation of his body to the world in which he lives.

His physical structure, and the nature and power of his senses, show that he was either adapted by creation to this globe already existing, or that the globe was fashioned and placed as it now is in anticipation of the being that was to inhabit it. It is impossible to consider the mutual relations of man as a physical being, and this world, to each other, without recognising design in the varied adjustments —design involving the highest wisdom to devise, the greatest skill to execute, and showing the greatest benevolence as characteristic of the designer.

It was impossible for us to trace this relationship without having thrust upon us the varied adaptations having reference to a higher nature than is possessed by any mere animal. This higher nature of man requires a separate discussion; but for the present we pass to the consideration of the lower forms of animal life, and of the vegetable kingdom, to show their adaptations to the world, the adaptations of the two kingdoms to each other, and of the parts of each individual to meet its own wants and necessities.

We have among the lower animals all the general adaptations which we find in man, but varied according to the peculiar position which the animal is to occupy. It is impossible to study any one of them without constantly learning more and more of the perfection of its relations to the world. Each one is not only provided for in general, as an animal, but he is specially provided for as that particular kind of animal. It is impossible to point out one in which continued observation has not detected increased harmony of adaptation between the world and the wants of the animal, as determined by the very idea of his structure. When we have so far understood the structure of an animal as to feel that we have reached the fundamental idea in his creation, we expect all subsequent study will realize that idea more perfectly. If the fundamental idea is a fish, an animal to live in water, and breathe by gills, then every possible variation which we can find will never be a defect, but some modification of the leading plan for carrying out more fully the main idea in connection with some special condition of life. No kind can be found so apparently abnormal in form as not to show wisdom in its fitness for some particular condition of life; no modification of organs so strange, that the naturalist will not look at once for its purpose, and expect to find conditions of life for that animal fully indicating the wisdom of the change in structure. Since there is perfect adaptation for each species and each variety, the number of forms specially provided for thus becomes so great, that anything like chance is excluded. That five hundred thousand different kinds of beings could be perfectly provided for, so that the ingenuity of man cannot suggest a single improvement in reference to any one of them, not only proves design originating from a high intelligence, but leaves no plausible ground for any other explanation.

We have seen that the world is either fitted for man as a sentient being, or he is so adapted to it as to secure enjoyment by the very process of living. In this respect he does not differ essentially from the other members of the animal kingdom. But his enjoyment as a physical being is so linked with that enjoyment which the world in all its relations secures to his higher, intellectual, and moral nature, that it becomes as difficult to separate one source of enjoyment from the other and assign the exact proportion to each nature, as it is to separate those natures from each other in their wonderful blending in the constitution of man. There is, therefore, a certain distinctness gained when treating of the adaptations of the lower animals to the world, which it is impossible to secure when treating of the complex being, man. In the lower animals we find nothing beyond adaptations to this world. They are physical beings only. There is nothing to be eliminated. On the other hand, we can learn the completeness of their adaptations only by observation. For our experience is rendered an imperfect standard on account of this very complexity of our nature.

We propose in the remainder of this lecture to treat mainly of those relationships by which whole classes of animals are fitted to the world, and reserve for a distinct chapter many of those special adaptations by which particular species or varieties are fitted for unusual conditions. But in treating of the adaptations of animals to the world, we must include their general relationships to each other, because their very existence often depends upon such relationships.

The waters are the home of a large proportion of the animal kingdom. In them we find a vast range of animal life beyond the reach of ordinary vision. The microscope may open wonders in a drop. And when we multiply the multitudes of animate beings that dart across the microscopic field by the drops in the pool or on the ocean's surface, from which our drop was taken, computation is impossible and imagination fails to conceive of the numbers that swarm upon the earth. What variety in form, what varied structure and mode of life are found among these atoms of the animal kingdom! We cannot expect yet to understand all their uses and relations. But not one can be found that has not perfect adaptation to the place it inhabits. It glides or rows through the yielding element apparently as intent on pleasure, certainly as intent on securing the means of living, as the highest tribes of land or water. There is adaptation of means to ends in the structure of each one of this multitude of different forms, so that we might find evidence of design even in the structure of organisms so minute and simple as these. But if they were all of one form, and that the most simple which can be found among them, we should still recognise in their very existence an evidence of wise design in the adjustments of the different ranks of the animal kingdom. They confessedly stand at the lowest step of sensitive life. They have wonderful powers of multiplication. They or their germs may even float in the air, so that multitudes are ready to spring into existence wherever the proper conditions of their life can be found. And if we believed, with some, in their spontaneous generation, we should still consider their perfect adaptation in the scale of organic beings as evidence of design. Many of them are so minute that they can feed upon nothing but organic solutions or the finest forms of organic matter just ready to decompose and pass into inorganic gases. They thus stand ever between the organic and inorganic world, the lowest scavengers of nature, to live upon its organic particles, while they themselves become the food of other larger and higher forms of animal life, and they of others, until the mighty whale, the largest animal on the globe, and man, the highest in rank, both are indirectly indebted for a portion of their food to the labors of these unseen atoms of life that turn back inorganic matter into higher channels, preventing the formation of poisons and ministering to the wants of higher beings.

Rising one step higher, we have the great division of radiate animals, the builders of coral domes and islands—the soft jelly-fishes and the starfish tribe. This group alone will furnish material for study for ages to come, but enough is now known of its general adaptations to excite the wonder of every naturalist.

One little body floating through the water fastens on some solid substance, and straightway, by the very law of its growth, a coral tree or coral dome begins to rise. He divides and subdivides or buds till the community numbers thousands. And to each kind is given a distinct form. And these forms so mingle together that coral reefs rise above the ocean and become islands for the abode of man. These little animals, of varied form and of varied nature, are all fitted to some condition of the ocean. The waters bring them their food and the materials of which their reefs and islands are formed. Amidst the constant rolling waves they find their appropriate home. They have power to gather their food from the clear waters, and, by the very law of their growth, to chisel from the overburdened sea the invisible blocks of which their Titanic masonry is composed. What infinite skill was required to adjust all these kinds to their appropriate places, and to fit them for their appointed work!

Nearly allied to the coral builders are the jellyfishes, many of them apparently but little more than vitalized water. But among them we find the same perfection of adaptation. One floats through the water by the gentle pulsations of its whole body, another cuts it with hundreds of glistening cilia, and others still float by air-sacs and are wafted by the winds. Each has its own habits of life, and each has a structure and mode of locomotion fitted to its wants. The means are entirely different, but they in each case secure the end in seuh a manner as meets our approbation. We feel that all the adjustments are complete, that the animal has been perfectly provided for.

The starfish tribe would at first sight seem to be most helpless. But one who has seen the Echinus climbing smooth rocky walls with his delicate sucker feet, or the starfish folded around the oyster or mussel, which, notwithstanding their stony shells, fall an easy prey to him, will never cease to wonder at the adaptations of means to ends among these apparently unfortunate and imperfect members of the animal kingdom. Each member of this group might be selected as a special study and important link in our proof; but it is enough for our present purpose to see that here there has been no less care and no less wisdom manifested in creation than among the higher tribes.

The next grand division in the animal kingdom is the mollusk or shell-fish. The most careless observer is struck with the variety and beauty in color, form, and finish, exhibited in a cabinet of shells. But the shells, beautiful as they are, and full of instruction as they are to the careful observer, are still but the mere outward coverings, and are no more to be compared with the animals that secreted them than the case of a watch is to the perfect combination of wheels and springs which it incloses. We are almost necessarily compelled here to depart somewhat from our prescribed course, for it is by a multitude of special adaptations that this grand division is fitted for the varied condition and mode of life so noticeable among its different members. What different forms of shells may be found upon a single beach; and for every form of shell there is a distinct animal structure and mode of life! But for each one shall be found as perfect adaptation in its structure and instincts, as though that were the only shell-fish in existence. They may be so unlike, that one form shall not even suggest another to us; but when each one is presented, it perfectly commends itself to our judgment in all its relations. The pinna was made for the waves, and her wide, thin shells would seem to be the sport of the waters. But she spins long silken cords, beautiful and strong, and with these glossy cables anchors herself securely. The saxicavas bore into the corals and solid rocks to form a secure resting-place. The myas and kindred tribes bury themselves in sand. The pearly nautilus finds water-tight compartments built in his tiny vessel by the very law of his growth. Before the Argonauts sailed, or the ark floated upon the waters, this modern invention of ship-building was freely used in adapting shells to the wants of their occupants.

Another group, not less remarkable for complexity of relation, are the articulates. The earth-worm that gropes in the soil, the crustacean of the waters, and the countless host of insects, make up this grand division of the animal kingdom. The earth-worm is perfectly fitted for his mode of life. His brothers, made to inhabit the ocean, are perfectly adapted to that place. Some move freely, well provided with organs of locomotion, while others secrete for their protection a solid tube of lime, exposing only those organs used in securing food and purifying the blood. The study of each one of these low forms of life shows a distinct but beautiful adaptation of means to ends; a perfect provision for these humble beings. The crustaceans are the most active scavengers of the ocean. They show wisdom and skill indeed in the perfect joints and varied arrangements of the shelly armor with which they are clothed; but we recognise a higher purpose and more comprehensive relation in the work they were appointed to accomplish—the purification of the waters by the swift destruction of all decaying animal substances found in them. They have been aptly called the insects of the ocean.

Among the insects proper we have another exhaustless list of special adaptations. But one who had never studied their structure or instincts for a single day, could not fail to recognise their general adaptation to the world. It is thrust constantly upon the attention of the most careless observer. He may not know how the thing is done, but he cannot fail to see that it is done. Thousands of different kinds swarm around him; some making day, and others night, the time of their activity. He may regard many of them as pests, but the very fact that they defy all his schemes for their destruction, shows that they are provided for by nature; and so provided for, that the combined efforts of all the men in the world could not extirpate a single insect species. Some live in water, some on land; some fly by day, some by night, and some never fly at all. Some feed upon the honey of flowers, some upon the vilest refuse of the shambles; some upon living plants, others only upon dead, woody fibre. More than a hundred thousand different kinds are known. In this vast multitude of species, what varied forms and natures, what varied instincts and relations to other beings ; and yet each general and special adaptation is perfect in harmonizing all their wants with the structure, the instincts, and relations of this vast host.

The highest type, and that which foreshadowed man when it first appeared upon the earth, are the vertebrates. It embraces the fishes, the reptiles, the birds, and mammals. These higher forms of life are well known, and each type suggests great beauty of adaptation. What is more perfect in its kind than a fish—the salmon, or the shark ! What architect or artist would have the presumption to suggest a better model! How form and fin are fitted for the element in which the animal is to live ! The feathery gills float in the water and sweep out oxygen to purify the blood. The eye is fitted to light coming through the water. And corresponding to every varied instinct, there is change of form to perfect the adaptation.

The loathsome reptile is not less perfect in his kind, though to us often an object of abhorrence.

The snake, without feet, darts like an arrow, and crushes his prey by tightening folds. And most of the reptilian tribe, unable to supply their wants in winter, bury themselves in dens or mud, and nature kindly puts her benumbing hand upon them, and reduces or suspends the vital action till the returning spring gives them another scene of activity.

In the birds, we have an entirely distinct type, but how perfect in its kind ! Aside from the general adaptation by which the bird occupies a distinct place in the animal kingdom, there are numberless special adaptations apparent here, by which every species is fitted for its peculiar condition of life. The form of the bird is as perfect for the air as that of the fish is for the water.

Its bones are hollow, to give it lightness. Its lung capacity is increased to meet the great draft made upon its powers in flying. To give it strength of flight, the muscles are thickened and strengthened, absolutely piled up, around the base of the wing. Need I speak of the fine adjustment of every feather, the eagle's eye, and the varied form of foot and bill to meet the different instincts and conditions of life?

Among the mammals, we find the highest forms approaching man in perfection, and therefore presenting those general adaptations which we have already considered when treating of him. But there are curious forms and varied conditions of life which demand relations entirely distinct from those found in man. The mole is made to pierce the earth, the whale to sport in the waters, the elephant for the jungles of the torrid zone, the white bear for the icebergs of the polar seas;—each one is fitted by instinct, power of endurance, and structure, for the place he is to occupy.

The otter is fitted for both land and water, and has a coat that the water never penetrates. The seal has no protection against the water from his fur; but he and the whale are both clothed with a thick layer of blubber beneath the skin, giving protection from the cold and buoyancy in the waters. This burden of fat, which would weigh down a land animal, is a float to one moving only in the ocean.

Thus we find one animal perfectly fitted for burrowing in the earth, and he comes out smooth and unsoiled as does the mole from the sand and dirt. One delights in heat, another can endure nothing warmer than icy water or the iceberg itself. The walrus and seal, the whale, the polar bear and reindeer, all find a home in the icy north, and each has a mode of life and structure peculiar to itself. But the form, the organic structure, the food, the adaptation to climate, and the instincts, all harmonize. Each animal is a study by itself; each one is wonderful in the harmony of its relations to the world.

Not only are animals fitted for every zone, but by their organic structure or functional change they are fitted for the change of seasons. As winter approaches, Nature thickens the coating of fur; and when spring returns, she plucks out the surplus coating to fit them for the summer months. For those animals, like the bat, the marmot, and the bear, whose food fails in the winter, Nature provides as for the reptiles already mentioned. They enter their dens as winter approaches, and a deep sleep falls upon them; a sleep by which the vital action is changed. The circulation becomes slow, the temperature of the body lowered, and the animal, with its vitality reduced to the lowest point, lives upon its own fat till spring calls him forth again to new supplies of food and new enjoyments. Without this provision these animals would perish in a single winter, and the species become extinct. But Nature has not left them unprovided for. Their vitality is like a burning lamp. In winter the wick is turned down so that the spark of life may remain, and that is all. This hibernation is no ordinary sleep; it is peculiar, and it is something over which the animal has no more control than he has over the change of seasons.

In these general adaptations, we must not forget the relationship of these animals to the length of the year. Were the winter essentially longer than it now is, these hibernating animals could not survive, excepting those rendered quite torpid like some of the reptiles. Those animals that lay up stores of food for winter would find themselves in want. The thickening of the coat and its loss are not the effect of cold and heat, but a change in the system whose machinery has been adjusted to the clock-work of the stars.

We come now to speak of a new principle of adaptation which has been only incidentally referred to. Thus far, we have spoken mainly of fixed relations; those growing out of form, anatomical differences, and functional peculiarities. In regard to all these, the animal is like a plant, plastic in the hands of Nature and entirely passive. He is thrown into the world with a certain structure externally and internally, and to this structure he must conform in some measure, necessarily

The mole cannot pursue insects in the air, nor the whale seek his food upon the land. The structure of both determines where they must live. But in addition to the peculiar structure and functions of each animal, by which, like a plant, he is fitted to the world, there is given to each one an instinct in harmony always with his structure, by which he becomes an active thinking agent, and thus voluntarily adapts himself more perfectly to the world. Instinct simply supplements structure and functions, putting them to the best use, and making a higher type of life possible than could be manifested by structure and function alone. The bee has a structure fitting it for gathering honey, and the rings of the body have the function of secreting wax. Instinct is needed to impel the bee to gather the honey, and to form the scales of wax into the honey-comb. And it is impossible to conceive of any complexity of structure in the bee, or perfection of function by which the varied results of the bee-hive could be secured. But instinct, utilizing the structure and function, exactly harmonizing with them, secures perfect results—most admirable adaptations.

We wish now to inquire more fully what this instinct is, and how far it is proof of design in the creation of these animals. We have no intention of completing the subject here, for we must refer to instinct again, in treating of special adaptations and the mutual relations of the animal and vegetable kingdoms to each other.

Instinct.

Instinct may be defined to be that principle of action implanted in the animal by which he provides for himself, and the continuance of the species. It controls the animal. He acts under its guidance always in a uniform manner under the same conditions, and without instruction. If there comes to be any variation or apparent change in this instinct, it is for a specific purpose; and the change or modification of instinct is as much under law as the change in form and structure by which new varieties are originated from the same species. It is this uniformity of instinct that gives uniformity of action to the same species of animals all over the world. It determines what the animal shall be as a sentient, voluntary agent. This description might be enlarged, but I am inclined to think it covers instinct proper.

Although it is difficult to draw the dividing line, we must recognise in some animals an intelligence distinct from instinct, and higher; an intelligence by which they enter into certain relations to man, comprehend his wishes, understand his commands, and form attachments to him. They must have a degree of intelligence to understand so fully as some of them do intelligent man. If any choose to say that we have here simply higher manifestations of instinct, then we must enlarge our definition; for many things comprehended and done by domesticated animals are neither necessary for their own existence, nor for the continuance of the species. When the watch-dog guards his master's treasure, it is for man and not for himself that the work is done.

There is in all animals an organic or vegetable life, which they have in common with the plants. In the lowest forms of animal life we can hardly recognise anything higher than this organic and functional action. There is certainly but the mere glimmering of instinct needed, because in the lowest types structure and function can complete the adaptation of the animal to the world without the intervention of volition. What needs the oyster more than the plant? So far as we can judge, it has no more conscious relation to its young than the tree has to its seed. The production of its young is simply the result of organic change, the law of its growth, like the budding and blossoming of the tree. The movement of the shell seems to be voluntary. Certain it is that volition is reduced to its minimum, and consequently instinct, since instinct is always connected with volition. We must, then, in animals of such low type, recognise mainly adaptation of structure and function. But, one step higher in this division of animals, we see marked cases of the relation of instinct to specific structure—the absolute necessity of the combination of the two to secure the well-being of the animal. The *Natica*, a shellfish found on our coast, can hunt his prey in the sand. He feeds upon other shell-fish, sometimes upon his own kind. He is armed with a long, rasp-like tongue, and instinct teaches him to use it, in piercing the shell that is closed in vain against him. Without this instrument he would be powerless; with it he would be just as powerless without the instinct to use it as he does. But the instrument and the instinct combined constitute an important adaptation of the animal to the world. They are evidently as much the parts of the same plan as are the different organs by which the vital processes are carried on.

It is only when we come to those animals where provision for their young calls instinct into play, that it becomes most marked; though in many cases we are compelled to believe that the acts of the parent in providing for its young are no more understood by that parent as having relation to its young, than the tree consciously provides for its flower when it folds it in the bud. Certain acts were needed to carry out fully what organs and functions commenced but could not complete. A blind impulse is upon the animal to perform those needed acts. And that impulse we call instinct; an impulse of a voluntary agent indeed, but an impulse so strong that it becomes like a wheel in machinery, which is so important that it makes the machine what it is, and without it all would fail. There is, on the part of the animal, will to do the act; but, so far as we can see, no desire to refrain from doing, and oftentimes no more knowledge why the thing is done, than there is in the flower when it bends itself towards the light. What knows the cicada, the so-called seventeen-year locust, that has burrowed as a grub in the earth for half a human generation, when it comes forth to deposit its egg in the limb of the oak, that in due time, after her own death, her young will find their resting-place in the earth? She obeys a blind impulse. The limb is pierced and the egg deposited. She has by instinct made use of both structure and function of organs, and thus completed her adaptation to the world in preserving the species. This is only one instance from a great number in which the parent never sees its young, and never can see them, and yet provides completely for them.

And the young cicadas that hatch from those eggs after their parents have perished and disappeared, find their way to the earth, and there, under the guidance of this instinct, provide for themselves; Nature taking care that the development of all the thousands shall progress so uniformly, that when seventeen years have passed away, on a given day they are all ready to come forth for their few gala-days of life. As they come forth only at the end of seventeen years, and then live only a few days, it is necessary for the preservation of the species that they should all come forth at the same time. They are like ten thousand chronometers all set to run seventeen years, and all the changes in form are accompanied by change in instinct, so that when the years have revolved, structure and instinct have completed their work, and the ten thousand chronometers are all found in perfect adjustment.

The *tent-moth* also lays her eggs upon the apple-twig, closely packed and varnished to protect them till the warmth of spring wakes the young to life, when the new leaf is ready for their food. But the mother dies when her instinct has completed the relations by which the species is to be continued. While forests of trees invited her by their slender twigs, on no tree did she put an egg that would not the next spring put forth a leaf fitted for the food of her young.

Many fishes make long journeys to deposit their eggs in places fitted for their progeny ; and when that work is done, parental solicitude ceases. The parent returns to the ocean, and the young fish, when hatched and grown to the proper size, knows the way to the great deep as well as though its parent had remained to act as guide. Nay more, it knows when and where to go, as by a divine knowledge. The thousands that go out for the first time find their feeding-grounds, and never forget to return when the time comes for them to deposit their spawn. Some species seek the cold, and some the warm waters. Some seek the fresh streams, and some the salt ocean ; each one seeks the proper condition for its young, which it is never to see, and to which it probably has no conscious relation. The impulse is upon it, and it obeys. It leaves its accustomed haunts, where would seem to be the most natural place for breeding, and seeks out a far distant location to which instinct guides it. This impulse was given to complete its relation to the world, and is the same evidence of design as the form of the fin or the structure of the gill. The wisdom of the design and the skill of the designer are shown by the perfection with which instinct supplements function, and thus completes the adaptation of each species to the world.

In the bird, instinct goes further still; and in every case there finally comes to be a conscious relation of the parent to the young. It hardly seems possible that all the acts that relate to the young are performed with a consciousness of the coming parental relation. Undoubtedly the migration of the bird is as much a matter of blind impulse as the migration of the fish. We judge so because we see the bird following such a uniform line of action in other respects. In certain things, birds of the same species act under the guidance of instinct with as great uniformity as the same species of trees in the arrangement of their leaves, or the pattern of their flower. So that while the act is truly voluntary, it is as certain to take place under similar conditions as any organic change in a plant, and the act is performed by a wisdom and skill given, and not acquired. The bird that has never seen a nest will build one as all its kind have done before, selecting the same class of materials and combining them in the same manner. If there is any conscious relation to the young that should lead to the preparation of the nest, how can we account for that impulse that thus, without instruction, induces every bird of the same species to build of the same materials, to select similar situations, and to weave those materials in the same manner? A hundred different species of birds of the same size, and, so far as we could judge beforehand, equally well accommodated with the same kind of nest, will build a hundred kinds; but a thousand birds of the same kind, without concert, in different parts of the world, some old, having built many nests, some young, now building for the first time, all without instruction, build exactly alike—the young as skilfully as the old. What but a divine wisdom and skill guides the architects of the air? The bird that has never before seen an egg, sits upon the nest until the young birds appear. What tells her that in that egg is a germ of life that the warmth of her body will wake to activity? Up to this point we cannot but regard all her actions as blind, and unconscious of their end, as the act of the fish and the insect that are never to see their young. As she works perfectly to secure an end, and is yet entirely ignorant of that end while she works, she must be under the guidance of a wisdom not her own. Nor does it alter the question whether that wisdom be the result of an impulse constantly imparted to her, or the certain, uniform result of her organization. But when the young bird appears, it needs in its helpless state a parent's care, and the instinct of the parent becomes quickened and rises to a higher plane by a conscious relation, while the almost unconscious instinct of the young instantly responds to this higher instinct of the parent. The mother brings food, and every bill in the nest is raised and opened to receive it. The old partridge flutters like a wounded bird in your path to attract attention, and gives the note of warning, at which every one of the brood vanishes as though the earth had swallowed them. Every fowl knows the hawk to be an enemy as far as he can be seen, though seen now for the first time.

In the large majority of these cases, and in others that might be mentioned, it is impossible to refer the act of these animals to previous instruction, to experience, or to conscious relation. The impulse is upon them; they act, they know not why. We see that those acts are for the actors the perfection of wisdom. We know the wisdom is not in them. It must be in Him who implanted the impulse.

Among mammals, of course excluding man, we find instinct taking a still wider range. It does not work with that almost mathematical precision seen in the bee and other lower animals; but while the animal remains in a wild state, it is so perfect and uniform in its action that every species is distinguished for the same habits, and every individual of the species under its direction seeks the same end for himself, and seeks it in the same way. The beaver, the otter, the fox and the marmot, the lion and the whale, remain essentially unchanged in their natures and uniform in their modes of life from generation to generation. The wider range of their instinct is seen when they are brought into new relations. They are then found to have greater variety in their adaptation than the lower tribes. In many of them, there seems indeed to be an intelligence quite distinct from instinct, which is called out especially when they are brought into constant conflict with man, or when they are subjected to his control and act under his direction.

But this instinct in the higher animals may itself take so wide a range as to be mistaken for intelligence by the casual observer, though just as distinct from it as the blindest instinct of the lowest tribes. The muskrat burrows in high banks along the rivers, and one who had seen him only in such places would suppose this to be his only mode of life. But if he cannot find banks, then he builds a house of mud and weeds in the open air, upon some stump or knoll, or shallow place in the water. This house, seen for the first time, would strike an observer, who had seen this animal before only among the steep banks of rivers, as the work of no mean intelligence, adapting itself to new conditions. But that house is built on a specific plan, and is just such in all particulars as all muskrats would build in any part of the world, when shut out for the first time from the high banks in which they had been accustomed to burrow. That house is then the work of instinct; an instinct that certainly covers two modes of building, and perhaps others. The same thing is undoubtedly true of many animals. Their instinct is not entirely exhausted in its resources by their present condition in life; and thus, when thrown into new conditions, they often meet them in a manner surprising to us. And therefore we hear of change of instinct, or the development of new instincts. But if the animals are sure always to meet these new conditions in the same way, they plainly act under the guidance of instinct; for intelligence acts in no such fixed directions.

Among these higher tribes, then, we find all that is needed for the animal's good, for the individual or for the species. In the youngest, it is sufficient for its wants, because it is supplemented by the instinct of the parent. It is simply more varied in these higher tribes because their relations to the world are more varied. And if, in some animals, we recognise intelligence, we always find it subordinate to instinct, so as to work in the same line for the animal's good; so that instinct, and not intelligence, controls the animal. In every kind, from the highest to the lowest, we find the thinking being just high enough in its mental powers to inhabit the body in which it is placed, with mind enough to use that body. Mind and body are both fitted to each other, and both work together in perfect relation to the world. They are parts of one comprehensive plan, perfect in its conception and execution; a plan that commends itself to the wisdom of man, so far as he can comprehend it, but higher, vaster, and more perfect than he could himself devise.

LECTURE IV.

SPECIAL CONTRIVANCES—PRESERVATION OF SPECIES.

Special adaptations.—Functions.—Cases mentioned by Paley. —Ball and socket joint.—Cuttle-fish.—Terebratulas.— Leech.—Gnats.—Bees.—Spiders.—Variation of substance according to their instinct.—Silk-worm.—Lobsters and Crabs.—Rattlesnake.—Birds.—Fitted for flight.—Oil gland—Structure of birds of prey.—Water birds.—Form of bills.—Grebe and Loon.—Waders.—Woodpeckers.—Development from use considered.—Homologous structure.— Limbs of animals.—Teeth.—Whales and Rays.—Crop of birds.—Preservation of species.—Definition of.—Multiplicity of germs.—Distribution of seeds.—Springs, balloons, hooks, barbs.—Same end secured by diverse means.— Vitality of seeds.—Fertilization of flowers.—Growth of plants supplementing instinct.—Carnivorous animals limited in number.—Destruction of animals provided for.— Suffering and death.—Goodness of Deity to be vindicated. —Man's enjoyment and suffering on different grounds.— Present discussion confined to lower animals.—Suffering never inflicted for its own sake.—Enjoyment in excess of suffering.—Death secures parental relation.—Sum of enjoyment increased by succession of animals.—Introduction of carnivorous animals increases the sum of enjoyment.— Disease.—Provision for its alleviation.—Design may show cruelty.—Apparent cruelty often real benevolence.—Creator Infinite in His attributes.

THERE seems to some minds to be great evidence of design in special adaptations. A loop, or hinge, or lens, is easier understood than the harmonies which embrace the relations of whole classes or kingdoms of nature. It is in the skilful presentation of special adaptations that the excellence of Paley's Natural Theology mainly consists. Very little can be added to the examples he has selected for illustration. The most of them are still recognised as good, and most of them are so plain that they were as well understood in his day as now, with all the advance in science. We shall not, however, confine ourselves to simple structure; for the function of an organ may be as special in its adaptation as structure possibly can be. Among the strongest cases mentioned by Paley, is the ligament within the hip-joint, fastening the ball and socket firmly together. It is a strong case, but this contrivance did not appear for the first time in man, nor is it confined to the higher animals. Some of the sea-urchins, dug out of the old geological formations, have their spines fastened to them by a ball and socket joint of most exquisite workmanship, and a ligament to hold the joint in place. This special contrivance appeared just as soon as an animal was created whose general structure and habits called for it. It has been continued from that time to this, and is now found in members of the animal kingdom furthest removed from each other in their organization and rank.

Among the shell-fish, we find almost every species with some special adaptation of structure corresponding to its instincts and mode of life. The cuttle-fish is a combination of special adaptations. He has a syphon tube, through which he forces a jet of water, that, by its reaction, enables him to move with great rapidity. He is also provided with an ink-bag, from which he ejects a cloud of colored fluid, and thus baffles his foe by the rapidity of his backward motion, and the inky screen that he raises before him. His tentacles are lined with miniature air-pumps, by means of which he fastens securely upon his prey. There is the nicely-fitting receiver, with its yielding edge, adapting itself to various surfaces, and there is the piston and the muscle to move it. In some species, a sharp claw rises from the piston and enters the victim by the very action that draws him firmly against the suckers; and the two longest tentacles, thus fastened upon their prey by the double action of pressure and sharpened claws, are held firmly together by other suckers, like forceps by the rivet, so that no instrument that man could devise would be so perfectly fitted for its purpose.

The silken cords by which the pinnas and mussels anchor themselves have already been described. The perforated shell of the Terebratula, through which the fleshy anchor-cable is drawn, is of similar character.

Among the articulates, the examples of special adaptation meet us on every hand. No more perfect lances are found than those that arm the leech for his bloody work. If we cannot see the use of all the structure for the leech in his common mode of life, no one who has seen him fasten upon his prey with his miniature cupping-glasses, make the incision and deplete the veins, can regard the whole animal other than as a special and most perfect instrument for bloodletting.

The voracious gnat that robs our veins does it by an instrument fine as a hair, but certainly wonderfully fitted for its work.

The proboscis of the bee is just the instrument needed for extracting honey from the flower. Her sting, with its bag of poison, cannot be improved upon as a means of defence.

The spinneret of the spider—little bags perforated with a multitude of holes—is perfect as an instrument; and the material from which this delicate thread is spun, is beyond all human power to equal. With this curious magazine of material, ever ready to be drawn into silken cords, one species suspends himself in air, swings from wall to wall, and spreads his net for his insect prey; another lines his dwelling with softest tissue; and yet another fashions diving-bells that defy the action of the water. The main design of the instrument is the same, but the work is varied according to the instinct of each species. The nature of the substance is somewhat varied too, undoubtedly; but the spinneret and silk-producing fluid, both adapted to each other, appear in every case a special adaptation to the creature's wants. And when the spider has twisted his hundreds of threads together, man still seeks for this cable for the cross-lines of his telescope, because he can spin no single thread as fine. The silk-worm is provided with a similar material from which it spins its cocoon, a temporary resting-place for itself while passing into a higher form of life. The lobster and crab are provided with a solid armor completely fitting all their limbs and joints ; an armor so solid that growth would seem to be impossible. But nature gives them the power at certain seasons of throwing off this solid case, and after a rapid expansion of the body, of secreting another covering adapted to the increased size.

The fang of the rattlesnake is the perfection of an instrument for his cruel work. It is a tube, but the end is flattened upon one side so as to bring the point to a keen edge ; and the poison, ever ready, is driven out by the very blow that makes the wound. This fang, so essential to the animal to supplement his instinct, is liable to be broken by his savage blows ; but nature has placed the germs of others in the same socket, to grow and take the place of the one lost. His rattle, which gives the warning before he strikes, is a curious piece of mechanism, not made for the animal ; but being so perfectly fitted for its work, and so in keeping with the instincts of the animal, we cannot but regard this as a special provision that this deadly reptile might not needlessly destroy life.

The whole bird tribe is a marvel of special adaptations. The whole external structure, which characterizes birds, is itself a special adaptation to the external world ; and when we consider the means by which this perfect relationship is secured, we are delighted by the skill manifested in the whole plan, and the perfection with which that plan is carried out.

Flight is secured by the most skilful mechanism of feathers, and the accumulation of muscle around the shoulder of the bird. What can be more perfect in its mechanism than each feather of the wing, —its hollow elastic shaft securing lightness and strength? Then we have the skilful joining of all the lines of the web, and that combination of barbs and hooks that has ever challenged the admiration of men. The position of all the feathers is such, that by expanding the wing, they cover the greatest extent possible with no openings between them. The muscles are not only of great strength, but they are so arranged that the wing strikes the air at the required angle to enable the bird to rise and completely control its motions. And then observe the compactness with which the instrument is folded away when not in use. The great expenditure of muscular force is provided for by the great lung capacity, the whole viscera even being bathed with air.

The bird by instinct trims its feathers, when the web has been broken; and because the feathers are too long, and not of a structure like hair, to receive from the body the oil which they need to preserve their gloss, nature has provided a never-failing bottle of oil on the back of the bird which instinct has taught it how to use.

In the bird of prey we find the sharp, hooked bill for tearing its victim, and sharp talons for seizing it ; both perfectly fitted for their work and harmonizing with each other.

In water-birds we find the web foot for swimming, and bills fitted for their mode of life. The wide-billed ducks have strainers on the sides of the mouth, because they gather their food from the mud and water. The narrow-billed sheldrake has the sharp saw-teeth which his instinct teaches him to use in holding his fishy prey. In those birds whose habits confine them mostly to the water, like the grebe or loon, the leg is thin as a knife, that it may cut the water with as little resistance as possible, and each toe is an oar of most exquisite construction. The feathers of such birds are waterproof. The waders, like the herons and snipes, are provided with long legs and long necks to harmonize with them in pursuit of prey and in flying. The feathers on the legs of these waders do not grow down to the middle joint as in other birds, but keep out of the way of the water like sleeves well rolled up. So perfectly are the bills of all birds adapted to their instincts, that from the bill alone the habits of a bird one had never seen could be judged of with great accuracy. The woodpecker is the best and most familiar example of this special and harmonizing structure. Its sharp bill is for piercing wood ; its foot, with two toes in opposite directions, is just fitted for clinging to the limbs on either side, or upon the bark. Its tail-feathers are stiffened and sharpened at the points to act as supports ; its tongue is barbed like a steel spear. What a perfect specimen he is; the general plan is perfect, the details are perfect, the execution is perfect. That tongue that cannot utter an articulate sound, speaks in a language which every reasonable man must understand. It was not only skill that planned those barbs, but it was a higher skill that so organized the stomach and whole system of the bird that the blood should carry to the tip of the tongue just the materials needed to form that spear. And when one talks of development through use, it is incumbent upon him to show some ground for believing that use of an organ can, not only change its form, but can so affect the system that it shall provide entirely new material to complete the change.

It is impossible to observe so many skilful and beautiful arrangements as are combined in the structure of birds, without admiring the wisdom and skill of their Creator. The feather in all its parts, the oil gland, and the crop, are all special adaptations, and all of them combined for the same purpose, to fit the bird for its place in the animal kingdom, to carry out first the leading idea of a typical bird. And then by special adaptations, we have the typical bird modified, giving us the countless varieties, each one fitted for its sphere of life, and altogether apparently exhausting the possibilities of bird-life. So many light, aerial ships are to be launched—and what a wealth of contrivance in the distribution of force, and in the rigging of each little craft! What man could suggest a single improvement in the structure of one of them, to better fit it for its instincts and mode of life? Let him consider the eagle that seems never to tire, while he rises beyond the reach of vision; and that gem of beauty, the humming-bird, as suspended in the air he sips the honey like a bee from the flower; and in the whole winged tribe, consider the perfect adaptation to their place by special contrivances, and he need not go further in search of the handiwork of infinite wisdom and skill.

We find in each of the four great divisions of the animal kingdom a series of homologies, or likeness of structure. The organs are constructed upon the same plan, but modified for specific use. It is this unity of plan and variety of modification that especially arrests our attention as the work of a wise Being. The wisdom is shown in devising a plan capable of such infinite variations, and skill is manifested in giving such variety as shall adapt the organs to the use of animals so diverse, without once swerving from the plan in which the grand idea is embodied. Among the vertebrate animals, this unity of plan and diversity of execution are most easily understood. The fin of the fish, the wing of the bird, the claw of the lion, the foot of the ox, and the hand of man, are identical in their plan of structure; but the plan is modified to such an extent to meet the wants of each species, that to a casual observer there would seem but little, if any relationship between them. But when their bony parts are compared, their similarity is not only apparent, but we are struck with admiration at the permanence of the plan which appears through all the modifications. Some bones are lengthened, some are shortened, and some are indeed wanting; but enough are left to give an outline. The pectoral fin of the first fish in the Silurian seas, in the dim geologic ages, was the first sketch of the hand of man which Nature introduced upon the globe. And from that simple sketch she never varied; but the plan became more definite and perfect, and higher in its use, as higher animals were introduced, till an organ was produced that is a fit servant of the intelligence with which man is endowed.

In the teeth of animals we have a marked adaptation to the instincts and desires of the various species. The *Rodents*, of which the beaver and squirrel are well known types, have their cutting-teeth almost as hard as steel upon the front, and softer upon the inside, so that constant use is sure to give them a sharp, cutting edge. And because these teeth are subjected to such constant wear, they are made to grow continuously. We see here a need to be supplied, and the structure of the tooth and the unusual condition of growth are both combined to secure the needed result. We referred to the early introduction of the ball and socket joint in the Echinus for the joining of his spines upon his shell. The same animal has the teeth constructed on the same plan as the Rodents, though they are five in number, and move concentrically.

In carnivorous animals, the teeth, in form and

position, are fitted to cut and tear. Their points are sharp, and those in the upper and lower jaws pass each other like scissor-blades. In those that feed upon insects, fine, sharp points fit into corresponding indentations.

In herbivorous animals, the modifications are numerous, but always adapted to the food. In the horse, the layers of hard and soft material alternate in the crown of the tooth, so that under constant use the surface of the tooth is like a millstone that is picked by the very process of grinding. And in the moose and deer that browse, the tooth grows sharp upon the outer edge like a chisel. The mouth of the Greenland whale is another marked case of adaptation in an animal for the food upon which he lives. This largest animal upon the globe feeds upon the minute mollusks and crustaceans that float in countless numbers in the northern seas. For such food, teeth would be useless. His huge mouth is fitted with a strainer formed by the fringes of the whalebone plates. By this curiously constructed net he gathers his food from the waters.

In the mouths of some rays and other fishes that feed upon shell-fish, there is a solid pavement of bone, both above and below, for crushing the shells. In birds where no teeth are found, and the food is mostly solid seeds, a compensation is found in the crop, in which the food is held for a time and gradually dropped into the powerful muscular stomach fitted to grind as well as digest.

Natural Theology.

We have thus given some of the more common examples which show that, in addition to that machinery of structure and those chemical and vital changes common to all animals, by which they are fitted to the world, there cannot be a single species found among the complex animals, where there cannot be pointed out some special adaptation, by which it occupies a particular place, or performs some function peculiar to itself. These adaptations remind us of the ingenuity of man; they often suggest contrivances to him; they are never such that he could improve upon them for the purpose intended. We might enter the vegetable kingdom with the same result, but enough will appear respecting this in our general discussion.

We have selected examples at random. But we might add, that the whole progress of science is simply a more perfect unfolding of adaptations, general and special; and our work with them is done, when we have shown that each species has received the special care of the Creator. And this brings us next to notice the preservation of species.

We regard each species as a distinct and original creation. It embodied some distinct idea; but, for our present purpose, no particular theory of the origin of species is needed. The first provision for the preservation of species which attracts our attention is the multiplicity of germs produced. It seems as though there had been a calculation of chances, and those organic beings whose conditions of life expose their young to destructive agencies, were made prolific to an amazing degree. In some of the lower forms of animal life, where there is no care for the young, the eggs are counted by millions. The same general law is true of plants. Their seeds, as a general thing, are food for animals, and are exposed to destroying agencies, and their productiveness seems in proportion to the chances they must run. Who can compute the thousands of acorns that must have fallen from some of the old oaks that count their centuries of growth?

Among the plants we find special contrivances for the distribution of their seeds, that must be reckoned as one means of preserving species. The *Impatiens* opens its capsule with a sudden spring which scatters the seed far from the parent stalk. The cranesbill does the same, except that each seed is held by its own little spring, which is ready to throw its seed when ripe, like a stone from a sling. Numerous seeds are edged with delicate membranes, like the maple and elm, so that every gust of wind scatters them broadcast upon the earth. Others still sail on silky balloons constructed with most exquisite skill. One dandelion-seed would seem to be enough to cut up all atheism by the roots. Its finely spread balloon, with its seed hanging like a miniature car as it floats through the air, is certainly a piece of mechanism perfect for the end in view. The seeds of other plants are armed with hooks, barbed like finest spears or hooks of steel. Almost every person who has rambled in the fields or woods in autumn has been annoyed by the seeds of vile weeds that fasten upon his clothing. But when he pulls them off and casts them from him, he has accomplished nature's purpose, the distribution of the plant. The detested burdock fastens its whole packages of seeds upon the passer-by with its multitude of polished hooks, so that the ripened covering is sure to be ruptured before it can be unfastened, and thus its seeds are scattered upon the soil. These are a few of the examples of that special care which Nature takes, that the germs of life which she has prepared may be scattered where they may find the conditions of their germination. We can hardly help recognising design in the distribution by means of animals, and by the waters of the ocean ; but these may by some be regarded as accidental. But when we see the machinery of springs, of balloons, and cunningly-formed hooks and barbs, we recognise a purpose, and the means wisely adapted to carry out that purpose. We see the same thing aimed at in both kingdoms. We see the end secured by means the most diverse, so unlike that one would never suggest the other, much less do they impress us as resulting from any process of development.

   Still another provision is found in the great vitality of certain seeds. Some of them have germinated after having lain for centuries. It is no uncommon thing to find the seeds in old fields springing up with vigor, when the soil is turned and they are brought under the influence of the sun and air.

We shall incidentally, in other connections, point out many of nature's plans for the preservation of species. Instinct brings the bee to fertilize the flower, that but for her would fail to produce seed, so that in time the species would become extinct. The tree provides for its young by a law of its own growth, and the animal by instinct makes provision for its young wherever peculiar conditions are needed for their preservation. The vegetable kingdom sometimes supplements that instinct, and provides by special growth both food and home for the insect young. So perfectly are all these means adjusted, that, so far as we know, no animal or plant has become extinct in modern times except through the agency of man.

But it is not enough that the species should be preserved; there must also be a balance of species. Too great a preponderance of one kind would be attended by injury or destruction of others. The number of each species must be determined by its relations to other organic beings. Carnivorous animals cannot be more numerous than herbivorous. Birds of prey must be few in number compared with those upon which they feed. There is thus a certain limit fixed to the relative number of different animals, by the amount of food fitted to sustain each kind, and by the climate which they can endure. But nature has not left all to push on to the utmost bounds of possible existence. She has plainly set limits to the power of increase among the great destroyers of animal life, that the species which she has created may not struggle for existence in vain. The animals that live by the destruction of others are not less in number because only a few can possibly survive. They are less by creation, by the law of their increase. The larger and more destructive any animal is, the less rapidly does it multiply. So that while nature evidently makes provision for the destruction of animals by others on a vast scale, it is not a part of her plan to increase any species without supplying adequate food for its support. The tribes that are most prolific are followed ever by multitudes of enemies, so that their number shall not be unduly increased. Some few examples there are, like the locust tribes, that show us what might be the result were there not the well arranged balance which so generally prevails in nature.

In order to secure the balance of species a mighty machinery is at work, bringing suffering and death. We recognise design in the machinery; but what shall we say of the goodness of a Being whose wisdom reaches its end through pain and suffering, however perfectly the end may be secured?

We may speculate on the possible constitution of animals by which they might be freed from pain and suffering. But it is not certain at all that such a constitution is possible in a world like this, without at the same time diminishing the capacity for enjoyment. And if we accept the present animal constitution as a wise and good one, then the destruction of animal life can be fully vindicated as a manifestation of goodness.

Disease and Death.

In considering this subject, we will, for the present, exclude man. For though he is liable to pain and death like the meanest animal on the globe, he has a moral nature, and claims to be immortal ; so that it is possible to put pain and suffering on entirely different grounds when considering man, from what we can when considering the lower animals. Man's highest enjoyment or suffering is certainly not connected with his physical system. He can in his moral strength despise both pain and death. We shall have occasion to refer to this subject when treating of the adaptation of the world to the moral nature of man. But for the present, we wish to inquire what can be inferred of the character of the Creator, from the pain and death of the lower animals.

The two main points which we wish to make are these :

First.—That by death among the lower animals, a greater amount of enjoyment is secured to them as a class than could be secured without it.

Second.—In disease and all methods by which death is produced, no case can be pointed out in which suffering is plainly inflicted for its own sake.

If it can be shown that happiness among animals is in excess of misery, and that there are provisions made for relieving pain and curing disease, then the burden is on those who doubt either the existence or perfect benevolence of the Creator, to show that there is not a wise and good reason for the existence of so much pain and suffering as are found in the world. They are here; but since no case appears where they are inflicted for their own sake, we infer that their existence is compatible with the highest benevolence of a Creator, who through those means may be able to secure the best results upon the whole. If we take any class of animals, there is no question but the amount of their physical enjoyment vastly surpasses the pain and suffering which they endure. The majority of animals have a lifetime of physical enjoyment with but a single pang, or the suffering of a few moments, when death comes. But the question returns, why should the pang of death come at all, and how is increase of enjoyment secured by it? We answer:

First.—Any constitution of animals that excluded death would exclude the parental relation. And the love and care of offspring are a source of delight to all the higher tribes, and we have no reason for supposing that there may not be enjoyment connected with reproduction among the lower tribes, even where there is no conscious parental relation.

Second.—In consequence of death, we have new generations coming each year into existence for enjoyment, instead of the continuance of the same individuals for ever. There is no question but the sum of animal enjoyment is increased beyond computation by the succession of animals upon the globe.

Third.—The number of animals that now exist is vastly greater than could exist if all were vegetable feeders.

If now we grant that these animals have more enjoyment than suffering during their existence, any method that increases the number of animals adds to the sum of animal enjoyment in the world. If we consider the vegetable-feeders that are destroyed, their destruction by carnivorous animals cannot be reckoned a misfortune to them as a class. It shortens animal enjoyment in the individual, but it saves individual suffering in the end, and increases the sum of enjoyment for the whole class Many more individuals among vegetable-feeders come to maturity now than could find food if all were allowed to live the full term of life. We thus have the enjoyment of several young animals for a short time, cut off in a moment, instead of the enjoyment of one animal living a much longer time with weakened powers of enjoyment and suffering in the end from hunger and weakness of old age. There can be no doubt in which way the greatest amount of animal enjoyment is secured. Old age to man is desirable, cheered by the companionship of friends ; and disease itself may prove a moral blessing. But for brutes, old age and disease are not thus mitigated. And provision has been made that among wild animals they should be impossible, or of the shortest possible duration. When the powers of an animal have been weakened by old age or disease, some watchful enemy is generally upon his track, and his sufferings are ended in a moment. By the introduction of beasts and birds of prey, then, animals are destroyed with less pain than by disease or old age, and their destruction is a source of enjoyment to the destroyers. Granting, then, that the mere capability of suffering is no proof of malevolence, the introduction of carnivorous animals certainly shows a benevolent Creator. For by this provision we have a saving of suffering to one portion of the animal kingdom, and at the same time an increase of enjoyment for another. But we have also death from disease. It would certainly be difficult to show benevolence here, were there not plainly provisions made for the alleviation of suffering. And all that we feel bound to show is, that suffering is not inflicted for its own sake. That there is design and plan in disease, has been of late fully illustrated. Indeed, were there not, the study of diseases would be hopeless. But design does not by any means always imply benevolence. It may show cruelty as well. Yet sometimes there may be apparent cruelty where there is the fullest benevolence. It is easy to see the design of the surgeon, as he severs the flesh and bone of the limb apparently sound. It is to cut off the limb. And if we saw the operation now for the first time, and knew nothing of surgery, and nothing of the cause of the act, it would seem to us unmitigated cruelty. But if we saw the operator first put the patient into an insensible state so as to diminish pain, and then tend him carefully till a cure was completed, we should have good grounds for supposing that the operator was not a malevolent being; but on the other hand, we should reasonably infer that there was the controlling principle of benevolence in the whole transaction, even in that part which seemed most cruel.

Now the animal system is liable to pain from disease and accident. This fact standing by itself, would look like malevolence in the Creator. But since there is provision for counteracting disease and diminishing pain, even among the lower animals, we not only have a right, but are bound to infer that the Being who gave the capacity of suffering and allowed disease, did so for a wise purpose, and with no malevolent design. Certain it is that remedies have been provided in nature both for the alleviation of pain and the cure of disease. And if a bone is broken, nature has her machinery ready to join the fractured portions together, and so surround their roughened points that suffering shall be brought to an end. Amidst all the pain and suffering among animals, then, we see benevolence in the provisions made for their alleviation. We see that physical enjoyment among animals is vastly in excess of suffering. We see no case where suffering is inflicted for its own sake. With all these evidences of His good-will before us, we cannot believe that the Creator takes pleasure in suffering. And if he does not take pleasure in it, we see enough of His wisdom and skill in securing results to be sure that the pain and suffering incident to animal life have a wise purpose, or He would not allow them. It is not needful for our present purpose to discuss the possible theories why they are allowed. The machinery of this universe is vast. The machinery at work on our globe is complicated beyond measure. It is not strange that, when contemplating a part, there should seem to be want of adjustment; and that in our self-sufficiency we should impugn the wisdom of the Ordainer, and distrust His goodness. But when we wait, when we have looked long, has our patient, careful search ever detected a mistake? The more the machinery is seen, the more complete all its parts appear, the better seems its adaptation to the end in view. Of what human works can this be said? They appear perfect at the first glance, but careful looking reveals imperfection in construction and defect in execution. Who but a Being infinite in all His attributes could so adjust all animal life upon the globe as to secure the continuance of the species He had created;—could so establish their relations, as by the very law of destruction and death to secure the greatest enjoyment?

We have necessarily turned aside somewhat for this brief discussion, but we have done so with a purpose; because when we return again to consider the provision made for man, we wish him to stand entirely disconnected from the lower animals, that we may consider him as an intellectual and moral being. It seemed proper to speak of the destruction of the lower animals in connection with the balance of species which depends so largely upon it.

We have now seen the adaptation of man and all other sentient beings to the world—a series of adaptations implying, certainly in the Creator, the attributes of a personal being ; the highest wisdom and skill controlled by benevolence, even in connection with pain, disease, and death. It is only in the structure and instincts of animals, and in the provisions made for them as sentient beings, that benevolence can be shown. But the other attributes of the Creator are clearly manifested in plant life, to which we next turn.

LECTURE V.

ADAPTATION OF PLANTS TO THE WORLD.

Design in plants seen only in organization.—Natural selection.—Provision made by plants compared with instinct.—Wisdom manifested by instinct referred to the Creator.—Relation of plants to earth and air.—Polarity.—Structure of leaves.—Fall of leaf.—Structure of wide-leaved trees.—Of evergreens.—Position of buds.—Mathematical order.—Symmetry and welfare of tree secured.—Variety of habit.—Fitted for soil.—Climate and place in the solar system.—Power of the bud.—Young fruits.—Structure of buds.—Food stored up.—The potato.—Beet and Parsnip.—Century plant.—Orchis.—Solomon's-seal.—Structure of seed.—Perfection and variety of machinery.—Relation of plants and animals.—Effect of each on the air.—Vegetable kingdom subservient to the animal.—Its support.—Oak galls.—Plants respond to the insect's instinct.—Fertilization of plants by insects.—Squashes.—Forget-me-nots.—Orchids.—Results.

IT is a remark of Paley that design is perhaps less apparent in the vegetable kingdom than in the animal. This may be true, but the argument for design in plants has certainly some advantages. Evidence of design in plants must be sought for exclusively in the structure and function of their organs. There is no mind, no instinct. All changes in them, and all provision which they make for their individual welfare, and for their species, must therefore be the result of organization, and not of contrivance originating in thought, inherent in themselves. Where there is a thinking being, it is natural for us to ascribe to it a measure of wisdom in providing for itself and for its young, and we may imagine, as some naturalists have, that the adaptations of an animal grow out of conscious attempts to harmonize its relations to the external world. But with the plant, nothing of this kind can be claimed. The principle of natural selection may be insisted upon, and the claim made, that we find the present tribes of plants, only because they happen to be fitted for the place in which they are found; and thus they survive, while their kindred, with less perfect relations, have been destroyed. But the fact remains, that those plants which now clothe the earth are what they are from no attempt on their part to better their condition or to complete their adaptation to the world. They are what they are either by chance or by design in their creation. Any other supposition no man would pretend to make.

He may talk of some law by which they are fitted to their place by development. But he cannot believe that plants establish laws for themselves. If they are under any law, that law was established for them. Whether the adaptation of plants to the world is the result of chance, by which some favored ones have developed in the right direction, so as to maintain their ground against all destroying agencies, or whether they were created as they are, and all their relations established by an intelligent Designer, can only be learned from a careful consideration of their structure and relations. If it be said that the provisions which they make are analogous to those made by animals under the guidance of instinct, and that therefore their creation proves nothing higher than instinct in their Creator, we answer that instinct, even, cannot be regarded, by any fair consideration of that attribute, other than the power of seeking ends under an impulse. It often knows nothing of those ends; and, in many cases, when its work is most perfect, it knows nothing of the relation of the means to the ends. It does certain things as the common mechanic might bore a hole, or make a mortice, where it had been marked by the master-builder, without knowing anything of the place the timber was to occupy in the structure. But if there is any wisdom apparent in the choice of ends, and in the choice of means to secure those ends, that wisdom belongs to a being of higher rank than one of instinct. We must refer that wisdom back to the Being where it belongs, and not be misled by the number of secondary agents that He calls into action to work out results under His guidance.

The first relation of plants that demands our attention is to the earth and air. It is from both of these that the majority of plants draw their support. The root, as though loving darkness, plunges into the earth; the branch, with its leaves, seeks the light. This polarity of the tree is striking, appearing as soon as the germ begins to develop. Both branch and root are formed from cells of originally the same nature, for, under proper conditions, the root may put forth buds and leaves, while the branch, under the influence of darkness and moisture, develops roots. But the welfare of the tree demands that there should be this polarity, and here we find it ; a portion constantly plunging into the earth to keep the plant in position, and furnish it with those salts from the earth needed for its growth, and the opposite portion just as plainly seeking the sunlight and the air, having a structure just fitted for its work. The root divides and subdivides, stretching far through the soil, gathering in its richness ; while the leaves give increased surface for sweeping the gases from the air, and for preparing the crude materials for the use of the plant.

All the varied forms of leaves are such as to favor radiation, and thus to condense the dews upon them. The delicate but firm woody framework, like the vessel's spars, keeps the soft tissues stretched in place, that abundant surface may be secured with light weight.

We cannot but admire that provision by which all wide-leaved trees in the northern zone, where snows and ice abound, are prepared for the winter. Their leaves appear as by magic in the spring, but the stem of every leaf has its curious joint, so that when the summer is past and the leaf becomes ripe or is killed by the frost, it drops from the tree, and naked branches alone are exposed to the snow, and ice, and winds of winter. Further south, wide-leaved trees are evergreen ; but were they so in northern climes, with their present structure, the species would be destroyed. One single winter would ruin our elms, and maples, and kindred trees, if their leaves remained upon them. Their trunks divide into large branches, that in some old trees break down by their own weight. And these large branches, if loaded with snow and ice, would be torn from them by the winds, and decay and death would follow. But our northern evergreens, the spruce, the firs, and pines, were made to endure the frosts and snow without danger. Their whole plan of structure is different from that of the broad-leaved trees. Their trunks rise single shafts, never divided except by accident. Their limbs are disposed in circles ; they are small, compared with the size of the trees. They are not subdivisions of the trunk, but are fastened into it as pins are driven into posts. The well-arranged, bending limbs, remind one at once of a well-formed roof, from which the snow easily slides. Even when the ice gathers upon them, they are with the greatest difficulty broken from the trunk ; and if broken, their structure is such that harm is seldom done to the main shaft.

Here, then, we have all wide-leaved trees, like prudent mariners, furling their sails when the dangers of winter approach, thus presenting only bare poles to the wind, while most of the northern cone-bearing trees, as though conscious of the strength of their spars, keep every stitch of canvas spread and bid defiance to the storm.

Did the elm form the joint to its leaf and determine the time for it to do its appointed work before the frosts and snow ? Did the pine and spruce find by experience how their limbs must be fastened to the trunk, and that the trunk must be kept solid and entire—a single shaft? Did any force in nature establish these relationships by which the tree is not only fitted to the earth and air, but to the dangers of particular zones.

The position of the bud is also worthy of attention. Every plant has a specific form, and this form is due mainly to the position of the buds upon its stem. They appear in an exact relation to each other, which in each species can always be represented by a fixed mathematical expression. Since buds represent leaves and flowers and branches, not only the symmetry but the welfare of the tree demands that there should be some definite order or plan in their distribution. Were it not so, leaves might be crowded together on some branches and scattered far apart on others, and the same would be true of the branches on the trunk.

By this mathematical arrangement of branches and leaves, the beauty of the tree is secured, it has greater strength, and the leaves are best distributed for contact with the air. When the tree is injured or diseased, it sometimes puts out buds without order, but we see at once that they mar the beauty of the tree, and that the power by which it builds up a symmetrical whole has been overcome, for such branches never grow in any fixed relation to the parent stock. They grow like independent plants, while every branch that grows from the appointed place, at once bends itself in obedience to the parent tree.

A second matter of interest is the variety of habit in plants, by which they are fitted to so much of the surface of the earth. There are but few places where vegetation of some kind cannot be found. The variety of structure and of habit by which this is secured, is certainly worthy of an intelligent and wise Creator.

Not only does every zone have its vegetation, but every variety of soil has its own peculiar plants. The various trees may mingle together to form a forest, but the willows line the borders of streams, bind the banks together, and bathe their thirsty roots in the water. The grasses weave their carpet in the meadows; the dry and wet lands having very different kinds, which always find their own place without the aid of man. The humble lichen adorns the unyielding rock and the trunks of aged trees.

The fragrant lily lays its long roots beneath the waters, and floats its leaf and flower upon its surface. Some plants cluster near the ocean, and others fasten upon the rocks, where its waves can wash them; and others still plunge deeper down, and form gardens and groves beneath the waters. The feathery palm finds its home in the torrid zone; the hoary, creeping willow steals along beneath the snow towards the icy pole. Thus the earth is covered with vegetation, and in the vast scale of adaptations presented by the multitudes of species, every zone and every soil is provided for.

Not only are the plants fitted for every zone and

every soil, but they are also fitted to our place in the solar system. There is a direct relation between the cycle of growth in ordinary plants and the length of the year. The different zones have indeed seasons of very different lengths, but their plants either cannot grow in other zones at all, or if they do, they as a general thing still require the same conditions as they had in their own locality. There is for each species a proper season for the germination of the seed, or for the unfolding of buds already formed; a time for growth, and a time for maturing seeds or buds for the succeeding year.

There is indeed great power of adaptation, especially among cultivated plants, so that they are subservient to the artificial conditions that man can bring to bear upon them. But even under artificial conditions of the hot-house they have their cycle of growth. Such plants of the torrid zone as seem to have little annual change, show their adaptation by their power to endure the climate of that region. But among all the adaptations that can be pointed out, not one can be mentioned that militates against the statement that the plants upon the earth are adjusted in their changes and growth to our distance from the sun and our movements through the heavens. The unfolding leaf, the bundles of fibres in the trunk, and the maturing buds and fruit, all know their time by the earth's position among the stars.

How strange it is, that the early frosts have power to kill the full-grown leaf on our fruit and forest trees, but not even the icy fierceness of winter's cold can harm the young and tender leaf and flower folded in the bud. They have not yet done their work, and therefore they are preserved. But what explanation can be given of how it is done? They are carefully packed and protected indeed, and this has been regarded as an evidence of design; but the whole bud is exposed and frozen in spite of its skilful structure. The mature leaf, though protected with ten times the care, could not withstand the cold to which the bud is exposed. Is that power in the young leaf which withstands the frost any less wonderful than the structure of the leaf or bud? Is it any satisfactory explanation to call it natural, the nature of the bud? How came the bud by this nature? If we were left to reason on the subject, we should infer that the tender unexpanded leaf would be the first to feel the blight of winter. By what process of development was this strange power given to the bud, this unexpected superiority over the full-grown leaf? Is any other account so reasonable as to suppose this power was given by a wise Creator who understood the conditions of the globe, and gave to the plants, to the leaf and bud, the exact power they needed to meet those conditions?

The same peculiar power possessed by the bud belongs to certain fruits. The young acorns on some of our oaks, which require two years to mature their fruit, and the apparently tender seeds of the witch-hazel, defy the coldest winters. In fact, whatever part of the plant is required to live over from one season to the next in order to preserve the species, has this peculiar power of withstanding cold, although it may appear the tenderest portion of the whole structure. In most of the cases thus far mentioned the relationship of the plant arises from what is ordinarily termed the nature of the organs, but the action of these organs is also important. Many of the results produced by the functions of organs are so specific and so well understood, that they present strong analogies to certain acts of animals under the guidance of instinct or intelligence.

The loss of the leaf already alluded to might perhaps be reckoned among the instinct-like provisions which the tree makes for its preservation; but in this case it more resembles certain organic changes in animals in which they are mostly passive, as in the shedding of the winter coat in spring. The animal has no power to produce this change, though he may be indirectly an actor. The snake could never slip out of its skin, nor the lobster from its shell, nor the ox remove his coat, if there had not been a provision in the organization and function of each for a periodical loosening of the scales and shell and hair.

But as by the animal, certain provisions are made from instinct for its own welfare and that of its young; so in plants we find analogous provisions made, as though they were sentient beings.

Some provisions made for the maturing, protection, and early growth of buds and seeds, are of this nature.

The structure of all leaf-buds is essentially the same, and in some of our trees, as in the horse-chestnut, they can be examined without difficulty. The delicate leaves all formed, are closely packed together in softest down. They are then covered with closely fitting scales, and these again by a coating of insoluble varnish. Mechanically, the whole contrivance is perfect, and the work most skilfully done. In adapting means to ends, the structure of the bud is not surpassed by any work of man.

But that bud is first to put out leaves, and these leaves are the organs for elaborating sap. How shall the tree, stripped of its leaves, supply itself with food while pushing out the myriad of new leaves from its buds? Like the instinct-guided bee, it has laid up provision for the time of need. When it has nearly finished its growth for one year, it makes provision for the year that is to come. In the axle of the leaf, the bud is set which, another spring, is to unfold in leaves and elongate into the branch. While this bud is fashioned and set in its place, food is also stored up in the tissues in form of starch and sugar and other organic materials for the support of that bud while expanding its leaves. The same principle is seen in a more striking manner in some of our cultivated plants.

The potato is only a thickened underground stem. Its eyes correspond to the buds upon the common branch; and the store of starch, so nutritious for food, was placed there to develop those eyes into stems at the appointed time. When the potato sprouts in spring without contact with the earth, the stalk feeds upon this store of food gathered for its use. The beet, and parsnip, and other kindred plants, produce an abundance of flowers and fruit, but not till the second year. The first year, the whole energy of the plant is spent in providing a large succulent root stored with sugar and other organized materials. The second year, its whole energy seems to be spent in producing an abundance of fruit, and now it draws upon the collected stores of the first year, and thus produces results which would be impossible, were it compelled to elaborate its food when suddenly needed by its multitudes of flowers and seeds.

Other plants are many years, instead of one, in making this provision. The so-called century plant and others in their thick leaves store up vast magazines of materials, that are used with astonishing rapidity when the time comes for them to send up their stems and produce their fruit. The same process may be observed in many of our perennial herbaceous plants, that do much of their curious work beneath the soil. The broad-leaved orchis and the Solomon's-seal are examples. They provide a large and vigorous bud as parent of the next year's plant, and while a portion of the old root decays, the remaining portion is packed with food to send up from that bud now hidden in the soil, a vigorous plant in the early spring. These provisions are for the plant itself, and only incidentally for the young plantlet which it is to produce. To see this apparent parental care most fully manifested, we must examine the seed. In it is the germ of the young plant. But that germ has no power at first over earth or the gases of the air. It is shut out mainly from both. For this helpless state a provision has been made. Around the germ, or in some way connected with it, the parent plant garners the food which shall support the germ, till large enough to provide for itself. The kernel of grain does not fill till its germ is fertilized. But when that is done, when a centre of life is formed, a new plant is there; and then the starch, and sugar, and oil, are furnished by the parent stock for its support. All this action is organic, but it is a perfect adaptation of means to ends. The machinery by which the results are reached is as complete in its structure and action as it is possible for us to conceive of. This provision is not made in one plant alone; but, in some form, in all.

It is not one kind of material that is provided, but many. The work is not done by one method, but by methods almost numberless; and yet every one of those methods commends itself most fully to our judgment. There is not a single case in the thousands that we could improve upon, for the welfare of the plant. We cannot believe that this varied machinery and these diverse methods result from the development of some force in nature, or organizing principle. We cannot, without doing violence to our own mental constitution, regard these as any other than the provision of an intelligent Creator, whose ways are perfect, whose wisdom and skill are infinite.

Between the animal and plant there is a still more striking series of adaptations than between either of them and the inorganic world. They develop in opposite directions; so that the more perfect the plant and the more perfect the animal, the further removed they are from each other in their structure and nature. The likeness of one to the other is only one of remote analogy. And yet in their most perfect state, when by their nature they are most widely separated in their organic structure and in their conditions of life, it is often apparent that they were constructed with direct reference to each other. The first relationship which we notice is the perfect balance which has been established between them in their effect upon the air by their chemical action. Everything thrown off from an animal as waste material is not simply waste to him, but is either a poison to the air, or capable of soon becoming so. The carbonic acid from the lungs, and all the excretions formed by the waste of tissues, fill the air with poisons.

But upon all the waste materials rejected by the animal system, the plants live. They sweep the carbonic acid from the air by their multitude of leaves, draw it from the soil by a thousand rootlets, and gather up the various organic compounds as they are ready to change to poison, and in the wonderful laboratory of their leafy tissue, they unlock and recombine the elements, giving back to us in woody fibre, in starch and sugar, in the nutritious grains and delicious fruits, those very materials which but for them would have generated deadly disease. They then throw back from the leaves the liberated oxygen, partly at least in that active form known as ozone, in which it is most efficient as a purifier of the air. Not only do the plants thus stand ready to save animals from the effect of their own poisoning influence upon the air, but they seem to have committed to them the task of protecting animal life from the poisons produced by general decomposition, both by gathering up the poison and also by some of them showing by their very presence the existence of poisons, and thus warning intelligent man of his danger.

On the stagnant pool the green film gathers, to many appearing the cause of disease, but in reality the safeguard which nature has prepared ; a thin veil with chemical power which she has spread over such places to gather up and condense a portion of the poisons, and to be a token of their presence. Around our southern swamps she has hung the long moss in rich festoons upon the trees, and woven the thick barrier of climbers, through both of which much of the air is strained.

The plants are thus more than a sign that poisons are generated there ; they feed upon and destroy them.

In studying these relationships, it soon becomes apparent that the vegetable kingdom is in general subservient to the animal. The lower is made to serve the higher. Plants are directly or indirectly the support of all animal life. No animals, unless it be some of microscopic size, have power to live upon inorganic matter. If they have power to assimilate it at all, they have no power to assimilate a sufficient portion to sustain life. We have around us an abundance of all the elements upon which we daily live, but we have no power to take them in their common form. If left to ourselves we must starve in the midst of plenty. The plant feeds upon these elements or their inorganic compounds. Plants are the chemists, constantly working for the welfare of the animal kingdom, bringing the elements within its power. If plants were destroyed, animal life would cease. For, though carnivorous animals may destroy others of the same kind, yet in the end we come back to those animals that live upon the fruits of the earth.

There are some curious adaptations in the function of certain plants, that show the relationship of one kingdom to the other, and this general subserviency of the lower to the higher kingdom. Certain insects sting the oak and other plants, deposit their eggs in their stems or leaves, and then leave them there for the young to be developed. In some cases the young insect simply bores into the wood and forms a dwelling and finds food for himself. The only adaptation here seems to be in the fitness of the material in which the egg was deposited by instinct, to supply the wants of the grub while actively providing for himself.

But what can be more curious, I might truly say what more wonderful, than the different kinds of oak-galls or oak-apples, which are formed by the oak wherever the egg is deposited!

When the egg is placed in its tissues, the oak at once by the very law of its being diverts a portion of the nutriment elaborated to enlarge its own trunk or fill its fruit, and forms a curious dwelling-place for the young insect, and not only forms the house but furnishes food. No animal by instinct ever fashioned a more curious structure for itself or its young than the unthinking oak forms for the egg of its insect enemy that has been thrust upon it for protection and support. And these dwelling-places, though always built alike on the same kind of tree for the same insect, differ according to the kind of insects for which they are built. Other plants present the same phenomenon, and plants entirely unlike botanically. On some of the rose-bushes, these insect-houses are built and ornamented until they are almost as beautiful as the opening bud itself. The stalk of the golden-rod forms a large ball, in the centre of which you are sure to find the larval insect housed and provided for, or the empty tenement from which he has escaped to a higher form of life. These are but single examples of the adaptation of plants to the wants of the insect tribe. But every naturalist will recall a great number of kindred cases, in which the plant responds to the instinct of the animal, and completes, even at its own expense of vital energy, and sometimes in a most elaborate manner, the machinery that is needed to perfect the work which the instinct of the animal has commenced. What chance should lead those insects to deposit their eggs in the very plants that are so ready to act the part of nurses, and supply by special provision all the wants of the young that come from those eggs ? How came these plants of different kinds to respond in these various ways so perfectly to the need of their animal foes ? We wonder at the provision which they make for their own young plantlets, we admire their general adaptation to the wants of the animal kingdom as food and purifiers of the air ; but when we see them building on one unvarying plan a dwelling-place for the insect young, and storing it with food, we cannot but recognise a power higher than that of insect or plant—the Creator of both, who ordained the laws of their being, who implanted instinct in the one, and made the other the willing servant of the higher form of life.

There is a variety of contrivances by which insects fertilize plants. The structure of the flower and that of the bee are often adapted to each other, as much as the key to the lock. The honey poured out in the flower attracts the insect, and in his endeavors to reach the precious fluid he indirectly benefits the plant. We might regard this as a matter of accident were there but a single instance of it, or the same structure for all flowers. But when we see thousands of species of plants of varied forms, with their parts so arranged as to secure fertilization by the aid of insects, and the drop of honey placed in the flower to attract them, we not only recognise design, but in a provision of such varied nature the idea of chance is excluded. If no honey is secreted in the flower, then it will be found that means have been provided adequate to produce fertilization without the aid of insects. There may be an abundance of pollen, and such a structure that the wind can do the work, as in the Indian-corn and pine, or some special arrangement of the parts of the flower to secure the result. It will be sufficient to mention a few cases from the many, of structure having reference to the action of bees in the process of fertilization. The cucumber and squash are good examples. These vines produce two kinds of flowers—the staminate or those producing the pollen, and the pistillate which produce the fruit. For the growth of these fruits it is necessary for the pollen to be transferred from one flower to the other. As the flowers are at considerable distance from each other, and protected from the winds, probably not one case would occur in a hundred flowers of the transference of pollen without the aid of insects. These plants therefore would seem defective if we consider their own structure alone. If left to their own action, the species would die out. In the Sandwich Islands, where no bees are found, it is necessary to fertilize the large squashes by the labor of men.

Where bees are found the work is completed by them. In each flower upon these vines, there is a tiny cup of honey, carefully covered, but the cover so thin in three places that the proboscis of the bee pierces it with ease. While gathering the sweets of the staminate flower, she becomes covered with the pollen dust, because the stamens are so placed in the narrow tube of the flower that she cannot steal away the sweets secreted there without loading herself with the fertilizing powder. When now she lights in the pistillate flower, she takes its honey; but in her eagerness, scatters from her wings and body the pollen grains upon the pistil, and thus secures the growth of the fruit.

When we examine the structure of these flowers, their relation to the size of the bee, and consider the fact that the honey, of no use directly to the plant, but a draft upon its energies, is ready to attract the bee when the pollen is fit for distribution, we see a provision for the welfare of the flower of such a nature as to secure the enjoyment of a sentient being. The bee is not only provided for by following her instinct, but the following of her instinct is essential to the plant. They were both fashioned with reference to each other. In our pretty spring flower, the forget-me-not *(Oldenlandia cærulea)*, we find a curious relation of the seed-producing organs. The stamens are always either much longer or much shorter than the pistil. When the bee visits a flower with long stamens the pollen is attached to the base of the proboscis; when he visits a flower with long pistil, this pollen comes in contact with its stigma, and at the same time the middle of her proboscis is becoming covered with the pollen from its short stamens, to fertilize the plants with short pistils. But the most remarkable cases of special adaptation are found among the orchids which have been so carefully studied by Darwin. Many of the species cannot possibly fertilize themselves, and if shut out from insects, fail to produce seed. One, the *Orchis pyramidalis*, may be taken as a type of many in its special adaptations by which its structure and functions, the structure and instinct of the insect, are all combined to produce the needed result. The structure of the flower is such that the proboscis must enter in a given direction ; this brings it in contact with the packets of pollen that adhere to it by a viscid fluid, that has the chemical property of rapidly becoming solid when exposed to the air. The packets of pollen bend over as they dry, so as to take the exact position they ought to take to strike the stigmas of the next flower. Those stigmas are covered with a viscid fluid to which the grains of pollen adhere, and the work is done. What a complicated arrangement is here, and yet how perfect the result ! First, there is the form of the flower that guides the proboscis aright ; second, the position of the pollen packets all ready to be withdrawn ; third, the glue by which they are firmly fixed to the proboscis ; fourth, their hygrometric action, by which in drying they bend just far enough to bring each one in contact with the two stigmas of the next flower the insect visits ; and lastly, the glue upon the stigmas sufficiently strong to rupture the packets of pollen and hold sufficient of it to fertilize the seed.

But it may be asked, what need of all this machinery? Would not as great wisdom as well as design be manifested by a more simple contrivance, such as is found in other flowers that fertilize themselves? Among other answers which might be given, is this: It is undoubtedly a means of preventing the formation of varieties in such plants in a wild state, and thus secures distinctness of specific forms. The design manifested in all that relates to varieties will demand our attention before these lectures are closed. We have now endeavored simply to show that a result is reached in a manner implying wisdom and skill in the adaptation of means to ends.

LECTURE VI.

PRODUCTION OF VARIETIES AND THEIR FINAL CAUSE

Origin of species.—May be varied for a wise purpose.—Living and fossil forms, parts of one whole.—Four plans of structure.—The rocks the true record.—May be mistranslated, but not changed.—Unity of plan in the Divine mind.—Changes that favor development theory.—Quotation from Darwin.—Variation considered historically.—For a definite purpose.—Adapts species to wide geographical range.—To man.—Definition of varieties.—Cause not known.—Quotation from Gray.—Final cause.—Reference to man.—Beauty of crystal.—Difference in kingdom of life.—Organs of plants.—Anthers.—Petals.—Double flowers.—Propagation of double plants. — Fleshy fruits. — Idea of beauty in some plants.—Of fruit in others.—Two series according to lines of development.—Corn. - Sugarcane.—Potato.—Tomato.—Indications in wild plants.—Exceptions.—Some plants for a double purpose.—Vegetable kingdom for the animal.—Appears primarily for itself.—Multitude of germs.—Grains of wheat represent food and plant life.—Use of soft fruits.—Plants and animals constructed for man as an intellectual being.—Increase of beauty not for the plant.—Varieties offer condition of continual progress.—Development theory not Atheistic.—Incurable scepticism.—Geology must explain origin of species. — Law of variation, evidence of design and wisdom.

IN our last lecture we considered some of the relations of plants to the world—the varied structure and nature by which different kinds are adapted to soil, to climate, and to our place in the solar system. It was also shown that plants have an obvious relation to the animal kingdom, not only in counteracting the action of animals on the air and in furnishing them with food, but also in their adaptation to the structure and instinct of animals, completing, as they often do by their own growth, in a specific manner, the work which the instinct of the animal commenced. It was shown that the structure of the insect, its instinct, and the nature of the plant growth, are all three often needed to complete the relation of the animal and the plant to the world, so that certain species in both kingdoms may be preserved.

There still remains another characteristic of organic beings that has given rise to much discussion among scientific men. I refer to the production of varieties, or different kinds, from the same stock. The fact is not only acknowledged, but modified forms are springing up almost every year in the animal and vegetable kingdoms. We do not propose to discuss the scientific tests that are proposed for distinguishing species from varieties; but we wish to show that the power of producing varieties is one of the means by which organic beings are better fitted to the world, and to the wants of man, and that in the nature and final results of many of these changes it becomes apparent that the wisdom of their production cannot be vindicated on any other supposition than that they were made with direct reference to man. This might involve the whole discussion of what constitutes a species, and how species come into existence. We have not time to enter fully upon that discussion. As to the origin and permanence of species, the best naturalists are not agreed. We accept the theory of a distinct creation for each species. Each species thus represents a distinct creative idea. The species may be varied for a wise purpose, without losing its essential characteristics. Thousands of new kinds of apples have been produced from the same stock, but no fruit was ever raised from an apple-seed that would be mistaken for a peach or pear ; so that there has not been shown to be the slightest tendency in the apple to change to any other kind of fruit. This is what we mean by saying that the creative idea is never lost amid all the changes in the production of varieties. We do not regard the doctrine of the distinct creation of each species as essential at all to the argument for the existence and attributes of God. We accept it on purely scientific grounds, believing fully that science and the Bible here agree. But we must acknowledge, whether the species have come into existence by direct creation or by secondary causes, that there is a systematic connection running back through all the geologic ages. The animals in the rocks belong to strange forms indeed ; but in all their strangeness, they yet show connection with those now living. But it is the same sort of connection we should expect to find among the creations of the same Being, who with wisdom and skill varied His work only according to the conditions in which it was to be placed. He has indeed His own distinct types running back as far as animal life is found. And the ancient tribes are so allied to those now existing that the fossil and living animals make one grand whole, the lines of the great plans of creation never crossing. Each plan is like an order in architecture, giving diversity in execution, but never entirely losing its identity. The marked difference in the plan of structure in the four great divisions of animal life, in which plan can be fully recognised, is a great point against development theories; and even in the same division it seems impossible that all the diverse forms should have originated from one. Who can persuade himself that all the different kinds of shells that can be found upon any beach, were derived from the same stock? But it is said that they shade into each other, and so attempts have been made to ignore all dividing lines as drawn in nature. We acknowledge the existence of the intermediate forms, and we admit that varieties have been mistaken for species; but notwithstanding this, as science advances, distinct plans of structure stand out in clearer light, and we believe that distinct plans of creation and distinct creations of species will be recognised as the teachings of the rocks of the earth. They are the great historic record of the change in animal life; to them must be our final appeal. And we feel thankful for such a book as this; a book which will be more and more read while the world stands—a book which no man ever has altered, and no man can alter. He may mistranslate it; but the text remains unchanged, and coming generations may read for themselves.

Whatever theory we may adopt as to the introduction of species on the globe, we must all acknowledge the same order of succession in animal life. From this there is no escape ; for that grand old volume, the earth, is full of these forms, varied as the strata of rocks rise one above another. And what a grand history is here recorded of creative power! What wisdom, skill, and unity of plan are revealed! The mountain-tops and the deep valleys unite in declaring that the march of animal and vegetable life, through all the vast ages of rock formation, was under the guidance and power of a Being who saw the end from the beginning, and moved on the grand succession, from the lowest forms of the Silurian age to the creation of man. We believe this unity of plan was in the Divine Mind alone, and that the varied tribes were the direct creation of His hand.

While we believe this to be the teaching of the rocks, it is freely acknowledged that there are changes in organic beings that favor the development theory. Distinct kinds of plants and animals have appeared within the historic period. In fact, new kinds may appear every year, as is well understood by every intelligent gardener. These new varieties are regarded by some as incipient species, which in time will become permanent in form and take their place among those that are now recognised as species. And since we find so many kinds of plants originating from the same stock, all our apples, for example, coming undoubtedly from one kind, what might we not expect as the result of this variation continued not only through the thousands of years that history records, but for the unmeasured ages of geologic time? If greenings, and russets, and Baldwins, and hundreds of other kinds, can in a few years be originated from one kind, why might it not be found, if we could go back millions of years, that oaks, and pines, and elms, and peaches, all came from the same stock? This is the question which a real believer in development propounds to us. We see similar changes constantly going on in animals as well as in plants.

How very unlike the different breeds of horses, all springing from the same stock! Now since the different breeds of horses have, within comparatively few years, sprung from the same stock, if we could go back millions of years, why might we not find that horses and cattle and beasts of every kind sprang from the same stock?

This is the second question which the real development theorist puts to us; and then to be consistent, he adds: since man as a physical being is an animal, if we go back far enough, why may we not find him to be a branch from the same stock, making his way up by development through the line of monkeys to his present high position? And that we may know just how it is supposed this variation may be brought about, I quote from Darwin, the great champion of the modern development theory:

"In North America, the black bear was seen by Hearne swimming for hours, with widely open mouth, thus catching, like the whale, insects in the water. Even in so extreme a case as this, if the supply of insects were constant, and if better adapted competitors did not already exist in the country, I can see no difficulty in a race of bears being rendered by natural selection more and more aquatic in their structure and habits, with larger and larger mouths, till a creature was produced as monstrous as the whale."

We have in this extract a good illustration of the changes in structure which it is claimed can be produced by use of organs or by habits of the animal.

The principle of variation of species and natural selection, say the development theorists, is enough to account for all the distinctions we observe in those kinds that are recognised as species. Now let us see how this fact of variation stands historically. When we point to the rocks as proof of distinct creations, we are told that this record is only imperfectly read as yet, and so the transition forms have not been found. When we appeal to living forms, we defy them to produce a single instance in which anything but an apple has been raised from an apple-seed. Untold kinds of apples have been produced, but we wait for the first fruit to be raised from an apple-seed that the most unlearned in botany would not know to be apple. The same constancy of species is found in all our fruits that vary most. We see by this that in all the variation, there are certain bounds beyond which it cannot go. It never blots out the creative idea in the plant. And the same is true of animals. Has there, in all the variations, been a single instance where the type of the animal was really changed? Would not all horses be recognised as horses the world over? We find in all these cases certain distinct lines beyond which variation never goes. When it is said that the horse and the ox may have come from the same stock, not a particle of historical proof can be given in support of it. And when it is said that man descended from the apes, it is a mere gratuitous lowering of human dignity.

Now the fact of variation being granted, we believe it can be shown that it is not accidental, but that it works for a definite purpose and within prescribed limits. As this variation among organic beings is a strong point with those who would either theorize God out of the universe, or rob Him of the character of a Creator, except as one acting through secondary agencies, creating thousands of defective forms to die out, for one perfect enough to hold its place in the world; in fine, of those who would in any way ignore the Bible account of creation—we shall be justified in treating the final cause of varieties at considerable length. And in doing this we shall have to introduce other material, that we may show how variation harmonizes with other characteristics to better fit the species for the world. If species were the direct creation of a wise Being, as the Bible declares, we should expect to find them endowed with properties fitting them to be of most use in the world, and that those most needful for man would have powers and capabilities adapting them to his nature as a physical and intellectual being. We think it can be shown that the power of producing varieties is the great means of adapting species to a wide geographical range, and to the wants of man as he increases in civilization and capacity to enjoy the beautiful and good. If this can be shown, we take the production of varieties from the category of chance, and show in it the highest, far-reaching, wise, and benevolent design.

Accepting, then, the common definition of varieties in the organic kingdom, we regard them as forms produced by the variation of species. The cause of this variation has never been explained. It was formerly referred to soil and climate, but probably the only account that will ever be given is: such is the nature of species.

It is a law written on the plant and animal, that in their development there shall be variation from the original stock, but only in certain directions. On this point we quote the language of a distinguished scientific man* who has lately written much upon this subject. It would be difficult to find in the writings of any other author all that we really know on this subject condensed into so few words:

"The former [*variation*] has never yet been shown to have its cause in external influences, nor to occur at random. As we have elsewhere insisted, if not inexplicable, it has never been explained; all that we can yet say is, that plants and animals are prone to vary, and that some conditions favor variation."

* Professor Asa Gray.

We thus confess our ignorance of the natural causes that produce variation. We propose to discuss its *final cause*. This implies that there is in it a purpose. If there is in the variation of objects in nature, a purpose, that purpose must have relation to the objects themselves, or to some other beings connected with them or in some way related to them. In all arrangements merely for the good of the object itself, final cause or purpose may be denied. It may be said that the thing exists because it happens to have a constitution fitting it for the mode of existence in which we find it. We shall therefore confine ourselves, in this discussion, mainly to those contrivances that seem to have relation to something out of the object in which they are found. But our special aim will be to show that all variation from original forms in the animal and vegetable kingdoms, especially in the higher kinds, is not in general for the good of the object in which it occurs, but for the good of other beings in some way related to it. We think it will readily appear to any careful observer, that much of the variation in both of these kingdoms has special reference to man as an intellectual and moral being. But we shall, for want of time, confine our present examination mainly to plants. It would be most natural, perhaps, to commence with the mineral kingdom, had we time for a full discussion of the subject.

And we might inquire : For what end is the beauty of the crystal? Certainly it is not for the crystal itself. We have great beauty in the primary crystal. But the law of secondary forms adds new beauty, by the variety it gives in modifying, with mathematical exactness, the faces and angles of the primary. We may be told that there is no design in all this arrangement of matter. It is so, is all that we can say. Because we admire the beauty of the crystal, and wonder at this law by which its beauty is increased, we are told that we are not to believe that the original beauty of the gem, or that the law of variation, was made for us, or with any reference to us. Nor are we to believe, necessarily, that they were made at all. *They are*—they always have been ; and they would be the same they now are, were there no intelligent being in the universe to behold them. We may believe that they have a purpose, or not. If one doubts it, there is certainly little room for argument. When the facts are stated, different minds will be differently affected by them, and argument will have little effect upon either class.

But when we study the kingdom of life, the facts that meet us are entirely different in kind. There is here a succession of beings, descending one from another ; there is a complicated machinery by which the individual is built up and preserved. It is certainly a legitimate inquiry : For what purpose is each part of these beings? For what purpose— or, if any object to this word—for what *use* are the various organs of the plant ? To answer this question is the work of the botanist. He examines the root, the stem, the leaf, the flower, and the fruit.

Use of Petals.

In this investigation he has been successful, so that most of the plant machinery is now understood in its relations to the individual plant, and to the succession of plants.

Who doubts the use of the root and leaf in taking up and elaborating nutriment for the plant? Who doubts the use of the anther in producing pollen, or of the pollen grains in fertilizing the seed? Although we may be uncertain about the use of some parts, it does not affect the certainty of our knowledge respecting those we have mentioned. But these are for the use of the plant. Let us push our inquiries further, and see if we can find in the structure of the plant any contrivances, or in its development any variations of form, not required by the economy of the plant itself. We omit for the present all discussion as to the method by which these were produced, or how they came to be; but simply inquire if there are such. For what purpose are the petals of the flower, the crown of beauty to the plant? Certainly they are not absolutely essential in the production of seed, for many plants are without them. And if in any case they are deemed essential, certainly the beautiful pattern of the petal, its numberless modifications and delicate tints, adjusted with masterly accuracy, are not necessary parts in the economy of plants. Of what use to the plant is that row of sterile flowers that adorns so many of our *compositæ*, the Rudbeckias, and helianths; or that curious circle of sterile flowers bordering the cymes of hydrangeas and some of our viburnums? We may be told that they have no use, or that these apparently useless parts will at some time be found to be of importance in the economy of the plant, aiding directly or indirectly in the perpetuation of the species, as the honey of the plant attracts bees, and thus secures the continuance of the species by the fertilization of the seed. We will go one step further, then, and ask : What end is subserved by double flowers? All agree that one use of the flower is to produce seed. But the perfectly double flower loses the organs of reproduction. The rose unfolds its stamens and pistils into petals, and thus gains in beauty, till it becomes the perfection of a flower, but always at the expense of seed. What use, in the economy of the plant, does the flower subserve when it can no longer produce seed ? It does not perpetuate the species, so that this variation cannot be for the production of new species, and more than this, it is a draft upon the nutriment that would otherwise go to build up the plant that produces it. By becoming double, the flower has ceased to be of advantage either to the species or the individual plant. But does nature thus defeat her own ends, and provide for the destruction of some species by the very law of their growth? Not at all. In every plant, which by cultivation is so far changed as to lose the power of producing seed, there is some other provision for the propagation of the plant, as by slips, by grafting, by bulblets, and the like. Nature seems thus to provide, in the structure of other parts of these plants, for the development of their flowers in the line of beauty at the expense of seed. And when annual plants become truly double, they at the same time become perennial.

Let us examine another group of plants, belonging to the same natural order as the rose. For what purpose is the fruit of the apple-tree, the pear-tree, and the peach? Their seed is evidently for the propagation of the species. But still we ask: For what purpose are the *apple* and the *peach?* The germ is in the seed or within the stone. The economy of the plant does not require that the covering of the seeds should be increased in quantity or heightened in flavor, for the seeds come to their fullest development in the unchanged native fruit. If the improvement in size and flavor is not for the seed, it has no relation to the plant. And probably no candid person will contend that the change in cultivated fruits which renders them more valuable to man, has any more relation to the wants of the individual plant, or of the species, than the milk of the mother has to her own wants. If this change has any purpose at all, it is for something outside of the plant. The seed is not for the plant that produces it, but for the species.

The change of covering, as already indicated, is of no advantage to the seed. Its increase in size is therefore a draft upon the tree, without having any relation to the species. So far as the economy of the plant is concerned, it is a mistake. The machinery is out of order. There is an absolute throwing away of material and of vital energy, and this goes on, as in some oranges and grapes, till no seeds are formed.

We are now prepared to introduce and illustrate certain propositions which seem warranted by plant development.

1. In some plants the idea of beauty is the most prominent idea, inasmuch as under the best cultivation the variation of these plants is always in the line of beauty either in the flower or leaf.

The beauty of the flower, the rose, for example, often increases at the expense of the reproductive organs, until the power of producing seed is lost.

2. In other plants utility of fruit is the prominent idea, as in the apple and the peach. Such plants, under careful cultivation, produce larger and more delicious kinds of fruit, without increase of beauty in the flower.

3. From these two propositions another follows: that the plants best known to us from long-continued cultivation can be readily divided into two great series, without reference to their botanical relationship, but according to their lines of development. In one series *utility of fruit* is the prominent idea; and in the other, *beauty of flower or leaf;* as under the best cultivation these series are developed in these two directions respectively.

The idea of utility is not manifested by fruit alone. The sugar of the sugar-cane constitutes its utility, while that of the Indian-corn lies in its grain. These plants, so nearly allied botanically, are developed in these two directions, according to the leading idea in their products. The apple and the rose already referred to, belong to the same botanical family; yet they are developed, in nearly all their variations, in opposite directions.

The potato has for its leading idea the formation of underground stems or tubers; while its brother, the tomato, has for its idea the production of a fruit corresponding in structure to the potato-grape. They show this in all their variations. In the pine-tree the leading idea is wood, and in the mint, essential oil. But in such plants as do not readily produce varieties the line of development is determined with difficulty.

4. Some plants in their native state give indications of the kind of change likely to take place in them by cultivation. The rose, for example, by its large corolla in comparison with the fruit, shows that change of flower is most likely to take place. In the apple, the large, fleshy fruit indicates a tendency to variation and improvement in that direction. The *viburnum opulus*, the *hydrangea*, and other plants, by the circle of sterile flowers, much larger and more beautiful than the fertile flowers, indicate change in the direction of beauty. Those beautiful circles of sterile flowers in some of our native shrubs, and the neutral rays of some of our compositæ, may be regarded as ornaments, rather than as of use in the economy of the plant. When, therefore, a new plant is brought under cultivation, there is little doubt in what direction it will vary, if at all. The increase

of beauty in the flower by doubling, and the increase of the fruit in size, beauty, and flavor, are of no advantage to the fruit itself, nor to the species; but in some cases they are a draft upon the plant for no purpose in its own economy.

5. Those plants that by variation lose the power of producing seed, can always be propagated in other ways, as by slips or bulbs. Nature, as though careful for the preservation of the species, never allows any plant, by its own law of growth, to lose the power of producing seed, unless she has given to it means other than the seed, for the perpetuation of its kind.

6. Variation is most common and rapid in those plants which are most useful to man for cultivation, and which must go with him over most of the earth. It may be said that they are most useful because they happen to vary; but their readiness to vary, certainly was not the cause of their first cultivation. They were selected for some particular good, as for fruit, or for beauty of flower, or leaf, or some other desirable property. The characteristic for which each one was first selected, is the leading idea of the plant; and in that direction all its variations under cultivation have tended. The rose, in all its varieties, is to-day cultivated for the same reason for which it was first cultivated, for its beauty; the apple-tree for its fruit, the sugar-cane for its sweetness, and so on, through the list of cultivated plants. We might multiply propositions and examples, if our space allowed. As they would not differ in kind,

they are not needed for the argument. Apparent exceptions to the propositions already stated may undoubtedly be pointed out, for it is well understood by naturalists that nature does nothing *per saltum*. Hardly a group of plants can be examined in which there will not be found one or more that the family description will not embrace, in all particulars. There are also some plants so valuable for several purposes, that it would be difficult to determine, in every case, the leading idea. They are made for a double purpose, and may develop in either direction. The apple-tree, with double blossoms, or the tomato, with tubers upon it, would not, therefore, with any candid person, affect the bearing of the propositions. If a law of nature is really discovered, all exceptions are either merely apparent, or if real, are found to be special provisions for some wise purpose. It is the general law of variation that we now wish to present for consideration, in the propositions just enunciated. If these propositions have any significance, to what do they tend? Certainly to show that the vegetable kingdom is not an end to itself. Men and animals do not make use of plants because they happen to be what they are; but the plants are constituted as they are, for the sake of the animal kingdom, and many of them with a direct reference to man as an intellectual and moral being. It is by the law of variation of species that they are most perfectly fitted for these high purposes.

In almost every department of plant life, the changes can be referred primarily to the good of the plant itself; and thus it is easy to say, and no doubt some believe, that there is in them no purpose other than the continuance of the species, if any purpose at all. The cereals—wheat, rye, barley, Indian-corn, and rice—furnish the great bulk of food for the human race. We have no doubt that most men will believe that they were made for this purpose, and not that they happened to be what they are, or that the primary object in importance was that they might propagate their kind, and that the support of animal life was no part of the plan, but accidental or subsidiary.

Yet there is much that seems to favor the theory that all the machinery of fruiting is for the continuance of species alone. If the germ fails to be fertilized by the pollen, no sugar, nor starch, nor gluten, is stored up in the seed for man. But when the pollen has touched the germ, there is power of independent life, and from that moment all the energies of the plant are taxed to store the kernel with food; but food for what? For whom? For the young plant, all agree. It puts in the seed the food which the germ needs for its support, till its roots and leaves are large enough to collect from the earth and air the crude materials and elaborate them for use.

For what purpose is the starch garnered up in the potato, and the sugar in the beet, the carrot, and the parsnip? We shall be told that they are stored up for the plants themselves, to supply the great draft made upon them in producing fruit. We cannot deny it, nor do we wish to do so. We love to contemplate the parent plant providing for every one of the thousand plantlets folded in its seeds, destined to beautify the earth when its own withered stalk has passed away. Would that men might learn a lesson from it, and provide for their offspring enough, and only enough, for their wants till able to provide for themselves. We can hardly help admiring the seeming prudence of the honest beet and parsnip, that industriously gather stores of food the first year for the flowering time, when both root and leaves would fail to supply their wants. In all these things we have been compelled to recognise a wisdom and a skill that thus arranged the machinery of the plant.

But in the very arrangement for the plant itself, there seems to shine forth a higher and nobler purpose. In the multitude of seeds, an apparent waste of energy, there seems to be a provision for their legitimate destruction by a higher creation. And if the grain of wheat fails to fill unless the germ is there, who does not see that it is better for man that it should be so? It is best for him that every grain of wheat should represent both so much food, and also a certain centre of new plant life. With what uncertainty would the husbandman sow his field, if perchance only one in a thousand of the precious grains scattered on the furrow would give the green blade, and, in time of harvest, the full ear! He who regards the support of animal life as the highest use of the vegetable kingdom, must also see that certainty of propagation is of prime importance in the plants already mentioned.

But we have perhaps too far prolonged this discussion on this provision in plant life, for the production of food. We readily grant that in the majority of cases, the food for animals is produced in a way that seems primarily for the benefit of the plant, as an individual or species. To some it may appear to be prepared solely for the plant. To this, however, we think there are plain exceptions; and among them we mention again our soft fruits, which are the envelope, or mere accompaniment of the seed. The seeds need a covering, it is true. But why should the covering of the apple-seed give the thousand kinds of this delicious fruit, of every tint and flavor, and varied time of ripening? Why do the pear and peach vie with the apple in the diversified forms and flavors they offer? Why does the strawberry enlarge its receptacle into that most delicious fruit? Why does the grape bury its seeds in such a luscious pulp, and sometimes form the pulp without the seed? That the perfection and variety of the soft portion of such fruits play any part in the economy of the plant, no one will probably contend. The pulp of the grape represents to man so much food. If it forms without seed, it is the cause of no indirect injury, as the filling of wheat-grains without the germ would be, because it never represents new plant life. If the soft fruits have no purpose except to cover the seed, their increase in size, and improvement in flavor, are a mistake. The native apple, in all its harshness; the frost grapes, which the animals allow to fall, with their seeds untouched, unless driven to eat them or starve; the peach, in its hard covering, and the button pear, which no cooking can fully conquer—all these are for the plant the perfection of fruits. Such fruits perfect and protect their seeds.

But our Black Hamburghs and Sweet-waters, our Pippins and Bartletts, are mistakes, and evidences of want of design in such plants, if they have no end out of themselves; for all these variations from the original stock either weaken the seed or invite to its destruction. Because they are of no advantage to the plant, must we grant that they are a mistake, or without significance? By no means. Nor do we think it possible for the majority of men ever to believe that we have not here a direct provision for the animal kingdom, as a whole, and for man in particular; a provision that shows wisdom, though through it plant-life is made entirely secondary. The continuance of the species must be provided for by some means, or its creation would be a failure. This being done, sometimes by one method, and sometimes by another, all the parts of the plant, not needed for propagation, may be modified for the benefit of this higher kingdom. It seems to us that all these modifications indicate this ulterior purpose, to which the interests of the plant, so to speak, are made to yield. We have no doubt, indeed, the three kingdoms of nature are all arranged with reference to man, especially as an intellectual and moral being.

We have already referred to crystallography, and we shall, in a future lecture, enter into the consideration of chemical combinations, in their relation to man. We never could see how the plan of structure, the whole science of homologies in the animal and vegetable kingdoms, could be fully comprehended by any one, without the recognition of a direct provision for man as an intellectual being. Animals and plants are constructed with parts apparently for no other purpose than to show their true place in the organic kingdom. We believe that they are thus linked together by homologous parts that they might be comprehended by man, that he might more surely trace the plan of the Great Architect.

We believe this also, without reference to the question whether these parts came to be as they are through secondary causes or by direct creation.

In the provision made for the increase of beauty in the flower by doubling, there is certainly no reference to the welfare of the plant, for beauty increases at the expense of the seed, the final cause, or one use of the flower, as all will allow. When we see this tendency to variation in such a multitude of flowers; when we see it confined to those plants having methods of propagation other than the seed; when we see this tendency conferring no possible benefit upon the individual plant nor upon the species; when we see what a source of enjoyment this law is to man in his highest cultivation, we might say, how necessary for that highest cultivation—can we doubt for what purpose this law of variation was given? Who can fail to feel that the plant is not for itself; but so far as it seems to be for itself, it is that it may exist; that it exists for a higher kingdom, and that the final cause of plant variation is found mainly in the wants of man, not only as a physical, but also as an intellectual being.

There is another significance of varieties, besides their adaptations to these wants of man, although to some it may seem a mere accident. We refer to the conditions thus presented to man for continual progress. In consequence of this wonderful law of varieties, there is opened the possibility of continued improvement; to reach the limit of this improvement is impossible. Were it true that each species produced from age to age the same identical form without variation, whenever each species was secured, all would be done that could be done in that direction. We have but one species of apple. From this have been produced hundreds of distinct kinds.

There might, indeed, have been as many distinct species created in the beginning. But even then, all that could be done, would be to secure the kinds created. In consequence of this wonderful law, the same end is reached as in the creation of numberless distinct species, and in a manner far better for man. From one species have sprung unnumbered forms; the next year may produce others still more desirable, and the next year others better still, and so on for ever. It is impossible for man to say that he has now the most delicious apple, peach, or pear, or the most beautiful rose, or the most prolific variety of corn possible. The next year a better apple, a more beautiful rose, a more prolific variety of corn may be produced, and this shall be true for ever.

There is thus laid in this law of the animal and vegetable kingdoms the surest condition of a continued progress in man. The possibility of better forms is ever saying to him, Onward! Upward!

In thus viewing the law of variations in all its manifestations, we have forced upon us the conviction that, while it sometimes has reference undoubtedly to the plant or animal itself in the preservation of the species in its higher manifestations, especially in the vegetable kingdom, it is for something out of the plant, and for a higher creation—the animal kingdom; above all, for man as a rational creature. If all these things were created by an infinitely wise Being, this is what we should expect. If they were created directly, we should expect it; if through secondary causes operating through myriads of years, we should expect the same.

And so at this point we are ready to say that we do not see the atheistical tendency of the so-called development theory at all, except so far as it has a tendency to remove us further from God in nature, and in this way make it easier for men to forget Him or doubt His existence. What difference can it make in our belief in the existence, the wisdom, or the power of God, whether he created the first oak as a tree or as a germ, that through secondary causes—the sunlight, the air, and the rain—should expand into the oak? The microscopic germ, with this force lodged in it, that determines the growth of the oak, the form and strength of every fibre, the outline of every leaf, the outward sculpture and inward structure of every acorn that shall cover it for a hundred years, is as much a proof of infinite wisdom and almighty power as the oak in its perfection. If one fails to be proof, the other must. If, to go further, we were to suppose a single germ to be placed upon this globe, which, with untold ages for its development, should give rise to all the myriad forms of vegetable and animal life, with all their wonderful relations to each other, as the germ of the oak develops into the tree; the root, the stem, the leaf, the flower, and the fruit, all unlike, but having a relation to each other—if we could believe that from one such germ all life upon our globe had sprung, would it shake our belief for one moment in God, or alter our conception of His character? Do we look upon the trees and the animals around us, upon our own bodies, as any the less the work of God, or evidence of His existence and illustrative of His character, because produced through secondary causes, than they would be if they came full grown from the hand of God, as we believe that Adam came? If one looks at his own body, and fails to see so much of purpose there as to imply a designer, then he would fail to see it if he were created full grown. There is a certain kind or degree of scepticism for which there is no cure; it is an incapacity to weigh proof. This may exist in connection with great learning and great power of scientific investigation. Where this defect exists, all labor spent in accumulating proof is labor lost. When you have presented one object to a man in clear sunlight and he cannot see it, you know he is blind, and no accumulation of objects will enable him to see. This principle was forcibly illustrated by our Saviour, when He represented Abraham as saying : " If they hear not Moses and the prophets, neither will they be persuaded though one rose from the dead."

We consider the decision of the question how animals and plants came upon this globe to be a matter of investigation as to facts. How that question will be ultimately decided we have no doubt. Biologists can throw light upon many dark points, but it is upon geology that we must mainly rely for facts. We have not seen any strong argument made out, none that leads us to believe that geology has yet given any satisfactory testimony in favor of the development theory. We have attempted to show that variation is what we should expect to find in species created by a wise Being. And if we are threatened with the authority of great names on the opposite side, we will not be dismayed while we have on our book-shelves the works of the same great men, in which the opposite view is most ably maintained. We can afford to wait, certainly, till they have refuted their own arguments, unless we get new light in other directions. When the truth comes, we are not only bound to receive it, but are ready to do so.

We welcome all labors of the development theorists, and feel thankful for them. We welcome them as contributions to science.

We never read a more convincing work on natural theology than Darwin's book on the Fertilization of Orchids. We have no doubt that he and his colaborers are accumulating weapons that will yet batter down his philosophy and the leading theory upon which it rests. "We heartily adopt," says a distinguished scientific man, "the science of Darwin, but not his philosophy."

The distinction is a just one; and such a spirit will guide us safely. The subject of variations, which we have been discussing, has given rise to the development theory. We accept the facts of variation and the influence of "natural selection," but not the inferences that are drawn from them.

We see the need of variations for the best good of the world, for man himself. If provided for in the creation of certain species, and those species most useful to man, we see in this a mark of wisdom as much as in the adaptation of the parts of our bodies to each other, or of our bodies to the external world.

We regard, then, the law of variation as a means of preserving the species under certain circumstances, and as a means of better fitting beings for their various uses, and not as the creator of the being, nor in any sense the originator of the species.

Variation is the quality of a species, and not its producer. We see nothing yet to shake this belief, and we see no theory of creation more simple or plausible than the Bible account.

LECTURE VII.

CHEMICAL ELEMENTS AND THEIR MUTUAL RELATION.

Argument for design may rest on collocation alone.—Character of Creator learned from the very proofs of His existence.—Number of elements known.—Results secured by their nature and relative quantity.—Fixed laws of combination.—Neither matter nor force lost.—Pillars of organic life.—Evidence of design in the constitution of matter.—Equilibrium, how restored in the four elements.—Balanced affinity.—Nature of their compounds.—Oxygen specially considered.—Its compounds.—The air.—Original condition of matter.—Oxygen in the air a residual substance.—Essential to animals.—Helps form the tissues and secures activity.—Produces artificial light and heat.—Common and active state.—Ozone.—Affinity of oxygen varied by temperature.—Hydrogen.—Basis of flame.—Its inflammable compounds.—Combination of properties fitting it for a light-producer.—Combines with carbon to produce light.—Summation of properties.—Its fitness for organic structures.—Constant change in animal bodies.—Relation of hydrogen to nitrogen.—Nitrogen adds to weight of atmosphere.—Moderates the action of hydrogen.—Negative properties.—Nature of its compounds.—Carbon.—Different forms.—Supplements hydrogen in combustion.—As an element, always solid.—Coal.—Indestructible at common temperature.—Carbonic acid.

IN our last lecture we considered the law of variation among species, by which varieties are produced in the animal and vegetable kingdom. That subject completed all we have to say of the adaptations to the physical wants of the animal kingdom. The remaining lectures will be devoted mainly to the provisions in nature for the intellectual and moral constitution of man, and to the Bible as a part of those provisions.

But before we consider these higher adaptations, we wish to go further still in our investigation of the physical universe, that we may see that we can reach no depth where evidence of the being and character of God is not found. As we commenced with man, and have followed organic life through the animal and vegetable kingdoms, we come, naturally, in our course, to the chemical elements which make up, not only the earth, but all of those beings we have been considering.

The argument for design certainly would be conclusive, if the science of chemistry were unknown. That argument can rest on the collocation of matter alone; on results worked out by means of it. A curiously constructed machine might be studied in reference to the end for which it was made, without any knowledge of the materials of which it was composed. The hands of a watch, marking the hours, minutes, and seconds, upon the dial-plate, would be to us proof of design, though we had never looked beneath the dial-plate to learn the material or even the combination of wheels and springs by which the result is secured. In fact, all the different kinds of clocks and watches equally show design although no one can tell how much skill has been manifested in their construction till he sees the work, or witnesses the results.

So the structure of the eye might be understood by an anatomist, and its evidence of design and the mechanical skill manifested be appreciated by an optician, though he knew nothing of the chemical elements that composed it, and had never heard of atomic weights or chemical formulas.

But the deeper we go in our study of Nature, the more perfect the proof becomes for the existence of God, and the more full are the revelations of His character. And by the very process of proving His being, we learn His character, for we only know that He is, in the study of nature, by learning what he is. There is now no field of physical research in which the knowledge is more exact than in chemistry; and there is no department of science that shows more plainly the being and character of God. The proof may not be so tangible as in some of the special contrivances found in the animal and vegetable kingdoms; and being of a more general character, it may not be so satisfactory to all men. But every argument here has the advantage of not being weakened by any development theories. Matter remains as it was. Chemical affinity is the same now that it was when the foundations of the earth were laid. There is in it no volition, no organic law of development. There is no possible indication of any change in the quantity of matter, or in its laws of combination.

When we consider that the living species of animals now known number half a million at least, and the species of plants are numbered by hundreds of thousands, with such diverse appearance and properties, we should infer that the kinds of matter composing them were very numerous. But these varied substances are merely combinations. The eye, with all its curious mechanism; the brain, the organ of the mind; the feather of the ostrich, the countless shells of the ocean and the land; the fruits and flowers, the healing balsams and deadly poisons—are all formed from but few of the elements that, under the control of chemical affinity, modified by the vital principle, produce these varied compounds.

Not seventy elements are yet known; and of these, not more than twenty make up the great mass of the earth's crust, and four of them constitute the greater portion of all organic beings. When we learn the small number of simple substances, we are at once impressed with the vast number of conditions under which they can appear in producing every inorganic and organic object upon the globe.

There is a wonderful fitness in the elements to produce results; and this fitness is secured both by their nature, and the quantity in which they were created. They give the solid framework of the earth, the water and the air, the plants and animals. This globe is what it is, not only because the elements are what they are, but because of their relative quantity. If the hydrogen which forms one-ninth of all the water on the globe had been much increased, there would have been more water; but no free oxygen would have been left, and animal life as it now exists would have been impossible upon the earth. If there had been less hydrogen to combine with the oxygen, or less nitrogen to mingle with it, the air would have been so rich in this element that combustion would have been uncontrollable. Had there been no potash, the majority of land plants could have had no existence; or if it had been found in small portions here and there upon the earth, what a scanty vegetation would have existed? And as animals depend upon plants for life, without this element as it now exists, land animals would be almost, if not entirely unknown. Men probably could not exist. The same is true of other elements, of which we are accustomed to think but little. If no phosphorus were found upon the globe, none of the higher plants could grow and mature their seeds, none of the higher animals could exist.

The bone and brain of man must have this element. Now it is easy for one who has never studied this subject in the light of chemistry, geology, and physiology, to think of the earth as a huge conglomeration of matter, supporting plants and animals, and to suppose that it might have been very different from what it now is, and still support them; but it is not so. The want of a single one of the abundant elements, of oxygen or hydrogen, nitrogen, carbon, calcium, phosphorus, or potassium, would have left the earth a dreary waste. Any essential variation in the quantity, or distribution, or chemical power of any one of them, would have entirely changed the face of nature. What chemist can gather a spadeful of soil in any portion of the earth, and find in it these elements, as he will, so essential to plant and animal life, without being filled with wonder at the accuracy of that great chemical experiment when the world was made? And when he has learned from geology by what means these substances have been spread over the earth, and so prepared that they may be ever present in the soil, his wonder is not diminished, and he needs what has been called the "capacious credulity of an infidel," to believe that anything but Infinite Wisdom and Power could produce the result which he sees. The poetic language of Holy Writ has for him a literal meaning: "*Who hath measured the waters in the hollow of his hand, and meted out heaven with a span, and comprehended the dust of the earth in a measure, and weighed the mountains in scales, and the high hills in a balance?*"

He finds an answer in the elements. These elements, so wonderfully constituted, so nicely balanced in quantity and so carefully distributed by the geologic forces that have continued to act since the foundations of the earth were laid, give not only the conditions of sensitive life, but all that sensitive life can desire. Man, the lord and master of the animal kingdom, finds in the combination and power of the elements the support of his life, the means of enjoyment in the exercise of all his senses, the means of improvement in the use of all his powers.

We learn also, that these combinations in the production of distinct objects is no matter of chance; that the objects around us are not mere accidents, here of one composition, and there of another. Limestone is the same the world over, containing so much metal, so much oxygen, and so much carbon. Give the chemist the weight of the stone, and if it be pure, he will tell you how much of each element is present, as well before he analyzes it as afterwards. Matter remains unchanged in its kind, and its laws remain the same; so that every gem, when it is crushed, or melted, or dissolved, has only changed its form. Neither the elements that composed it, nor the forces that arranged the particles, have changed. All that is wanted are the proper conditions, and the gem will reappear. Decay and fire may destroy the form of the animal, tree, and tender plant; but from every one goes forth the material and the energy, that, under the control of the vital principle, shall produce the same kind of organic structure, or its equal, in quantity of matter and chemical force.

So in the ceaseless changes on our planet, in the grand succession of life and death, that, like successive waves, sweeps over it; nothing is lost, nothing ever has been lost, and nothing gained.

Nothing of chance has been found, or can be found. The elements are the alphabet of the material world, and chemical affinity and vitality the great, unwearied compositors, that set in type the thoughts of God, which He would reveal in the material universe. And we have in the constitution and laws of matter, as convincing proof of design as in the type of the printing-case, that, in the hands of the skilful compositor, goes through the numberless changes known in the art of printing.

We shall have occasion, in another place, to speak of the law of chemical combination in relation to mind. In the present lecture, we shall confine ourselves to the consideration of some of the results of that law, and to some of the elements and chemical compounds that play an important part in the economy of nature, especially in relation to man.

And the first elements that force themselves upon our attention, are the four which are the pillars of organic life. While many other elements are called into play in building up and supporting organic beings, they are so small in quantity compared with oxygen, hydrogen, nitrogen, and carbon, that these are properly regarded as the pillars of plant and animal life. They not only supply material for building up the living structures, but they also furnish the conditions of their existence. The water and the air are their products, and without either of these on the globe, organized beings could not exist. We are struck with wonder and admiration at the fitness of these four simple elements for the part they play in this globe, in transforming it from a barren rock into an abode of beauty, and a place of animal and intellectual enjoyment. If there is design in the collocation of matter, in the adaptation of parts in created beings, the manifestation of wisdom and benevolence in adorning and peopling the earth, we can hardly fail to inquire if there is not also evidence of the same personal attributes, somewhere apparent, in the materials with which all these marvellous structures have been formed. And when the inquiry has been fairly made, the answer has been fully and explicitly in the affirmative.

There is nothing absurd in supposing matter to have existed, in some form, from all eternity. But when we have studied the elements in all their relations and adaptations, it is impossible for us to believe that matter came to be what it is without an ordaining intelligence. Such relations of quality and quantity have appeared as to show, most conclusively, that the elements were adapted to the reign of life upon the globe. And the combination of so many substances, with such a range of affinities, could not be supposed to exist, working harmoniously to the same end, the sustaining of life, unless they were created for that purpose. To believe that they happened to be what they are, would demand the utmost credulity.

We can but glance at some of the properties and compounds of the four elements already referred to. So essential are they to life, that it was not only necessary that they should be well distributed, like other substances, in the beginning, but since such vast quantities of them may be consumed in a single place, they must also have the power of easily restoring the equilibrium, or of returning to any portion of the earth from which they may be taken. This requirement is remarkably met by their constitution, either in the simple, or the compound state.

Three of them are gases so permanent, that no mechanical power that man can bring to bear upon them can reduce them to the solid or liquid form. Oxygen and nitrogen are free, uncombined gases, floating over every inch of the globe, as atmosphere, bathing every object, and under the pressure of their own weight permeating every porous substance. Hydrogen is not found uncombined; but in its compounds, especially in the vapor of water, it is almost, if not quite, as constantly present as the atmosphere itself. Carbon, the fourth element, differs entirely from the other three. So far from being a gas, it is one of the most fixed of all bodies; no heat yet brought to bear upon it having caused it to take the form of vapor. But when united with oxygen it floats away in the air, and as carbonic acid, forms itself an atmosphere for the earth.

These four elements are, then, ever present in every portion of the earth. No matter how many tons of them are taken up by the green herbage of the field in a single day, at its close there may be just as much of each one of them hovering over it and resting upon it as though not a single grain had been gathered in over its broad acres. These elements mingle together in the whirlwind and the storm. They float together in the gentlest breeze. Every breath of air that fans the cheek, or moves the aspen leaf, bears these four elements as inseparable companions. They combine and recombine under the chemical power of light and heat and the electric flash, and thus they are ready in every place, at every moment, to renew the face of the earth.

The affinity they have for each other is so nicely balanced that under the action of living beings they are decomposed and recombined to form organic compounds ; and when these compounds have performed their allotted work, they are decomposed into other compounds of gaseous form, to float away, until again imprisoned by the roots or spreading leaves of the forest, or the tender herbage of the meadow ; and then again they return in ceaseless circuit to the inorganic, air-like state.

Each of these elements is worthy of careful study, for its relation to the other three, and for the part it plays in the economy of nature.

Oxygen is the most abundant element on the globe, and has the widest range of affinity. Nearly, if not quite, one-half of all the solid crust of the earth is composed of this gas, in combination with metallic and metalloid substances. And here we are struck with the numberless series of compounds which oxygen gives, without which the earth would be entirely unfitted, in its mineral constitution, for the support of vegetable, and consequently of animal life. The deepest rocks which the convulsions of the earth have thrown up from its very framework, are made up chiefly of the oxides of metals and silicon. And every sandstone, slatestone, and limestone that makes up the sedimentary rocks, is simply a combination of this gas with other elements.

The quartz pebble, and almost all the gems, borrow their hardness and varied tints from combinations of this same element. The sand that smooths the rugged rocks, and a large proportion of all the salts upon which plant life is dependant, are oxides. Remove the oxygen from our globe, and it would be left a metallic ball, mingled only here and there with metalloids in combination. Then eight-ninths of all the waters that fill the oceans, roll down in mighty rivers, and permeate the earth, is oxygen. Thus far it appears in combination.

It has seized upon the metals and turned them to stone ; on hydrogen, and formed the waters. In no one of these substances would its presence ever be suspected, were it not for that searching analysis by which the chemist unlocks every element from the chains with which its own affinity has bound it.

But in the air we have it uncombined. It is diluted with four times its quantity of nitrogen ; but there is no chemical union between them, and the oxygen is unchanged.

No chemist can study the rocks without feeling that there was a time when their particles were brought together to form the compounds which they now present. The oxygen that forms the granite was undoubtedly once free and uncombined, and the oceans of water once floated in space as separate gases. But when the great experiment was made of bringing these elements together ; when the compounds of the rocks and the waters of the oceans had been formed ; when oxygen had spent its fury on all the elements which it has since held in its unyielding grasp, the oxygen of the air was undoubtedly left as a residual substance. For, notwithstanding the strong affinity of oxygen for other elements, the amount of each element which it can hold in combination is unalterably determined. When every metal and metalloid that forms the crust of the earth had received its portion, the oxygen of the atmosphere was so much of one material in excess in the world-making experiment.

Nor do we regard this as in any sense a mere lucky accident. Certain it is that the whole range of life upon the globe, depends upon the fact. We regard this excess as one of the predetermined conditions of the experiment which was tried to prepare an abode for sensitive life, and which was, therefore, tried in such a manner as to secure the end in view; for the free oxygen of the atmosphere is as essential to life as the rocks, and soils, and water that form the earth's crust. The result is the same as every chemist sometimes aims at in his work in the laboratory. He pours in one element or compound in excess. The great Architect of the universe who ordained the chemical power of oxygen, ordained also the quantity of materials upon which it should act to form the rocks and oceans; and when the eternal balance was poised, to determine the proportions, provision was made for the atmosphere. Oxygen was not only the great preparer of the globe for living beings, but it plays such an essential part in sustaining life, that the early chemists named it vital air. No animal can live without it. It not only enters into the tissues, forming in the higher animals bone, and muscle, and nerve, but it is also the great purifier of the animal system, combining with the worn-out particles, giving them the form best fitted for elimination from the body. And by this very process, it gives that power to the system which volition calls into play in every movement of the body, and exercise of mind ; and as it burns up the organic compounds, it becomes the greatest agent in securing in the body that degree of warmth which the functions of life demand.

It is also the producer of artificial light and heat in all ordinary combustion. Practically, artificial light and heat would be impossible without just such an element as oxygen is. We have indeed light and heat from the combination of other elements, but their products are generally solids or noxious compounds. It may be said that hydrogen and carbon, the other elements concerned in ordinary combustion, show as much design as oxygen ; and so undoubtedly they do. They were created in reference to each other ; and the office of each, and the perfect adaptation of each one for that office, we shall endeavor to show in another place. But all will agree that oxygen is the great heat and light producer. In vain were our coal-beds formed, or the veins of the earth filled with oil, were it not for the free oxygen of the air. For without this, they could give no more light and heat than the granite of the mountains, or the waters that gush from their sides.

Professor Cooke, in his extended work on Religion and Chemistry, has forcibly presented the evidence of design in the two states of oxygen. In its ordinary condition it seems harmless, uncorrosive, bathing the most delicate organs without injury; but when roused to activity by a certain temperature, it devours with the fury of a demon, and never rests till nothing more is left to be destroyed. Under certain conditions, this element becomes so changed that it has had applied to it a new name, ozone, from the supposition that it was an entirely distinct substance. Some particles of this active, corrosive form of oxygen are ever floating in the air, so much diluted as in general to prove harmless to living organisms, but ever ready to unite with decomposing particles of organic matter, and thus more perfectly fulfil its mission as the great purifier. When this subject shall be more fully studied, we have every reason to believe, from late experiments, that new proofs will be brought out of the evidence of design in adapting this peculiar condition of oxygen to the welfare of the animal kingdom, and especially of man.

There is another characteristic of this element that seems to have special relations to the wants of man. Its affinity varies in its intensity for different substances according to the temperature. With iron, it unites so readily, that particles of pure iron, properly prepared in fine powder, glow with heat, and are changed to oxides, simply by dropping through the air; while charcoal, at the common temperature of the globe, remains unchanged for thousands of years. But in the heat of the furnace its relative affinity is completely reversed, so that the oxygen rushes from the iron ore to the heated carbon, leaving the iron in the metallic state for the use of man. It is proper here to state, that this is only one example of the change in the relative strength of affinities by change of conditions; taking advantage of which, the chemist is able to unlock every compound, and produce results entirely impossible were the affinities of all substances increased or diminished alike, by any change of condition. The materials of gunpowder are ground and pressed together, and yet the chemical affinities of the compounds remain, at ordinary temperatures, unchanged. The oxygen still clings to the potassium, holding even the nitrogen with a firm grasp. But a single spark of fire reverses these affinities in an instant, so that there is an interchange of elements; new compounds are formed; the solids change to gases with terrible explosive power.

When we see an element transforming the globe from a ball of metal to the rocky crust of our earth, forming its gems and soils, its oceans that beget the springs, the rains, and dews; when we see it entering into the structure of every living thing, and essential to animal life for every moment; when we see it prepared in such quantity that when it had formed all needed compounds, just enough was left to carry on the processes of life; when we see its relation to light and heat, its passive and its active state, and its change of affinity under the temperature which its own combination produces, so as to set free the metals and other substances most useful to man—can we fail to recognise in it the work of an Infinite Intelligence?

The second element of the group, hydrogen, is never found as a natural product in an uncombined state. It would be impossible for any considerable quantity of it to exist mingled with the free oxygen of the atmosphere, without chemically combining under the influence of electricity, and other agencies brought to bear upon it. In all the processes of nature, in which hydrogen is liberated by decomposition, it is liberated as a compound, or it unites with some other element the instant it is set free. Its most abundant compound, water, is formed by its union with oxygen, so that what we shall hereafter say of water will have as much reference to one of these elements as to the other. But hydrogen has of itself properties of paramount importance to man. It is in almost every instance the basis of flame. Any incandescent gas is flame; but strike hydrogen from our list of elements, and artificial light from flame would be almost impossible. It is hydrogen that fills our gasometers, and, flowing through the iron arteries beneath the streets throughout the city, shoots forth its jets of flame wherever the wants of man demand it, almost turning night into day. It is hydrogen, that, stored up in the petroleum for countless ages, now flows through the thousand openings in the rocks, and gives to the whole world abundant means of light It is hydrogen in the oil of the whale that gives it such value, that the leviathan of the deep is hunted among the icebergs of the north. The blazing wood upon the hearth-stones sends forth in its flickering flame the cheerful light of hydrogen. The palace and the hovel are alike its debtors.

It is so abundant, and so combined with other substances, that no science was needed to prepare it for common use. In wood and oil it has ever been at the command of the most illiterate savage. These substances gave him light as well as heat, he knew not how.

It remained for modern science, after wood and oil had supplied the wants of man for thousands of years, to show the nice balance of the hydrogen affinities with other elements, so that it should be ever ready for use in its most available form.

It was only when the demands of civilization called for a more extensive use of flame, that science was needed to set hydrogen free in large quantities. It cannot improve its quality over that which the wax and oil gave the ancients, before the science of chemistry was known. It is only by a combination of many properties that hydrogen thus supplies the want of man in the production of artificial light. First, we have the strong affinity of this element for oxygen, by which flame is secured. Second, its affinity for other substances with which it is found in combination, so nicely balanced that the heat produced by burning one portion shall be sufficient to set free another portion, and so on until the stock of hydrogen is exhausted. A common lamp or candle is a gas-manufacturing apparatus where the burning of one portion of the gas, while it gives light and heat, as though that were its only office, is setting free another portion to renew the flame. The flame is constantly consumed, and yet never growing less. A third property of hydrogen that fits it for illuminating purposes is, that its product with oxygen is water, which, intensely heated at the instant of its formation, passes off in an invisible form, neither obscuring the light nor doing injury to the air. But hydrogen alone is not sufficient to produce light. It gives flame and heat, but there is a want of brilliancy. Even the compound blow-pipe flame, giving the most intense heat produced by combustion, would be almost useless of itself for illumination. And here we have another remarkable property of hydrogen, that fits it for giving light. Whenever it is produced by heat, from organic substances, it brings off in combination with it a portion of carbon. This carbon is set free as minute particles of charcoal in the hydrogen flame, and for a moment these thousand points of white hot carbon glow with intense heat, and give us the light of the common flame. The next moment they are burned to invisible gas, while another series takes their place. How nicely all these affinities must be balanced. Suppose the affinities were changed so that the carbon should burn first, we should have heat, but no sufficient light. Or if the affinity of hydrogen were too strong to be set free from combination by the heat of its own combustion, then flame, as now ordinarily obtained, would be impossible. But the hydrogen having the power to bring off carbon in the form of gas, and then to drop the particles in the heated flame an instant before they are consumed, we have the light-giving machinery perfect. So far in the production of flame, we are sure of the chemical changes. And if we consider the nature of hydrogen when set free; the substances with which it is found in combination; the process by which it secures constant flame; its affinity for oxygen; its power of bringing away with it the particles of carbon needed to give light; its process of burning, by which the particles of carbon are caused to give light till others are ready to take their places, and its harmless product—water;—when we consider all these, we not only recognise a substance admirably fitted for an important place among the needful things bestowed upon man, but its fitness is secured by so many distinct conditions, that intelligence and wisdom are necessarily inferred from such a provision. Hydrogen being one of the constituents of all organic beings, we naturally seek to learn its fitness for this purpose. There are many things connected with physiology that we do not yet understand. But we know it is a law of all animal bodies that their particles shall change. The human body is like the constantly consuming flame. Its particles are dissolving and vanishing, while others, prepared from the constant supply of food, take their

Nitrogen. 197

place. We may not fully understand why this constant change should be necessary. But we know that it is necessary under our present constitution, and that by it heat and muscular power are both produced. And since this rapid change of particles is necessary for the body, we see how beautifully adapted hydrogen is for the important place it occupies in the animal system. Its oxidation evolves more heat than the same weight of any other substance; and its product, water, is not only readily eliminated from the system, but it aids in bearing away the other substances that in the form of salts must be eliminated by solution.

Hydrogen has also important relations to nitrogen, so that in the decomposition of nitrogen compounds, and probably also as water in the air, it forms ammonia, and thus brings nitrogen into the most favorable condition for the nourishment of vegetation.

The third element to be considered is nitrogen. Design may be learned from results as well as from the means by which the results are produced. As already intimated, a clock would indicate design by the movement of its hands marking the hours, though its wheels were never seen. It is by its results, rather than by knowledge of the methods of its changes, that we must recognise design in nitrogen. We are not, by any means, so sure of its methods and conditions of combinations as in the case of the two elements already considered. It constitutes four-fifths of the atmosphere, but as a portion of the atmosphere, it seems to have no direct relation to animal life. It has mechanical relations to them, and the wing of the bird and of every flying thing has been fashioned with reference to it. For if the nitrogen were gone, the weight of the atmosphere would be so changed that very few, if any, of the winged animals could sustain themselves in it. But chemically considered, nitrogen is an inert body mingled with oxygen, the life-sustaining element, to moderate its force by dilution. But, why it may be asked, could not the oxygen alone suffice, since that alone takes an active part in sustaining life? Certain it is, that organic substances, as they are now constituted, could not exist in pure oxygen. It would prove too stimulating for animal life, and combustion would be terrific beyond description.

We may therefore properly say, that the chemical relations of organic beings have been adjusted with reference to the amount of nitrogen in the air, although it exerts no direct chemical action upon them ; for both of the disastrous consequences just mentioned as resulting from an atmosphere of pure oxygen, would follow simply from the quantity of oxygen breathed, or that would come in contact with the flame in a given time.

When the oxygen is diluted with four times its quantity of this inert gas, its strong chemical power still remains, but only one-fifth as much can be brought into action in a given time on a given space, as there would be were the atmosphere pure oxygen.

We have here all the advantage of the strong affinity of oxygen in producing light and heat, and in supporting life, while its action is beautifully regulated by the nitrogen with which it is diluted. We see, then, its fitness for a constituent of the atmosphere, by its very negative properties. It has no taste, nor color, nor odor; and its affinity is so sluggish, that though mingled with oxygen in an aerial ocean more than fifty miles deep, rolling on the whole earth, only the minutest portions of it ever combine with that oxygen. We cannot conceive of any change that could be made to compensate for the loss of nitrogen in the atmosphere, unless oxygen were increased in quantity, and weakened in its chemical affinity. And there is no end to the confusion that change would introduce into the relation of the chemical elements most useful to man. To meet his wants, oxygen must have the power it now has to combine, and it must be mingled with just such a body as nitrogen to control its combination.

Nitrogen is confined mainly to the air, to organic beings, and to those compounds that, small in quantity, but widely distributed, seem like a special provision for the food of plants and for the use of man. Most of its compounds are soluble or easily decomposed. They cannot therefore make up any portion of the permanent crust of the earth. In fact, it is chiefly in those countries where rain seldom falls, or in places entirely protected from rain and running water, that they can accumulate. It is on the rainless islands of South America that we find guano, a compound rich in nitrogen; and in similar places, in caves, and beneath old buildings, we find an accumulation of nitrates.

We have no direct evidence, then, of the presence of nitrogen on our globe in its earliest history. It is only when we find the remains of organic beings, that we have data for inferring its existence. It may have been brought into its place among the elements that compose our globe, after oxygen had struggled with the other elements, and changed them by its Titanic grasp into the materials that have hardened into stone. Certain it is, however, that nitrogen is essential to all the higher organisms.

It is the nitrogen compounds of plants that chiefly form the food that builds up the animal body and supplies its waste. For this purpose it is well fitted by its weak chemical affinity, and the nature of its compounds. It is easily broken up in every combination, and the resulting compounds being soluble, are most readily eliminated from the system. Its compounds naturally formed by decomposition are volatile, and thus being disseminated by the law of diffusion in the air, are ever present, to be washed down by the falling waters for the nourishment of plants. And small quantities of its compounds are undoubtedly formed by the action of electricity and other agencies in the atmosphere itself, so that this inert element is slowly but surely brought under the power of plant life, and through plants it takes its appointed place in the highest organic forms.

Its weak affinity gives rise to explosive compounds of the utmost importance to man. Gunpowder is not alone for war. It is a great engine of power for the progress of civilization. It not only secures civilized society against the inroads of barbarian hordes, by giving greater war power to civilized man, but by its agency he makes his way through the mountains, and overturns the hills by the roots. The works accomplished in our day through the agency of gunpowder are truly marvellous. Gun-cotton, which may be used as a substitute for powder, and the percussion-cap that ignites them, are both nitrogen compounds. So weak is the affinity of this element when held in the solid state in combination, that by percussion, or the direct application of heat, its compounds are instantly broken up; and this gas, which no mechanical force can compress to a solid, leaps particle from particle, and crushes the solid rocks, or hurls the deadly shot and shell.

We find this element, then, perfectly fitted for its place in the atmosphere and in organic beings. We see its compounds so essential to living beings, tending to equilibrium, from their distribution in the air or by their formation in it. We find some of its compounds, like nitric acid and the peroxide of nitrogen, most useful to man in science and art, so corrosive and poisonous, that were they to be formed in abundance, they would destroy all organic life upon the globe. They are simply combinations of that nitrogen and oxygen which float together in the air, and are kept from forming these compounds abundantly by their nicely-balanced affinities. But wherever a strong base is found like potash or lime, there nature allows nitric acid to be formed in large quantities; because, uniting with these bases, it not only becomes harmless to organic life, but remains a reservoir of nourishment to plants, and an important product for man. We say the base causes the nitric acid to be formed by its presence, and the older chemists called that kind of action catalysis; but if no man can satisfactorily explain it, he must admire this curious relation of chemical substances, and admire the beautiful and beneficial results secured by it. It is one of the safety-valves, one of the regulators abounding in the machinery of nature, by which action is modified and changed, so that the machinery of nature never gets out of order; by which the inorganic world, even, seems to become organic in its vast system of chemical and physical changes, so as to prepare the materials and present the conditions needed for all organic beings, as the human system prepares the various secretions and throws them from the body, or pours them out where they are needed for further use.

We find this element also giving rise to a series of substances most explosive in their nature, by which man becomes terrific in war and powerful in conquering the earth. There is much remaining for us to learn respecting it; but of all that we do know, not a single characteristic can be pointed out that does not seem a special provision for some important purpose.

Every organized being and every organic product

contains carbon as an essential constituent. This element is among the most familiar and most useful in its relation to art and science. It would challenge our admiration for the benefits it bestows upon man, if not a particle of it entered into the composition of our own bodies. But some of its highest uses arise from the fact that it takes its place among the ever-changing particles of the animal system, and is thus constantly oscillating between the two great kingdoms of nature, now appearing in organic products, and then again by combustion or decay rushing back under the power of chemical affinity into the inorganic form. Like oxygen, already described, it exists, even in its uncombined state, under forms so different in all their physical properties, that nothing but chemistry could convince us that these different-appearing substances are one and the same element.

As the diamond, carbon is the hardest and most beautiful crystal known. As coal, in its various forms, it is one of the chief combustible substances. As plumbago, or black-lead, it is soft to the touch, so that its dust is used to prevent friction; and in strong contrast to coal, it is able to withstand the intense heat of a blast-furnace without combustion. Certainly the diamond, flashing with light, as though miniature suns, stars, and rainbows were gleaming through its facettes; the coal upon the glowing grate; and plumbago, one of the softest solids, defying heat and oxygen—are three wonderful forms of existence of the same substance.

They are no more wonderful, indeed, than the different conditions of oxygen; but as carbon is a solid, its different conditions are recognised by the sense of touch and sight, as well as by their chemical relations.

Carbon, like hydrogen, is a constant element in ordinary combustion. They beautifully supplement each other. Hydrogen is a permanent gas; carbon, on the other hand, in a pure state, is always a solid. It is this physical property of carbon that secures to us the vast accumulations of combustible materials in the earth, so essential to mankind in developing the arts of civilized life. The inexhaustible beds of coal are a wonder to the world. They have remained for thousands of years comparatively unused and unknown. But now they become the very basis of material prosperity. If other combustibles would in part take the place of coal, how imperfectly they would do it, and how soon they would be exhausted! Our forests would vanish like frost-work before the sun.

But the mines of coal would never have been formed, if carbon had been other than a solid. The vegetation from which these beds were formed, having lost the other elements, was left as pure anthracite; or in connection with hydrogen and oxygen, gave rise to the different grades of bituminous coals. When we consider the dependance of·man in his highest state, upon these different varieties of coal, for producing light and heat, and working of metals, and for the generation of steam, we see wonderful adaptations in the nature of this element itself, and in its chemical relations to the other elements, to meet his wants; since, when buried under different conditions, it gives rise not only to coal, but to so many kinds of coal, each one fitted for a special use.

Another remarkable characteristic of carbon is its indestructibility, when in the form of coal, by all ordinary agencies. Neither water, nor the oxygen of the air, has power to oxidize it at ordinary temperatures. It defies such agencies for thousands of years. But when raised to a red heat, it not only unites rapidly with oxygen, but under proper conditions easily secured, the process is self-supporting. Its heat is of sufficient intensity to melt all metals on the globe that occur as oxides, and by its heat and affinity for oxygen, to reduce them from oxides to the metallic state.

We hardly need to show how unfitted it would be for its most important uses were it either a liquid or gas, or were it possible with furnace-heat to melt it. In smelting, it can be mingled with the ore in large or small pieces. Intense heat only increases its affinity for the oxygen of the air and of the ore. It remains solid, and firmly keeps its place, even while the melted iron flows through it. The portion that consumes instantly takes the form of gas, and is swept out by the heated nitrogen, thus keeping the products of the furnace pure and the surface of the coal constantly free for increased oxidization. If man was made to use fire, he must have two just such substances as hydrogen and carbon, both together giving light and heat, and the products of both taking the invisible form.

While carbon in the form of charcoal, or mineral coal, defies the action of oxygen at common temperatures, it has no such power in its organic combinations. In animal and vegetable tissue it seems to be in a state of unstable equilibrium, so that portions of plants and animals readily return to the form of carbonic acid. Who can help admiring this beautiful adjustment of affinities, by which carbon can become fixed and remain for ever unchanged until used by man, and also be so joined to other elements in animal and vegetable tissues, that when they are exposed upon the surface of the earth after death, they rapidly decompose, giving up their carbon as carbonic acid, needed to renew the face of the earth?

The properties of carbonic acid itself are eminently worthy of attention. It is heavier than air, but according to the law of diffusion of gases, it is rapidly mingled throughout the atmosphere. It is thus ever present, where vegetation is found, to supply it with the needed carbon. It is highly soluble in water, so that both rain and dew bring it down to be absorbed by the leaves and roots of plants. It gives to the waters percolating the earth greater solvent power for certain substances, so that they set free more readily the mineral salts needed for vegetation. When this gas has reached the tissue of the leaves, the strong affinity of its elements is overcome by the magic power of light, the plant is built up by retaining the carbon, and the oxygen is restored to the air. It combines with various substances to form salts so directly useful to man, that we can hardly regard them as other than a special provision for him. But before the creation of man, it played an important part in the animal kingdom. Nearly all the shell-fish and coral animals that filled the old oceans of geologic ages, like those that are now piling up their walls and towers among the waves, built their masonry of carbonate of lime. The vast beds of limestone and the quarries of marble are the products of carbonic acid gas.

Like the other elements already mentioned, carbon has a perfect fitness for its place in the animal tissue. In partial decomposition of the tissues, it forms soluble compounds, and finally it becomes a gas with such relations to the blood, the tissue of the lung and the air, that it is constantly set free from the system, while oxygen takes its place to produce the changes necessary for the continuance of life. We do not pretend to understand fully all those changes, notwithstanding our advance in animal chemistry; but we understand the results perfectly. We see carbon making a large part of our food. We know that carbon is consumed in the body by oxidization. We know that heat is produced, and that the compounds of carbon are such, that this element is as rapidly and easily eliminated from the body when it has done its work in the vital processes, as those elements that are permanent gases. We find it then a body with great diversity of properties and relations, but each property and relation apparently a special provision for the organic kingdom, and many of its properties evidently having reference to man himself. We have no doubt the diamond was made to delight man by its beauty, and that the coal was stored up for his use. If its affinities were different from what they now are, it would not withstand the agencies of nature as it now does, or it would defy them. But now it does service in untold ways for man.

How easily it is conveyed over the world when changed to gas! Having done its work as carbon, it must now be distributed and brought in contact with vegetation to perform its work anew. We need not recount all its nicely-balanced affinities, by which at a high temperature it combines like a giant in strength, and then under the soft sunbeam playing upon the leaf, relaxes its grasp and becomes an obedient servant under the ordinary power of life in an organic being.

These four elements now considered, were they alone known to science, would be enough to establish the proof of design in the constitution of matter. Every plant that clothes the earth, every animal on the land and in the waters, as well as the unnumbered tribes buried in the earth, declare the wonderful fitness of these four elements for producing the myriad forms of organic beings that have appeared upon the globe. We have not here simply a thousand chances to one in favor of design, but they are millions to one. For these

Conclusion.

four elements combine to form all organic beings, forming hundreds of distinct parts in each one, just fitted for their places. Their affinities are such that they answer perfectly the needs of the organic being through the whole course of its life, and when broken up and thrown off by the vital processes, they are alike prepared to appear in other forms. To create such elements implies infinite wisdom, as well as infinite power. To believe them to be uncreated would be possible only to the ignorant, or to those constitutionally unable to weigh proof.

Such a vast field here opens before us in the groups of elements, in considering their varied properties by which they are fitted for the part which each one plays upon the globe, that we need not go beyond the domain of chemistry to show the existence and wisdom of the Creator, and that His handiwork extends even to the dust of the earth. We might go much farther in pointing out the nature of the elements already considered. They show design in their adaptation to plant and animal life, as well as to the higher nature of man. The same is true of all the abundant elements that are well known. But many of them have such plain reference to the intellectual nature of man, that we shall refer to them only in that relation. And we have now come to that part of our course where the adaptation of the world to man's higher nature **must claim our chief attention.**

LECTURE VIII.

PROVISION FOR THE INTELLECT OF MAN IN THE STRUCTURE OF MINERALS AND LAWS OF CHEMICAL COMBINATION.

Preservation of man requires preservation of other beings.—The whole plan to be grasped.—Field of mind.—Animals remain the same.—Man's physical nature conditional for his higher.—Provision for our personality to be expected.—Personality of the Creator.—Mind seeks for the laws of nature.—Physical good never sought for by the great leaders in science.—Search for thought among ancient inscriptions.—Physical and intellectual appetite compared.—Mind of man and the order of nature from the same Creator.—Nature the great teacher.—Her models perfect.—Proofs of the provision for mind.—Minerals.—Mind must be taxed.—Language of Minerals.—Our work is to translate it—Perfectly adapted to the human mind.—Crystalline forms.—Progress of mind in unfolding them.—Fundamental forms.—Effect of crystalline force in the crust of the earth.—Beauty of crystals for man.—Taylor's description of the Russian jewels.—Bible language.—Chemical relation of the elements.—Power of the chemist.—Condition of progress.—Beyond the reach of development theories.—Man has increased in knowledge, but not in mental power.—Answers which nature gives.

WE have thus far attempted to show that this world is a creation, the work of an infinitely wise Being. We attempt to do this by proving that every object has a purpose, and that matter in its ultimate constitution shows that it also was created, being fitted for the structure and support of the varied organic beings on the globe. The constitution and the collocation of matter considered separately proclaim the same great truth; taken together, they give higher and grander views of the Creator's character than either could give by itself.

But we have considered the evidence of design in creation mainly in reference to physical organization, the preservation and growth of plants, the preservation and enjoyment of the animal kingdom. We have incidentally touched upon other and higher topics, but only incidentally, and never of set purpose.

If we commence with the highest created being that inhabits the earth, we find full provision made for his physical wants. But that very provision requires the creating and preserving of other organic beings lower in the scale, which are also provided for in the same perfect manner. And thus we find the provision for man including and absolutely demanding a provision for a complete series of beings, animal and vegetable, and they the unnumbered modifications and conditions of the inorganic kingdom.

It is not enough, then, for us to see the provision for one created being, however adequate that provision may be, nor for a single species, more far-reaching than for the individual. But we are to grasp, if possible, that mighty plan, all-comprehending as it is, by which all the species of plants and animals are suited to the globe, are related to each other as dependants or supports, so that the whole kingdom of life is preserved and all its parts joined and adjusted to each other. There is no doubt proof of design in the structure of the eye, the loop, the hinge, or the ball and socket joint; but it is in comprehending the magnitude and perfection of the plan by which all these varied contrivances make up individuals, and the individuals are adjusted in myriads to the globe, that we rise to the comprehension of the power and the goodness of the Creator. As in some great manufactory, we may see contrivance in every spindle that twists a thread, and in every pulley that turns a shaft, though nothing else is seen, yet it is only when we pass from room to room and see the snowy fibres passing through the maze of machinery, each process preparing it for the next, that we understand a more comprehensive design, that, from the ponderous wheel which rolls beneath the ever-falling waters, up through all the lines of shafts and belts and points of steel to the loom itself, forms one vast machine for the production of the web.

But in the works of God we have a field hardly entered by us yet in this discussion—the field of mind. For the lower animals, the world needs only to be adjusted to their physical wants, and their wants are the same in all ages. The lion, the eagle, and the insect, are unchanged for a thousand generations. They require to-day the same conditions they required ages ago. Under the guidance of instinct they provide food and shelter for themselves and their young. Beyond this they never rise, and to meet their physical wants the world is adjusted. But the physical nature of man is not the end of his creation. As the lower forms of life are conditional for the higher, so the physical nature of man is conditional for other and higher powers connected with his intellectual, emotional, and moral nature. Of the possession of these powers all men are conscious. And if this earth simply provides food, and shelter, and animal enjoyment for man, or if these are the paramount provisions, then he is an anomaly among the creatures of the earth, a being having powers the highest and noblest unprovided for.

But we have already recognised the evidence of the personality of the Creator in his providing for the physical wants of a person, especially in the creation and adaptation of the different parts of the human body. If a personal being, wise, and good, and powerful, were our Creator, we should expect to find as perfect provision for our personality through all the works of nature, as for our physical support and enjoyment. And this evidence of design we consider to be of the highest kind, because it constantly speaks of the personality of God, inasmuch as the provision is for our personality; and in the second place, there is no such necessity for this provision as there is for that for our physical wants.

We may, through the befogging speculations of development theories, believe that all animals and man himself have reached their present physical organization by a principle of adjustment by which they are brought into harmony with the forces and conditions of the natural world. But the wildest theorist cannot believe that the mind of man has gradually developed under the influence of those laws and evidences of mind in creation, which have flashed upon the world only within the last century. So far from their giving origin to mind, or influencing its nature, it is mind that seeks them out from the darkness of ages; seeks for them, too, in the very foundation and framework of the globe. It hungers for them before they are known, and seeks for them as for hidden treasures. The study of nature is nothing more nor less than the search for mind. It brings wealth, indeed, and the means of physical enjoyment; but the whole history of science shows that these were not the primary objects sought for by the great leaders in scientific discoveries in all ages.

They have ever been considered the dreamers and impracticable men; because ever pressing on in the dark passages of Nature's temple, reading her obscure inscriptions, they have had no products to show to those who can see good only in silver and gold and fruits of the earth. They have sought to commune with the Maker of the universe by reading the ancient inscriptions on its pillars and beneath its foundation-stones, as scholars bend with wearied eye and throbbing brain over the old mutilated inscriptions on the slabs and columns unburied in the East. These do not expect to find lessons of wisdom in the old inscriptions, which they have never read in other languages, nor to make discoveries in art and science which shall lengthen human life, alleviate its ills, or add to its comforts.

But in every line upon those old marbles there is the record of a thought, and whatever its value or worthlessness, they wish to throw its light on the great background of human history. It is the search for thought that leads men on, and dignifies the labor among the mounds of Nineveh; that redeems it from the charge of childish folly, and makes each new discovery a matter of universal interest.

To make such investigations is natural to man. Whatever gives evidence of thought, he wishes to understand. The field of thought is the home of a thinking being, the home of man in his highest and noblest state.

No exhibition of thought, unless connected with evil associations, can ever be regarded by him as useless. The very law of his intellectual being forbids it. He may not have so far analyzed his intellectual powers as to know why he is impelled to this or that investigation in nature. He may not be able to give a satisfactory answer to the one who demands the use of his study. But he knows there is a use, as he knows food strengthens his body, although he may be in happy ignorance of such an organ as a stomach, and have no knowledge of the peculiar office of carbon and nitrogen compounds. He cannot tell how the food acts, but he goes on eating, for his appetite demands it. In satisfying its cravings, the good of the body is cared for. It was given to guide men before science could guide them; and it led them in the right direction as surely before the days of Hunter and Liebig as it does now, with all the light of modern science.

So this intellectual appetite, that has led men to dig among ruins, to wipe the dust from the ancient inscription, to gather as a pearl every monument of human thought, to scan every form of matter as it exists in nature; the crystals and the flowers, the animals, from the largest to the animalcules, those now living and those sleeping in their beds of stone, —this intellectual appetite, not a thing of development, and depending upon conditions, but an original controlling power, has led men in the right direction. It has led them to labor, though unable to defend themselves from sneers, and unable to frame arguments in favor of what they knew must be right.

It is this fact in nature, its manifestation of thought, that has enchained so many brilliant intellects in its investigations from the days of Aristotle to the present time. This was the charm that bound them to their work and cheered them in their investigations. The power of this element has never been more fully recognised than in the late work of the great master in zoölogy, Agassiz, who sums each of his first thirty-three chapters as expressions of the thought of the Creator.

He does not, like the alchemist, claim that he has made the gold which he holds up to our admiring view. He presents the gleaming ore, and says: "Here I found it, where it was poured in all its purity by God himself."

We have now laid open broad veins in this rich mine, by centuries of patient search; but it was the particles of the same true ore, the thought of God, that led on the early searchers, though they found it in grains so small and scattered while walking upon the edge of the placer that the multitude could see nothing. But as the miner neither creates the gold which he finds, nor the gold fashions the eye that discovers it, so the mind of man neither creates the order and harmony which he discovers in nature, nor did the order and harmony originate the mind which discovers them. They are both the work of the same Almighty Creator who formed man in His own image, so that he should ever delight to revel among the works which the Infinite Intellect pronounced very good in the beginning.

The great minds of the world have walked with Nature as the scholar walks with the great master, listening as he unfolds his thoughts and deferentially propounding questions in every case of doubt. It was because in nature there was thought embodied; a constant unfolding of a plan drawn by Infinite Wisdom, and written out on every star and mountain, in all the tribes of land and water, in the expanding flower and glittering grain of sand —that they never tired of her communings, never grew wiser than their teacher, but felt themselves to be children to the last. We have but like them to enter the portals of this great temple and read the thought of its Builder in every separate stone and in its joining to others. Nothing is superfluous; and, so far as explored, nothing seems wanting. Every line, seemingly useless in the separate stones, serves to show their true place in the arch or dome. And not a single tint could be lost without marring the grand picture which the pieces all conspire to form. They are like the colored glass of some grand old cathedral window, forming a picture unseen by those who pass on the outer side of the temple, but to those within giving gorgeous tints and celestial groups.

We spend days and nights in our libraries communing with the great of the past ages, and we do well. It gives strength and beauty to the mind to drink in the thoughts of those who towered up as beacon-lights to the world. We make long journeys to see the works of the great masters; but in this temple of nature which opens its portals to us in every land, we are surrounded by works which the great artists have only rudely copied, and in these works we commune with Him who by wisdom hath founded the earth.

We argue that special provision was made in the world for the intellectual nature, because the mind here finds sources of delight; it is constantly urged to renewed investigations, it increases in strength by the work, and all the objects in nature are so related and conditioned as to satisfy the mind when the true relations are discovered.

We step first into the lowest vestibule of this temple, the mineral kingdom.

While design is manifested in single objects, it is mainly in the relation of objects to each other that design seems to have special reference to the mind of man. Wherever contrivance appears that has no possible reference to the welfare of the object itself, as beauty of sculpture, or where objects are hidden from the world, like the pearl or diamond, until brought to light by man, who is capable of appreciating and taking delight in their beauty; or where we find objects bound together by mathematical or physical relations, so that they are brought within the ready grasp of mind, and this principle running through the whole sweep of the three kingdoms, we see a more direct and far-reaching provision for the mental than for the physical constitution of man.

Chemistry has revealed to us more than sixty kinds of matter. All these elements occurring in a simple state, and their compounds existing as natural products, belong to the lowest department of Natural History, mineralogy. It is the same kind of matter as is found in the higher departments, but it is combined and controlled by inferior forces, chemical affinity being the highest force ever manifested in a mineral. We have in the mineral kingdom hundreds of substances making up the earth's crust, mingled in seeming confusion, and many of them of protean form. These are to be sought out and their true nature discovered under their

various disguises. At first view this seems beyond
human power. A vast globe is to be investigated.
Were there no order nor law in the structure of
minerals the task would be hopeless. For where
there is no relationship, the study of one object can
give no aid in understanding another. Any arrangement not founded upon like nature, is only an
arbitrary placing, which is no sign of progress in
any de, artment of science But all of these objects
in the mineral kingdom have a definite plan, and
each one has a relationship to some other. Upon
every one of them are stamped the characters
by which its nature may be known by those who
look with patient study. And nothing in the department of mind is given without labor. Any
scheme that should fail to tax and draw out the
mental powers, would so far be wanting in evidence
of design. We find here a system that leads the
mind on from one discovery to another, ever calling
for greater and greater power, and ever meeting
its highest requisitions by the perfection of the
relations when discovered. What more fitting provision than this can be conceived of? There is
engraven within the very structure of all the minerals of the globe a story, an autobiography, that
unrolls the more, the longer we gaze upon it. It is
perfect, for the writing is a transcript by their Maker
of the nature He has given them; not like the
daguerreotype, the very shadow, but the very thing
itself. It is the nature given by God, manifested in
all these sensible signs by which the thing is

known. So beautiful and so complete is this language, so valueless except in relation to man, so perfectly adapted to him as an intellectual being, and through his intellectual being becoming such a means of physical as well as intellectual enjoyment, that we seem to hear the voice of God speaking from the silent rocks more audibly than among the higher forms of animate nature.

A celebrated mineralogist was once asked how he knew that a certain body had fallen from the heavens, which he was giving thousands of dollars for, to enrich his cabinet of meteorites. His answer was: "I see the finger-marks of the Almighty stamped upon every part of it!" This might seem a bold expression, or as indicating some wonderful or unusual property in those bodies that fall from the heavens. But if such language could be applied to a meteorite, it is equally true of every pebble beneath our feet. To translate these marks, to read this language of the mineral kingdom, requires indeed the highest conditions of mental activity; but when read, it is a language not of our making, but simply of our translating. We have a multitude of forms, but each form perfectly defined; the sensible properties varied without limit, but all combined forming labels for every species in the mineral kingdom as perfect as the works of God ever are; a language the same in every part of the world; a language charming in its variety, beautiful in its accuracy and adaptation to the human mind.

The nature of this language we have already indicated, but we will examine it more in detail, because it is a part of that in which the whole book of nature is written. And he who would read the inscriptions on her grand old arches, and the poems in her grottoes, must not despise the alphabet even, which, meaningless by itself, is the only key to unlock those well-springs of knowledge which the unthinking multitude never enjoy, hardly knowing of their existence, though walking for a lifetime among them. And let not those who, with eyes untrained or with minds never roused to activity, see nothing but chaos and chance in the forms and properties of matter, deny the existence of such a language; and let not those who have labored hard and successfully in its translation mistake its beauty and completeness for their own work. We can present only the mere outline of this language; but enough, perhaps, for our present purpose. It is made up of the signs or characteristics by which minerals are known. These signs constitute the language which students of this department of nature have been for ages enlarging and enriching by discovering new minerals, and by studying with more care those already known. I need but mention these characteristics of the mineral kingdom, to have it seen that they tax every sense for their acquirement, draw out the mind by every avenue, pour in knowledge by every channel, and thus vindicate their adaptation to our intellectual nature by offering the conditions of rapid, well-balanced mental development.

The first of these signs is the crystalline form. And what a brilliant language is here introduced! We have been delighted with the beauty of its characters, even while unable to translate a single word, and perhaps ignorant that they were signs of a language, old as creation, and sure as the divine oracles. It sparkles from every grain of sand, glitters from every well-filled cabinet, and streams forth in joyous gushing beams from the "Mountain of Light." The precious gems, like the stars, have in all ages delighted men by their brilliancy. But it is in the study of their angles, the planes of cleavage, and the position of their axes, that the ablest minds have found a life employment, and seen the deepest beauties of the mineral kingdom. It is interesting to trace the progress of mind verging towards truth, peering into the myriad of crystalline forms, coming nearer and nearer to the true translation, sometimes reading a sentence correctly without daring to vouch for its truth, or able to join others to complete the story, until Haüy, by the fortunate crushing of a crystal, found in its broken fragments the primitive form, the first intelligible key to this hitherto obscure language.

Minds that had been groping in darkness, now saw light flashing from the very midst of that darkness. Then was called in mathematics, that ever-ready instrument of progress in science. Whole volumes were filled with problems relating to this department of nature. What were all those problems? Not the work of men, as we too often think

They were but lines in the translation of that Divine language, which needed for its completion the power of the whole human intellect. But the fact that this translation could be made into mathematical formulas at all, shows the accuracy and universality of this language written in the mineral kingdom. We are filled with wonder and admiration at the fact that amid the varied forms into which nature moulds the outer surface, as if to hide and protect from mortal eye as a secret charm the primitive form, the mind of man has been able to look beneath the cunning disguise. And when he has accomplished this, she rewards his labor by showing him that there are among crystals but thirteen fundamental forms from which all others can be derived, and of which they are modifications. Such a generalization is indeed evidence of the godlike nature of the human mind, and the existence of such materials for thought, such means of bringing the rocks of the earth by one grand discovery within the intellectual dominion of man, shows what provision was made even in binding the elements together, for man in his highest nature.

We might enlarge upon the evidence of design in the action of the crystalline force which separates the mingled materials, bringing particles of the same kind together, so that the metals and ores have been gathered in veins for the use of man, and the granite and marble fitted not only as the pillars of the earth, but for his service. We could hardly overlook the utility of this force in the hands of the chemist in producing some of the wonderful operations demanded by his science; but when we consider the beauty of form, the brilliancy of lustre, and the richness of color and the unchangeable nature of the precious stones, we can have no more doubt that they were made in reference to the intellectual and emotional nature of man, than we have that the fruits of the earth were made for his food. Was it chance that determined the constancy of angles, and the law of variation, so that the variety of forms might be without limit and yet perfectly within the power of man to comprehend and describe with mathematical accuracy? If the problem were given to meet the wants of the human intellect in the very dust of the earth, can the most learned philosopher conceive of a more perfect result than is found in the law of crystallization? And that law is only the expression, in our imperfect language, of what was written in all crystals when as yet there was no man upon the earth, when the elements were created and brought together. If it were also a problem, to provide for the love of the beautiful implanted in man, no higher provision can be conceived of than is presented in these unchangeable gems. Their beauty is glowingly set forth in the description of the Russian jewels, by an American scholar and poet. "The splendor of their tints is a delicious intoxication to the eye. The soul of all the fiery roses of Persia lives in these rubies; the freshness of all velvet sward, whether in Alpine valley or English lawn, in these emeralds; the bloom of all southern seas in these sapphires; and the essence of a thousand harvest moons in these necklaces of pearl."

Even the glories of the Holy City in the Apocalyptic vision could be set forth only in the symbols of gems. *Its foundations were of sapphire and emerald, of topaz and amethyst. And every several gate was of one pearl.*

I have dwelt at length on the form and beauty of the crystal, because these two elements have such plain relations to man in his higher nature, that it seems impossible to refer them to any blind principle or to any agency except the Ordaining Intelligence that created man, and made provision for his progress in knowledge, and to gratify the love of beauty implanted within him. The beauty of crystals has been a delight in all ages, for the great majority of them are so perfect even when they come from the earth that it is beyond the power of art to improve them; while their structure and forms are conditions for the later and higher developments of intellect, the conditions of progress without which the requirements of mind are never fully met.

And when we leave the domain of Natural History proper, which regards only the outward form and structure of minerals, and examine the chemical relation of the elements, our wonder is increased at the order and comprehensive law of chemical change and combination, by which the human mind has entered into the dark galleries of nature, and read her formulas, according to which the world was made, and by which all changes in earth and air are now going on. The unchangeable rocks, and the organic beings, that dissolve and reappear, have all revealed their structure to us. Not only the outward form of the crystal, and the cleavage of the rocks, and the organic structure of every plant and animal may now be known to man, but the relation of the elements that constitute the structure is unfolded to him, as if he were present when that relation was ordained, in the morning of creation. What higher proof that man is in the image of God, and that the Great Father has acknowledged that likeness and heirship in His works, than is seen by the chemist, who is conscious of his power to command the fire and the lightning, whose eye can pierce the structure of the granite, and all the deep foundation-stones of the earth; who has power to change the waters back to their elements; who can trace the chemical changes in the invisible air above us; conscious of his power, among the unnumbered compounds of nature and of art, to unlock their secrets and call forth their elements, like spirits, obedient to his will? What but an emanation of the Divine Mind could thus enter into the hidden things of creation? What but the ordaining, Divine Intelligence could bring all the works of the universe within the power of the human intellect? Do you say that there are heights yet to scale? I answer, yes; the hills must ever rise before us, or there would be an end to progress; but no hill appears more difficult to climb than those already passed. And never before did man stand on such mountain heights, with such a background over which he can cast his eye; with such a landscape before him, inviting to new discoveries, the whole conspiring to proclaim him the offspring of God, standing in the very midst of the temple reared by his Father's hand.

We are, in chemistry, beyond the reach of all development-theories, for the ancient mountains that have been waiting on their rocky thrones for long ages, while countless generations have come and gone, now invoked by the chemist's power, lift up their voices and declare the power and the laws of chemistry, the same to-day that they were when darkness and desolation were upon the face of the earth.

And the history of man declares that he has not developed any new faculties or powers under the influence of these laws. He was the same, centuries ago, when these laws of chemistry were unknown, that he is now. He has increased in knowledge, but is not changed in his nature by their discovery. The child, who has never heard of atomic weights, and whose ancestors have all been as ignorant of chemical science as though Dalton and Davy had never lived, may be just as ready to enter into its wonders, and to grasp its principles, as though his father were a Liebig, or a Bunsen. His power to grasp science, comes from a higher paternity. He is the offspring of God, and is thus ever ready to comprehend a portion of his Father's works.

In a former lecture, we referred to the change of affinity under varied conditions, as in the case of carbon, and the formation of nitric acid from ammonia, in the presence of a base to neutralize it. These are only isolated examples of changes of which every chemist avails himself in chemical analysis.

He learns in what condition each element is weak, and when it is strong; he learns the changes that every element produces in combination with every other; and as he questions Nature she gives unvarying answers in change of color, change of form, and in the evolution of light or heat or electricity. And when he finds the elements combining by exact weight and measure, and their order of affinity so established, that he can foretell the order and proportion of their combination when thrown together, and count with absolute certainty upon the composition and properties of every compound, he has another proof of the adaptation of the laws of matter to mind. The laws of the invisible atoms have been discovered by men, and those secret changes which constitute the basis of chemical science, ordained from the beginning of the world, are among the most certain subjects of human knowledge. It seems impossible that one should enter into the rich inheritance which chemistry now opens to her students without recognizing infinite wisdom in the relations of the elements to each other, and a provision in them for man as an intellectual being, that he might comprehend there the divine plan, and wield those elements for his own purposes, as his progress in civilization calls for new products and new appliances of matter and of force.

LECTURE IX.

PROVISION FOR MAN'S INTELLECT IN THE RELATIONS OF ORGANIC BEINGS AND IN THE CRUST OF THE EARTH.

Kingdom of life.—Mathematical law continued.—Orders of plants.—Animals.—Fossils.—All form one picture.—Science discovered.—Manifestation of thought in Nature.—Astronomy.—Enthusiasm of Naturalists.—Geology.—Present changes its key.—Provision for man's physical wants presupposes his intellectual nature.—Crust of the earth shows design.—Man multiplies his powers.—Properties of metals. Gold and Silver.—Platinum.—Mercury.—Iron.—Loadstone. —Metals essential to man's progress.—Fuel for man alone. —Power which Chemistry gives him.—Plants and animals made to minister to his physical wants through his intellectual power.

WE pass now to the kingdom of life. We have here the manifestation of a new principle that is connected chiefly with four elements, and gives rise to more forms than are found in the whole mineral kingdom. Vitality gives relations and developments entirely unlike those in the lower department, and not even suggested by anything found there. We have here the relation of parent to offspring, by which matter is moulded into a continued series of similar forms, not by a force in it, but by something higher than physical forces, giving us animal and vegetable structures in which perfection and beauty depend upon the constant change of matter, while in the crystal they depend upon its permanence. We have not here stepped beyond the limits of mathematical law, but it is obscured by more deviations than in the most complicated crystal. What myriad forms start up on every side! Let us sketch an outline of the picture, that we may see how utterly hopeless all attempts at science would be had not an Ordaining Intelligence fitted all things for the intellectual nature of man.

Here we see the plant of single cell, cradled in the northern snow; its kindred lurking in every pool—the fungus, scavenger among plants, feeding on decaying fibre—the lichen and the moss, picturing the broad rocks with fairy groves and rings—the grasses weaving their carpets of green and yielding their riches in almost every portion of the earth—the fir, dwarf birch, and willow, braving the mountain storms, or creeping almost to eternal snows—the pine, whispering its sad moanings in dark and gloomy forests—the oak, spreading its arms in strength—the orange and citron, loading the air with perfume—the broad palm, lifting its feathery leaves in quiet grandeur to the sky, and the algæ binding the ocean with one eternal fringe of rich and varied hues. Mingled with all these are thousands of other plants that adorn every landscape, as rich in product, as curious in structure, and as varied in form. And all these are ministering to a higher form of life—the animal kingdom, that, starting so near the vegetable kingdom that we cannot draw the dividing line between the two, bursts into a wealth of forms with sensitive life, ending in man, endowed with thought and reason, with power to understand this chain of beings, as he is their appointed lord and their connecting link with the Maker of them all.

Among these we know the polyp, that with radiate masonry builds its walls and mounds strong enough to shut back the ocean, and broad enough for nations to dwell upon.

The waters teem with fishes and shells, the air with birds and insects, the fields and forests with the higher tribes, and the rocks with the casts and figures of those that lived in geologic time. We reckon our species of plants and animals by hundreds of thousands, besides the vast numbers of the fossil series. A single species, among the cultivated plants, may come to be represented by more than a thousand distinct varieties.

It is in this field, among these countless hosts of the kingdom of life, that the human mind has achieved some of its greatest triumphs, in tracing the grand design by which the vast multitude of organic beings are so related in their plan of structure, that the whole series can be comprehended by a single mind. And when we add to the living forms the countless host that the rocks contain, we do not confuse the picture, but only make its shadings more perfect. All the labors of the army of naturalists have tended to this one result: to bring out order and system, not by creating them, but by reading the plan and discovering the grouping which

Nature has already made. She prepared the work so that the mind of man should be fully satisfied when it was comprehended. She prepared it in such a way that the best powers of the mind should be called out in discovering and comprehending it.

Nature never arranges. She does, indeed, put her symbolic language on every stone in her temple. But though the building is perfect to the eye of the Great Architect, it is a perfection of relation and not of position. Its blocks are like those so prepared in the mountain, that no sound of hammer or any tool of iron was heard when they were joined together. It seems chaos to man until that relation is perceived as it existed in the Divine Mind and is manifested in his works. The blocks are scattered where they were fashioned by the Creator, on every continent, the islands of the sea, and beneath the waters. Their true place is written in their structure; it is repeated in every change, from the unfolding of the germ to the perfect being. But it is the gathering up of these scattered fragments, so that their relation shall be seen by man, as they formed a perfect whole to the omnipresent eye in the first creation—it is this entering into the thought of God by the army of naturalists, that is the great triumph of intellect. This shows both the divine type of the human mind, and also the perfect provision that has been made for it in the organic world, that the whole plan of structure, and the manifold relations, should all be perfectly within the grasp of that mind, and be adapted to its nature; adapted to it in calling out its powers and in meeting its highest conceptions of wisdom and skill in the nature and perfection of the relations discovered.

It is this search, this gradual unfolding of the Great Master's thought, that has quickened the senses and strengthened the powers of Aristotle, Linnæus, and Cuvier, and of the long list of the dead and living naturalists almost equally worthy of mention. The record of single struggles and of single triumphs, had we time to recount them, would not only prove to us the intensity of thought, the taxing of the senses, and the broad generalizations through which each of the great naturalists has passed, but would show that every truth searched out and brought within the domain of science, by discovered relations to other truths, has repeated this higher, this sublime truth, which transforms the world from a mere machine to a living interpreter of God's character to man ; this truth, that all portions of the universe, its matter and forces, were so arranged in reference to the mind of man, that he might comprehend them and recognize in their Builder the omnipotent Being of whom he is the image.

And what part of the physical world is there which we can affirm to be beyond the power of man to unravel?

The stars, whose light in coming to our earth has darted for years through space—whose distance is more millions of miles than we can comprehend—are man's figures on the great dial-plate of the heavens. He predicts the changes of the planets, giving us a map of these heavens as they shall appear some night in coming ages. How perfect must be the image mind, that can thus comprehend and trace out the work of the Great Original!

In other departments, the work has not yet been so perfectly done as in Astronomy. But it has been well begun, although science is in its infancy, and much remains to be accomplished before man enters into the full inheritance of nature, which belongs to him as the offspring and heir of God. There have been mistakes, indeed; but each true student of Nature has in some points been successful. These mistakes have arisen because the life of one man was not long enough to read every sign correctly, or because he attempted to form an arch from the materials at hand, while the key-stone, perhaps, was fashioned on another continent, reserved as a discovery for some more fortunate workman.

In respect to material for study, Astronomy has a vast advantage over almost every other natural science. A man may station himself in any portion of the earth, and the heavens, as they roll over him, will give him the means of forming a perfect system of Astronomy; while one who would study the crust of our earth, or discover the relationship of plants or animals upon the globe, must either travel or avail himself of the labors of others who can bring to him the results of their explorations. And the labor to which men will submit, that they may bring the scattered blocks of this glorious temple together, till the eye of man can see the perfection of its work, and its beautiful proportions, is another proof of the perfect adaptation of these works to the higher nature of man. No other worldly good, but gold, has ever sent men on such long and perilous journeys. The gradual unfolding of the plan of nature so enchains the mind, that ease is forgotten and money despised, except as a means. It is never valued for a moment, compared with progress in this pursuit. Linnæus not only roused his mind and body to the work, so that weariness and disease were almost forgotten, but his pupils were fired with that enthusiasm which sent them round the world, to find for their teacher and for themselves, new lines in this book of nature.

There is one department of science, embracing, indeed, the whole range of Natural History, in which the most brilliant revelations were reserved for our day, and where the human mind has yet its grandest problems to solve in the material world. Slowly from the mountain and the valley did light break in upon the mind, and the great truth become established, that in the bosom of the earth, where there had for ages seemed to be mere chaos and confusion, there was a divine volume of stony leaves with strange inscriptions—the record of unnumbered organized beings, kept through long ages amid the convulsions of the globe, the warring elements of fire and water, all perfect for man the translator. He has already read enough to learn that the earth's true history is written in this volume, and that in this apparent chaos there is perfect order and a provision for man as an intellectual as well as a physical being.

The student of antiquities has no lexicon except some chance Rosetta stone, for reading the strange inscriptions on the bricks and slabs of those ancient, buried cities. Their engravers, and those who wrote and spoke the languages, are gone; not a single letter will ever be added to those already written. From them alone, unchanging and unchangeable, must a key be found by which the world can unlock their meaning. Not so of the history written in the rocks of the earth. No Rosetta stone is needed to throw light upon these inscriptions. The language engraven there, God is repeating every year in the sunshine and storm, and in the varied forms of animals and plants that live and die. This language the students of nature had already begun to learn. As they opened the leaves of stone, the forms were strange indeed, and antiquated, like the characters in the old black-letter volumes of our libraries, but the language was soon seen to be the same as had been the mother-tongue of naturalists for generations. The intellectual triumphs in this field are too recent to need mention here. The ablest leaders have still their armor on. But for fifty years, there has been no such field of thought as Geology; no study to which the universal mind has so turned; none that has thrown up such a background where thought can rest, or run back through the ages. No place in the universe can man reach where the footprints of the Creator can be more clearly traced than in the crust of this earth; no part of His creation has more manifest reference to man.

It may seem, at the first glance, that design in the structure of the earth's crust has special reference to man as a physical being. But we must not overlook the fact that some of the most wonderful provisions in the crust of the earth for man's physical wants, presuppose his intellectual nature, and his progress in civilization. There was a certain wise provision made for him, as there was for the whole animal kingdom, in the outline of continents, the mountain ranges and the river systems, and in the preparation of the earth for vegetation by the mighty machinery of the glacial period. All these provisions on a scale so vast, and with adjustments so perfect for the support of vegetable and animal life, are so plainly ordained by some comprehensive Intellect that saw the end from the beginning, and guided all the agencies through the geologic ages till the earth appeared in its present beauty, that we can only wonder that any mind can be satisfied to regard them as the accidental results of fire and water and living things. These have been mere servants in the Master's hand. We see that secondary agencies have done the work; but when we have traced the plan through the whole structure, that plan, according to which the earth moved on towards its present state, by a process like the growth and changes of a living being, until it was prepared for man, we find recorded in the rocks what Moses wrote, in substance, three thousand years ago: *And God said, Let the earth be prepared for man.* For this is a summary of the first chapter of Genesis. And we wish to show, that in addition to these provisions which simply make the earth a fit dwelling-place for the animal kingdom, there have been most wonderful provisions made for man alone ; but provisions that he can avail himself of only as he is an intellectual and progressive being.

We recognize this provision for the intellect in the nature of the various elements, and in their distribution. The metals, the coal and the oil, of each of which the earth holds inexhaustible quantities, are for man alone ; but he can avail himself of them only as he is an intellectual being. He reads the earth's history, translates her inscriptions, and thus becoming master of her secrets, opens her treasure-house and supplies his wants.

With these treasures and with this mind, behold the wonders that man accomplishes. He multiplies his power ten thousand fold. He drives his vessels against wind and tide. He lowers the hills and fills the valleys ; stretching the iron rail, he whirls along with breath of steam and sinews of iron that never tire. He speaks through the iron wire, and his friend hears the message though a thousand miles away. He peers into space with his telescopes, maps out the hills aad vallies of the moon, and measures the belts and bands of planets. He brings to light the hidden mysteries of the dust, and living forms too small for the unassisted eye to discern. He arms himself with thunderbolts, and with the deadly rifle and ponderous cannon he becomes terrible as a destroyer. All this he does because by intellect he seizes upon the provisions that have been made for him alone in the crust of the earth. As there is no limit to his intellectual improvement, so there is no limit to the provisions that have been made in the elements, and their combinations for this nature with which he has been gifted. If we consider the gathering together of the metals in veins in the earth, and the comparative quantity of each, according to its relation to the progress of man, we cannot fail to recognize a wonderful and perfect provision; a provision depending upon so many conditions, that we seem necessarily to infer an intelligent provider. Like the many cases already cited, so many conditions must meet to secure the result, that he alone is chargeable with credulity who refers such combinations to chance. If we consider the properties, physical and chemical, of the metals alone, we have a marvellous provision for man; a provision without which he would find no fitting means of embodying his grandest conceptions in material forms; no means of becoming lord and master of the earth; no means of manifesting those higher characteristics of which civilization is both the offspring and parent. In fact, without the metals mainly as they are, man would be like the bird without an atmosphere, though spreading its wings, doomed ever to walk upon the earth.

We have first the metals, gold and silver, almost defying the power of oxygen, beautiful and capable of being drawn into finest wires, and hammered into thinnest sheets. They meet the wants of man by gratifying the love of the beautiful, which they do, not by any conventional usage, or because they happen to be rare, but by an intrinsic beauty, and the power of retaining, for an almost unlimited time, the delicate work with which the cunning of the artist has enriched them. They also meet our demands in art and science and in commerce.

In platinum we have another noble metal, without which the chemist would feel his power wonderfully abridged. It seemed to be discovered just when the progress of science absolutely demanded such a substance. If the chemist had ordered a substance for his use, he could have hardly combined in it all the desirable properties which he already recognizes in this metal. Its infusibility is extreme, withstanding, as it does, the most intense combustion of the ordinary furnace, yet welding at a comparatively moderate heat. It almost defies the strongest simple acid, but yields readily to nitric and hydrochloric, mixed. It is one of the densest known substances, and yet is capable of being put into the most porous form of any metal known. These properties, which make it so valuable for apparatus, and the chemical nature of its salts, strike me as a wonderful provision; and I never look at the platinum ware of the laboratory, the crucibles, and foil, and wires, and other forms in which this substance is used, without recognizing a direct provision for the intellectual progress of man. I might, indeed, add the same of many other articles found there, but as I am speaking of the metals, I omit the other substances for the present.

In strong contrast to the metals already mentioned, is mercury, but hardly less useful and seemingly necessary for scientific research. Liquid, at common temperatures, it dissolves other metals, and by its aid the gold and silver are readily extracted from the ores. How difficult it would be to find a substitute for it in the thermometer, barometer, and many other instruments known to men of science! We know not where to look for a substitute; we could not well get along without it. It happens to be the very substance we want to complete the metallic series—very unlike all other metals—and, because so unlike, filling an important place among those materials which seem essential to human progress.

Too common, almost, to attract attention, is iron; but it possesses a number of properties, so marked, that it seems impossible they should be studied without producing the conviction that they were an express provision for man. It is hardly possible for us to conceive in what state man must have remained to this day without iron; how low in civilization, and how powerless, compared with what he now is. Before speaking of its properties, we cannot fail to notice the fact of its abundance. It is distributed in almost every portion of the globe; and, certainly, in such large quantities, that there will be enough for all mankind while the world stands.

They may weave their iron tracks like a net-work over the continents, span the rivers with iron arches, plough the ocean with iron hulls, stretch iron wires from city to city, cover the roads with iron cars, and build iron palaces, and yet the mountains of iron ore will hardly be diminished in size.

It might seem at first thought, that want of design is shown in the fact, that so useful a substance is seldom if ever found in a pure state. But a mine of solid iron would hardly pay for working. So hard a substance is it in a pure state, that huge masses would seem to defy the miner's power. But as a brittle ore, it is easily quarried, and is thus brought readily into the conditions most serviceable to man.

Its first property worthy of special notice is its chemical relation to oxygen and carbon, by which its ores so readily yield in the blast furnace their oxygen, unite with carbon, and become cast-iron, with the physical property of expanding just as it solidifies, so as to fill the mould and give the sharpest outline to the finest figures on the pattern.

If we consider it as cast-iron alone, we find it perfectly adapted to its purpose. As wrought-iron, it is obedient to the fire and hammer, taking the thousand forms which the workman demands, bending, yielding, and welding, and then, when cold again, holding the form he has given it with the power of a giant.

Combined with carbon it becomes steel. And what a multitude of uses the very word suggests;

Steel—Magnetism.

It may be cast in moulds, it may be made soft, like common iron, or hardened in a moment almost like the diamond. And between these extremes, any degree of hardness can be secured that the workman desires. He can divide the bar, and from one portion make a blade that shall cut the other part as though it were wax. He can obtain from it the most brilliant surface and the keenest edge; he can form the strongest links, and the most delicate springs, that, fine as a thread, for a whole lifetime shall never tire in controlling the delicate balance of the watch.

All these diverse properties in cast and wrought-iron, and in steel, fit this metal to become the great instrument of progress in the hands of man, but it is great to him only as he is an intellectual being. Its properties are developed, and its uses discovered, as in his advancing civilization he feels conscious of new wants. There are in iron, unbounded possibilities. But it is to all creatures on the globe, except to man, like the sand or rocks that make the soil.

I must not omit to mention the magnetic power of iron and its relation to electricity. One of its ores is the loadstone, which was for ages a mere curiosity or wonder to men in early days of science. But in that curious mineral was the latent power, that in the hands of man was to give him the magnetic needle, and in wider application, the magnetic telegraph. The needle of steel, touched with this mysterious stone, thenceforth became a guide to the mariner upon the deep, when storms and clouds shut out the friendly stars. And when the electric fluid was made to develop magnetism at will, and the iron wire was found to be a pathway for the lightning, the conditions and properties were becoming known, that in the end should bring distant nations as near together as neighbors of the same village. The transient magnetic power of iron, the permanent magnetic power of steel, either of which no man can explain, and all the relations of electricity to iron and air and chemical action, constitute the conditions of this grand triumph of man over the material world. No Arabian tales of magic power, in commanding demons of earth and air, can equal the power of man, who, sitting by his battery, calls, by the touch of the finger, "spirits from the vasty deep," and sends them with the speed of light with messages a thousand miles away. But iron is the most potent wand he wields. Take this from him and he is almost powerless.

What need of dwelling on the other materials, that either alone, or in combination, respond to the increasing demands of science and art? How every property possible to be conceived of as desirable, is found in some ore, or in its alloy. Who can recount the multifarious uses of copper, and lead, and tin, and zinc, and all their combinations, meeting the varied wants of man, but needful to him only as an intellectual being!

Nor is it to the metals, alone, that we look for this special relation to man, but to almost every element found in abundance on the globe. We have already referred to this adaptation to his intellect, in their chemical relations, thus making the science of chemistry possible. We regard every natural science, indeed, only as an expression of the relation of that part of nature to the mind of man. But in addition to this chemical relation of the elements to each other, so beautiful and satisfactory, there is an adaptation of each and all of them as servants of man, as ministering to his physical wants ; but ministering to him only because, by his intellect, he first subdues them, entering into the secrets of their nature, and thus finding in them means of perpetual improvement.

We have already referred, in another connection, to the evidence of design in the relations of carbon and hydrogen as fuel. But the very idea of fuel, as ministering to physical comfort, implies intellect. Fire is the servant of man. No race has been found so degraded as to be without it, and there is no history to tell of men who were ignorant of its use. No mere animal has been found with any power to secure it, or with any apparent knowledge of its use, except as a source of comfort, supplied to him by man. Fire is a provision for man alone ; and every provision in nature for combustion, is either without significance, or it has reference to the intellectual nature. The nature of carbon and hydrogen, the beds of coal, the fountains of oil, the accumulation of woody fibre in the trunk of the tree as heartwood, which is of no special service to the tree itself —all of these substances, with their nicely-balanced affinities, which we considered when treating of the chemical elements—all of these have relations to mind alone. If, then, we consider the physical provisions for man, we find the most abundant evidence that his highest physical good was to be secured only through the exercise of his intellect. The coal, and wood, and metals, and marbles, supplement his higher nature. They make a world fitted for a progressive being. They minister, in their natural forms, to the good of all organic beings ; but in their relation to man, they rise into another plane and supplement his power, as the hand of man, in its cunning, rises above the fin of the fish, or the wing of the bird.

At no time before in the history of the world was there anything like the proof of the perfect adaptation of the world to the higher nature of man that we have now. When before could he search the earth for treasures as he can now? He has but just entered into the fullness of this inheritance. When before had he the art of moulding these products into such unnumbered forms for his comfort and delight? He draws and moulds the metals into a thousand forms, and the sands are melted into crystal glass. He takes up a dull ore from the earth, and by the magic power of chemistry throws it back changed to the finest pigments. We admire the multiplied means of enjoyment which civilization now has at its command. We admire that power in man that enables him to compass the earth, and bind its forces, and make them his servants. But how powerless the intellect of man would be without materials fitted to his powers!

It is not in the crust of the earth alone that the intellect of man has been considered, but also in the structure of the animals and plants that now live. The fruits came to their perfection, and burst into that wealth of variety which we now enjoy, only under the fostering care of an intellectual being. The precious grains of the earth, prepared undoubtedly for man, can supply his wants only through the exercise of mind. They must be cared for ; the soil must be prepared, and the grains must be scattered, and the harvest must be gathered, by man. Nor is it yet proper food for him. The grains that supply so large a portion of the race are certainly a provision for their physical wants, but these grains would either perish from the earth, or be almost useless to man were he no higher in mental power than the lower animals. The guiding mind of man is needed to preserve and prepare them for his food.

Thus it is that every physical want of man in his highest state, is provided for, not by the products of the world in their natural state, as the lower animals are supplied, or as man may in some places be supplied while in a state of barbarism.

But man in his upward progress, finds ever opening before him new possibilities, new sources of delight and progress, in the elements and in the organic beings that abound on the earth. When we consider what man has done, in chaining the forces of nature, in changing the form of the chemical elements, in calling to his service the animal and vegetable kingdoms, making them all contribute to his comfort, giving food, and shelter, and clothing, all through the power of mind, we understand that sovereignty delegated to him by the Creator, when he said of man, *"Let us make man in our image, after our likeness; and let him have dominion over the fish of the sea, and over the fowl of the air, and over the cattle, and over all the earth, and over every creeping thing that creepeth upon the earth."*

LECTURE X.

PROVISION FOR THE EMOTIONAL NATURE AND THE VARIED INTELLECTUAL TASTES AND POWERS OF MEN.

Love of the beautiful.—Provision for it in nature.—Taste.—Fine Arts founded upon nature.—Poetry.—Bible language.—Painting and sculpture.—Music.—Conditions necessary for it.—Beauty of outline and color.—Clouds.—Crystals.—Plants.—Increase of beauty in leaf and flower.—Double flowers.—Microscopic animals.—Corals.—Jellyfishes.—Shells.—Their beauty not for themselves.—Insects.—Distribution of their color.—Vertebrates.—Beauty of fossils.—Grandeur and sublimity.—Emotional nature perfect in man ages ago.—Different intellectual tastes provided for.—Advance in science and art thus secured.—Sciences yet to be unfolded.

WE have considered, in the last two lectures, the adaptations of the world to the intellectual nature of man. This adaptation was shown to exist in that order and harmony, that mathematical and mechanical connection of the objects in nature by which the mind of man is not only able to grasp the plan of creation, but finds in the study of natural objects the constant source of mental improvement and delight. We also showed that the provisions made for the physical nature of man have reference to his intellectual nature, as it is only through mind that he can avail himself of the metals and forces of nature, and those products most valuable for food, raiment, and shelter.

But it is not alone the physical welfare of man, and that pure intellect which is satisfied with weight and measure and established relation, that have been provided for, in constituting the elements and the varied objects in the world. There has been given to man an emotional nature, one manifestation of which is the love of the beautiful. And for the gratification of this love there has been made most ample and special provision. We have made some reference to this fact in the subjects already treated of. For we can draw no dividing lines in the works of nature that shall completely separate one provision from another. Beauty and utility are in general so interwoven, that while we speak of one, the other can never be entirely ignored. But the provision for man, as a lover of the beautiful, is as ample and as striking as any other that has been made. Nature is to him the cosmos revealing a mind and speaking to the mind in its varied language of order, proportion, and grandeur, thus ever, awakening the emotions of beauty and sublimity. The faculty or constitution of the mind by which we perceive these qualities and enjoy these emotions of beauty and sublimity, is Taste. To aid in gratifying this faculty we have the fine arts, which are the creations of genius to supply the demands of Taste. But genius would be powerless without the patterns which the Great Master has given in the things he has created. As that is true science alone that reveals the relations established by the creative Intellect, so the whole history of the fine arts shows that God has here established immutable relations between the love of the beautiful implanted by Him in man, and the world which he has fitted up for man's abode. No genius can ignore this relation and succeed in any one of the fine arts, any more than the intellect of man can make a science. Those works of art have alone stood the test of time that approach the patterns God has given. The voice of the Most High speaks to the artist as to Moses in the building of the Tabernacle: "*And look that thou make them after the pattern which was showed thee in the mount.*"

All the creations of poetry, sculpture, and painting, are either reproductions of natural scenes and natural objects, or embellished by them. Glance for a moment at your favorite authors; the poet, whose sweet song charms and gives enjoyment by its refining power; the orator, whose words enchained every listener; and see how much they were indebted for their influence over the mind to symbols drawn from nature. Their words may be joined by the rules of grammar and logic; they may convince the intellect by the force of reasoning; they may arouse the will by the plea of interest; but when they would charm with beauty, they must reach forth for the gems and flowers of nature. The stars glitter in literature almost as they do in the heavens. The bands of Orion and the sweet influence of the Pleiades, and all the famous constellations, have beautified almost every language. There is force and beauty even in the language of the savage borrowed from natural objects. When the poet would sing of the Indians' legends and traditions he repeats them as he heard them from the lips of Nawadaha, as he found them

> "In the bird's nest of the forest,
> In the lodges of the beaver,
> In the hoof-prints of the bison,
> In the eyry of the eagle."

All along the stream of ancient song the beauties of the natural world are set in thick and sweet profusion, not gathered into clusters, but adding to the richness of the poetic imagery as flowers deck the meadows. And the soft numbers seem to flow like crystal streams reflecting the nodding verdure on their grassy banks. How beautifully are they braided into song as a chaplet for the tomb of the Grecian poet.

> "Ye evergreens, around the tomb
>   Of Sophocles your osiers braid,
> And ivy, spread thy pensive gloom
>   To form above the bard a shade.
> And intertwine the blushing rose
>   And gentle vine your leaves among.
> Thus gemmed with beauty shall your boughs
>   Prove emblems of his graceful song."

Poems in our own language speak as plainly of the power of the natural world to delight man by displays of beauty and of grandeur. To meet the demands of taste implanted in man, the sons of genius and of song have gone forth into nature for their subjects and their illustrations. So that every poet, worthy of the name, in every language and in every age, whether he would or not, has been a priest of the Most High, in making known the perfection of His works in their adaptation to the emotional nature of man.

If we needed higher illustration not only of the power of natural objects to adorn language and gratify taste, but proof that here we find the highest conceivable beauty, we should appeal at once to the Bible. Those most opposed to its teachings have acknowledged the beauty of its language; and this is due mainly to the exquisite use of natural objects for illustration. It does indeed draw from every field. But when the emotional nature was to be appealed to, the reference was at once to natural objects; and throughout all its books, the stars and flowers and gems are prominent as illustrations of the beauties of religion and the glories of the Church.

"The wilderness and the solitary place shall be glad for them, and the desert shall rejoice and blossom as the rose."

"The mountains and the hills shall break forth before you into singing, and all the trees of the fields shall clap their hands. Instead of the thorn shall come up the fir-tree, and instead of the brier shall come up the myrtle-tree."

The power and beauty of these same objects appear in the Saviour's teachings. The fig and the olive, the sparrow and the lily of the field, give peculiar force and beauty to the great truths they were used to illustrate.

The Bible throughout is remarkable in this respect. It is a collection of books written by authors far removed from each other in time and place and mental culture, but throughout the whole, nature is exalted as a revelation of God. Its beauty and sublimity are appealed to to arouse the emotions, and through the emotions to reach the moral and religious nature. This element of unity runs through all the books where references to nature can be made. One of the adaptations of the Bible to the nature of man is found in the sublime and perfect representation of the natural world, by which nature is ever made to proclaim the character and perfections of God. No language can be written, that so perfectly sets forth the grand and terrible in nature and its forces, as we hear when God answers Job out of the whirlwind. No higher appreciation of the beautiful, and of God as the author of beauty, was ever expressed than when our Saviour said of the lilies of the field, "I say unto you that even Solomon, in all his glory, was not arrayed like one of these;" and then adds; "If God so clothe the grass of the field"—ascribing the element of beauty in every leaf and opening bud to the Creator's skill and power.

Thus, in all the adorning of common language,

in poetry itself, and in the vivid pictures of divine inspiration, the sweetest note that strikes the ear comes from the landscape; the brightest picture is the landscape itself. All that Taste has ever demanded for her gratification, genius has here found; and if God is the author of both nature and the mind, here we should expect that among the crystals, flowers and sensitive life, the emotional nature of man would find one of its highest earthly gratifications. In painting and sculpture the human mind is striving for the same that appears in poetry and in the adorning of common language. It is the gratification of the love of the beautiful. Poetry, painting, and sculpture, have moved on together in all ages. They are the natural outgrowth of the human mind. And the great masters have gained their preëminence from their clear conceptions of nature, and the emotional in man, and their skill in selecting from one what should meet the wants of the other. The artist who can so combine the hints of nature as to make a perfect whole, need have no fear of being forgotten or neglected.

As nature is the store-house from which writers draw, and the pattern according to which they must work, so must this also be true of the painter and sculptor, who would trace upon the canvas and chisel from marble, figures that shall glow forever with the warm expression of life.

But if no line of poetry had ever been written, no canvas ever glowed with colors, and no sculptor had ever found the statue within the block of marble, we could not fail to recognize the provision that has been made in nature for us, as emotional beings, and lovers of the grand and beautiful.

We have referred to the fine arts only as evidence that men have in all ages recognised this provision, and that in all their attempts to appeal to the emotional in man, they have sought to follow nature. And when we rise into the higher spiritual sphere, we still are dependent upon nature's symbols, in order to express our conceptions of these higher beauties. The heavens and the earth, in their grandeur and beauty, as pictures of unequalled composition, are daily presenting new occasions for wonder and enjoyment; while each distinct object, that like the pencil-stroke, completes the picture, has its own power by its beauty or grandeur, to call out the emotions of the soul, and give its revenue of pleasure.

How much enjoyment comes to us through the sweet sounds of music! The ear was formed with power to mark the nice distinction of sounds; and bird and insect; the brook tinkling over its pebbly bed; the ocean, and the thunders, in their deep diapasons, give the elements of the sweetest and grandest melodies. If we consider music as an art, ministering to our enjoyment, we cannot fail to observe how many conditions are necessary in us, and in the physical nature of the elements, that this source of enjoyment should be possible, and so rich. The sense of hearing we have already considered in a former lecture; but all the common uses of this sense would have been answered without the power of appreciating music.

The sense of hearing is not absolutely essential to man. It is plain he might exist upon the globe without it. The race would, indeed, be vastly lower than it now is, for we are not to judge from what mutes become under the teaching of those who can hear, what a race of deaf mutes would be, if left to make progress for themselves.

Hearing is undoubtedly one of the important adaptations by which man, as a physical being, is fitted to this world; but the power to appreciate music is an entirely different thing. No necessity for it can be pointed out, if we consider man merely as an animal; it is simply and solely a source of enjoyment. As a condition of this enjoyment, we have the power of appreciating the music when it is produced; a power which does not belong to us necessarily, for some are without it. We have also the nature of material objects, by which sounds are produced. There is no necessity in the case that air, when vibrating, should produce sounds, and that it should always give the same power to the same instruments, in all parts of the world. There is no necessity that different kinds of wood and metal, and other materials, should give the variety of sound they do. In fact, the wonderful powers of all the instruments invented by men, to give sweet sounds, are proofs of the provision that has been made in the nature of things to gratify that love of music implanted in man, simply as a source of enjoyment.

The joy and the sadness which music awakens in the soul, like the light and shade that flit over the landscape, show how the emotional nature of man is provided for even in the vibrations of the air, by which music is produced. The rich, joyous sounds of the human voice, so sweet to the ear, the blending music of the organ, all waking the deepest emotions of man, by the power of sound alone, declare the provision that has been made in the mechanism of the ear, and the waves of the air, and in the pure intellect that combines them, for the delight of the emotional nature of man.

But in beauty of outline and of color, the most lavish provision has been made for our enjoyment. We can never think of the beauty of the evening sky as being a matter of chance. The starry concave seems to have too great power to gratify by its beauty, not to be a provision for this purpose; and this we may acknowledge, though we know that each star is a sun, and the centre of other systems.

The varied forms and tints of clouds give new scenes of beauty every day. What glories light up the morning and evening sky, as the beams of the rising or setting sun glance from the piles and lines of vapor that fill the upper air! One who has watched the varied beauties of the gilded morning and evening clouds in every clime, will acknowledge the beauty of the scenes, and the source of enjoyment which they are to every lover of beauty. We cannot regard that constitution of water that gives the glories of the clouds their gorgeous play of light; and the enchanting beauties of the rainbow, painted in the falling drops, as something necessary in the nature of things. It is necessary according to the present order of things, but such provisions, or such relations, are strong evidence that this order is the result of a plan. We know not why the forms and colors of crystals may not be part of the same provision. What sources of delight, as objects of beauty, are the crystals into which nature forms the minerals and some organic productions! We recognize in this selecting power of crystallization, a provision of the highest value to man in many respects, and we have already considered its relation to pure intellect. We have not only the selecting power, but also the beauty of form, as exhibited in the primary and secondary crystals, as well as the varied tints of all the gems. The precious stones are not beautiful on account of association merely, but are undoubtedly fitted, in and of themselves, to gratify our love of beauty.

When we come into the organic kingdom, the provision is still more striking. The clouds and the crystals may be lightly thought of, because they are simply exhibitions of the properties of matter and of light. But organic beings are on entirely different ground. They once had no existence upon the globe. Their beauty certainly is nothing fixed or necessary. In many cases, no possible use can be ascribed to certain forms, and the display of colors, except to gratify the love of the beautiful in man. It matters not whether we refer to the animal or vegetable kingdom, for the same design is apparent in both. In the vegetable kingdom alone, there is a wealth of illustration. There is beauty everywhere, and produced in such ways, that it is often apparent that it was the sole object in creation, while utility and beauty are in other cases conjoined. The beautifully cut edge of the leaf favors radiation, and is thus subservient to the welfare of the plant; but when we consider the varied outline of all the leaves, their increase in beauty, by cultivation, and their combination in the compound forms, we are delighted both by the great variety, and the intrinsic beauty of distinct forms, neither of which certainly is necessary. The same is true of the flower. We know what is essential to a perfect flower, that seed may be produced. But what human ingenuity could have ever devised the numberless patterns of the flowers? How is the mind charmed in some of the great collections, as at Kew, where royal wealth has collected plants from all portions of the world, and where, among the thousands of species, or among varieties that have been produced, not one can be found that has not in it some element of beauty? If we confine ourselves to the consideration of form alone, there is much to delight us, among even our common flowers. But when we add to form, the matchless coloring, how can man believe that such a provision for his enjoyment was made by any other than by a Being like himself; or at least, one that understood his constitution, and desired to gratify his emotional nature?

Look at the opening lily, as it floats upon the waters, and see the beautiful contrast of alabaster and gold! or at the nicely balanced colorings of a multitude of our flowers, where the tints are ranged in dots, or rings, with such precision as to delight us, not only by the rich coloring, but by the artistic relation of the colors to each other, and to the form of the flower. Who can believe that such beauty of form and color serves merely to attract insects?

It is among plants, also, that we find that special provision for the increase of beauty, as they are cultivated, and man becomes capable of appreciating beauty for its own sake. We refer to the doubling of flowers, like roses, and dahlias, and many others, that increase in beauty by this process, until they lose all power of producing seed, for which the flower seems primarily to be made. But no plant ever loses the power of producing seed, unless other provision has been made for its propagation; and when an annual thus changes, so that it can no longer produce seed, it becomes perennial. The whole economy of the plant in such cases seems to be arranged with regard to beauty, but with wise forethought for the preservation of the species. How nicely balanced the forces in the plant must be, that while it can produce seed, its course is run in a single year, but when the seed-producing power is lost by the unrolling of its organs into beautiful petals, there is power enough saved by the process to carry the plant over, and make its life continuous, that it may be propagated from the root.

Another remarkable evidence that this changing of flowers to increase their beauty was provided for in their creation, is found in the fact that those flowers, in which the stamens are large and ornamented, so as to make a distinct element in the beauty of the flower, seldom, if ever, become double.

In the animal kingdom we have everywhere apparent the same regard for beauty of outline and harmony of color. If there are monsters, it may be partly from association of their form with their natures, or because they occupy such a place in creation that there can be no beauty but that of adaptation. But when we have thrown aside all these cases in respect to which there might be difference of opinion, the great mass of animal life speaks of the same Divine Artist whose matchless skill has arranged the lilies of the field.

In the field of the microscope there is often a display of beauty that is wonderful. Animal and vegetable forms too small for the naked eye to discern, or if discerned at all, seeming like grains of dust, under the power of the magnifying lens, become perfect marvels in beauty of outline and sculpture. We have also the same exhibition of beauty and perfection of structure in the minute organs of larger forms of animal life. In some of our liberally endowed scientific societies we have a section of the society given to microscopic research. They gather the mud from pools in all parts of the earth, the dust that collects upon the sails in long voyages upon the ocean, the ooze brought up by the sounding lead from the deep bed of the ocean ; they seek in every hidden place for the minute in the animal and vegetable kingdom.

But in all their search, did they ever find one mark of imperfection? As they ply still greater and greater power with their improved instruments, is not the charm which so holds them to their work, the new beauties which every new specimen reveals to them? In one there is beauty of structure ; in another, of outline and sculpture ; in another of color ; and in another of adaptation ; so that the microscopist dwells in a world of enchantment, a world unknown to common men, a world of wonders by itself, but a world as perfect in all its parts and as plainly proclaiming divine wisdom and skill as the suns and planets that circle in space. Among all these patient observers we have yet to find the first one who claims that his microscope has revealed anything but perfection. To every object of beauty he applies the glass with one expectation—that greater beauties will be revealed by its magnifying power. In all the works of man, it brings out imperfections ; in all the works of nature increased beauty, without a single exception in the whole history of microscopic investigation.

If we advance one step further, we find the radiate division of the animal kingdom, the corals, jelly-fishes, and star-fish tribe. The coral animals, by their beautiful forms and brilliant colors, form gardens in the ocean, so beautiful that it is not strange that poetic fancy should locate in the coral-groves the dwelling-place of sea-nymphs, beings too beautiful for the upper air.

And when the gay color of the living coral is gone, and nothing but the solid stone-work remains, what graceful outlines and delicate sculpture the varied forms present! What human genius could devise the multitude of patterns which abound in a rich collection of these treasures of the ocean? The branching Madrepore, the domes of Astreas and Meandrinas, have each their own element of beauty, so that we feel at once that the idea aimed at has been reached. We may consider one form more beautiful than another, but not a single specimen can we select which we could improve in its style of beauty without changing its plan of structure, and making it another species.

We discover here a grand principle, further illustrated in the shells of the ocean, of which we shall by and by speak. While there is beauty in the living animals, the solid coral and the shells are to remain the permanent objects. The beauty of the animal cannot be preserved, as it can be in some of the higher forms of life. All beauty is gone in these lowest animals when life is gone. But the solid coral and the shells are so indestructible, that even the coral, which is hidden from sight, while the animal lives, is ornamented as though it were intended that the solid framework should be the permanent record and constant witness of the provision made in nature for the love of the beautiful in man.

Among the jelly-fishes, which are among the most evanescent of all beings, there bursts upon us another group of beautiful forms and colors. Nothing can surpass the beauty of a Greenland harbor, on some clear summer-day, when the varied species of jelly-fish are filling its waters. Their perfect forms and delicate tints make them beautiful as gems, though so soon to perish. While in the slow-growing coral we have its strong framework left to delight us, the jelly-fishes, like the annual flowers that beautify the earth every season, fill the waters with ever-recurring riches, for the lover of perfect forms and brilliant tints.

It would take us too long to mention every branch and division of the animal kingdom. Nor is there need of doing so. But in this lowest tribe, the radiates, the element of beauty so completely runs through it; beauty of outline and sculpture, and richness and perfection of coloring, both without any possible reference to the animals themselves, that we are forced to accept it as a provision for the love of the beautiful implanted in man. It gratifies this element of our emotional nature. It is such a provision for our gratification and enjoyment that we accept it as the handiwork of a Being who comprehended our nature, and had the desire and the power to gratify it. While He cared for the creatures themselves in adapting them to their place in the universe, He made them to subserve the higher forms of life, and finally to minister to the highest possible type, made in His own image. And it is not irreverent to suppose that the Creator delights in the physical beauty of His own work.

But this provision will be better understood and appreciated in considering the next division of animal life—the shells. What fancy can conceive of greater beauty, of its kind, than is seen in a cabinet of shells? The exquisite forms and ornaments, and the profusion of richest colors, are arranged for the most perfect artistic effect. Each shell among the thousands has beauties that no human fancy would ever have suggested, had not nature first furnished the pattern. The pearly nautilus and the brilliant cowrie, in almost endless variation, are there—the mother-of-pearl and the silvery pearl itself. Not one of these beauties is for the animal itself. The brilliant colors invite its enemies and thus favor its destruction. Can we see in them any other design than a provision for the delight of intelligent beings? Is it possible that we can fail to see in them design at all?

Among the insects we have equal exhibitions of the same rich artistic skill. Their structure and instincts were necessary for their existence, and therefore it might be argued that we find the perfect combination, because those species alone have survived for which ample provision was made. But no such reason can be given for the admirable balancing of colors, and the elaborate patterns embroidered on the wings of the species that flit from flower to flower on a summer's day. The wing itself is often a marvel of beauty in its outline, and then the combinations of colors are more varied and beautiful than can be found in any work of human art; the colors themselves are absolutely unapproachable. The colors alone would not strike us as so remarkable, were it not for their distribution to produce ornamentation. We are sure here that we have the work of nature pure and simple, and we are beyond the influence of that potent principle, natural selection, because it is a question of mere distribution of color. And when the principle is pointed out, we need but visit a collection of insects, or recall the fairy forms that have reappeared every year upon the flowers, to understand its force. We can recall the golden yellow wing, with a line of ebon following the wavy outline of the edge—the gorgeous blue and red of other species, with silky sheen, in rings and spots and lines,—and "beetles panoplied in gems and gold."

We need not multiply examples; for the same exhibitions of beauty meet us from the lowest to the highest ranks of the animal kingdom. The same idea is secured by means so different that it speaks of a great provision for the enjoyment of rational creatures. In the coral polyp and jelly-fish the color is generally in the animal itself. In the shell-fish tribe it is made permanent in the shell, which is solid as the stone split from the quarry; in the insect tribe, it burnishes the wings of beetles and tints the delicate scales upon the wings of the lepidoptera. In the vertebrates, it appears in the scales of fishes and reptiles; in the goodly feathers of the peacock and the ruby and emerald tints of the humming-birds, and thousands of other forms that swarm in the tropics. Take the fishes of the rivers or of the ocean, the birds and animals of higher type, as they come from the hand of nature, and wonder at the artistic display of color. It cannot possibly, once in a hundred cases, have any reference to the enjoyment of the animal. In some cases similarity of color to natural objects may protect the animal from its foes; but in the vast majority of cases color must be regarded as a gratuitous provision having no reference to the animal itself. Yet no one who studies it can fail to recognize design; and the only possible design in the harmony and balancing of colors, must be the delight of intelligent beings.

But just at this point I am reminded that this beauty did not begin when man appeared upon the earth to admire it. There is the same artistic skill, not only in adapting means to ends, but in the ornamentation also, among the geologic plants and animals, as appears now. We have no doubt there is a vastly greater wealth of animal and plant-beauty upon the earth now than in any previous geologic period. We are not sure of this indeed, but only infer it from the kinds that live now compared with those that lived then. But whatever tribes appeared had their beauty, and its traces are left in the rocks. We find this beauty of ornamentation even among the trilobites of the silurian rocks. And in any geological cabinet can be found specimens that were in their time not only beautiful in sculpture, but in color. In addition to the elaborate finish of the Ammonites, we have seen some in which the beauty of the shell remained as perfect as in the pearly nautilus just taken from the sea.

Among the plants there probably was little beauty of flower, but the leaf and every part needed for those early tribes of plants, was as artistically finished as the plants that most delight us by their beauty of outline.

Buckland gives a graphic account of the rich profusion of beauty in the petrified plants of the Bohemian coal-mines.

"The most elaborate imitations of living foliage upon the painted ceilings of Italian palaces, bear no comparison with the beauteous profusion of extinct vegetable forms, with which the galleries of these instructive coal-mines are overhung. The roof is covered with a canopy of gorgeous tapestry enriched with festoons of most graceful foliage, flung in wild, irregular profusion over every portion of its surface. The effect is heightened by the contrast of the coal-black color of the plants with the light groundwork of the rock to which they are attached. The spectator feels himself transported, as if by enchantment, into the forests of another world; he beholds trees of form and character now unknown upon the surface of the earth, presented to his senses almost in the beauty and vigor of their primeval life; their scaly stems and bending branches, with their delicate apparatus of foliage, are all spread forth before him, little impaired by the lapse of countless ages, and bearing faithful records of extinct systems of vegetation which began and terminated in times of which these relics are the infallible historians."

What use of all this beauty when, as yet, there was no intelligent being upon the earth? *He that formed the eye, shall not He see?* and He that implanted in man the love of the beautiful, shall He not take delight in His own works? For His pleasure they are and were created. But considering man alone, we have a satisfactory answer. We have before shown that in making provision for man's physical nature on the earth, his intellectual nature was necessarily considered. The highest development of man demands that he should study the earth's crust. The coal and the metals are hidden there, and he must find them. The remains of ancient life are his land-marks. The crust of the earth is man's possession, and there is the same reason why he should find objects of beauty there, as that they should be found among living forms. It is pleasant to contemplate, these provisions made for man in the early earth—provisions prophetic of his exalted nature, and of his progress in knowledge.

In the slight sketch we have been able to make, it must be apparent that ample provision has been made, in every department of nature, to gratify the love of the beautiful. The faculty of appreciating has been given, and then special provision has been made, in varied form and color, to meet the demands of this faculty, where no other reason can be given for their existence. But when we come to consider grandeur and sublimity, the case seems somewhat different. We can hardly feel that the mountains rear their heads that we may wonder at their majesty; that the thunder-clouds marshal their forces, and the ocean puts on the terrors of the storm, that we may witness the grand and sublime. We feel that these all are exhibitions of the great forces of nature, and that they all have a purpose, irrespective of man. But we cannot fail to recognize the design of a wise Creator, in implanting in us the faculty of comprehending these mighty works, so as to be filled with awe and wonder before them. If anything in nature brings us near to God, it is the grand and terrible. We worship neither the mountain, nor the ocean, nor the thunder; but in their presence the boldest atheist sometimes forgets his doubts, and stands humbly ready to adore.

Not only is there this ample provision made for the emotional nature, but the history of the race shows that this higher nature of man, so nearly allied to the moral and religious, was as perfect ages ago as now. While science, which depends upon long-continued and accumulated observations, could come to perfection only in later times, so as to give us any adequate conception of what the pure intellect is capable, this higher emotional nature showed its divine origin in the earliest historic times. If we want the highest type of poetry, we turn to Homer and the Hebrew bards; if the beautiful in form;

to the cunning work of the old masters. These flashes of the highest powers of man, shining out of the darkness of unstable civilizations, and in the infancy of physical science, show the fallacy of all development theories, when applied to the mind of man. As far back as we can go, in poetry, and sculpture, and architecture, and philosophy, we have evidence of as high type of mental power as can now be found in the world. They lacked the method in science, and the means of progress, which are the aggregate accumulation of centuries, but they lacked no element nor degree of power which we possess. The fact that men worshipped the grand and terrible in nature—the mountain, the sun, the fire, and the thunder—showed want of knowledge, indeed ; but it showed the power of the emotional nature, and the potency of natural objects and physical forces to call it into action, and thus to arouse the moral and religious impulses.

The last adaptation between nature and the mind that we shall notice, is the provision which has been made for the different intellectual tastes of men. There is similarity of mind enough to be a basis for mental philosophy ; but it is apparent that even in the same families are found children having a fitness for different intellectual pursuits. Without this variety of taste and power, advance in science and art would be slow, and vastly contracted in its range. How small a portion of science, of the fine or useful arts, can be mastered by one man ! The most gifted and most accomplished man in the world, has only to walk through the streets of any city for a single day, to see how small a portion of the knowledge possessed by all men he possesses, and how small a portion of the works of art he would be able to equal. Civilization, as we find it to-day, is represented in no one man; it is the aggregate science and art of thousands working in different directions. Some men may be turned in one direction rather than another, by chance; but progress, nay, the very existence of different departments of science and art depends, upon the variety in the constitution of the human mind. There is not only laid in nature the foundation of science in the very constitution of matter and in all its collocations in organic beings, but provision has been made in this variety of the mind, that all these sciences should take their place in due time as means of human enjoyment. These scientific possibilities remain unknown for thousands of years, like the coal and oil and other provisions for man's physical wants, till progress demands them, and then they are reached. Who can tell what sciences are yet enfolded within unexplored chambers of the physical world, where this busy mind dividing its work and increasing its power a thousand-fold by its different, distinct lines of action, shall yet penetrate? And when all these explorers return from the deep, dark galleries of research, the treasures which they bring forth become the property of the world, and the whole race, as it were, steps upon a higher plane. There is not only provision made for unlimited improvement, both in the constitution of nature and the constitution of the human mind as a whole, but provision is made for rapid advance, and for the special employment and happiness of the race, in the variety of taste and power which calls them to such different spheres of activity.

LECTURE XI.

THE MORAL NATURE OF MAN, AND THE BIBLE AS A NATURAL PROVISION FOR HIM.

Decisions of the moral nature.—Chief characteristic of man. —Conscience.—Implies accountability.—The existence of a moral governor.—Approval of conscience.—Public opinion. —Others suffer from our acts.—Malevolent feelings produce unhappiness.—Appetites.—Physical suffering from sin.—Labor tends to virtue.—The world as it is, best for us. —This world not enough for man's powers.—His immortality inferred.—Questions which we need to have answered. —The Bible a natural provision.—Adapted to meet the wants of man's moral nature.—Answers questions which nature cannot answer.—Forgiveness of sin.—Immortality brought to light.—With the Bible, man completely provided for.

WE have thus far traced the handiwork of a wise Designer through the three kingdoms of nature. Whatever field we entered, there we found evidence of wisdom, skill and power. The ends are wisely chosen, the means are skilfully adapted to secure each end, and the plans are on a scale of vast magnitude. When we consider our intellectual powers, we are not only conscious of our ability to comprehend these wonderful plans; but we find all the arrangements of matter, having reference to the mind of man, fitted to give constant exercise and unlimited improvement to his highest mental powers.

We find the world also corresponding to the emotional nature, giving objects of beauty, grandeur, and sublimity. We find it as completely fitted to the whole intellectual nature of man as it is to his physical nature.

But it is not enough for man that he is able to provide for himself food and raiment and shelter, or that he can revel in the enjoyment of intellectual and emotional exercises; for above all these he has a moral nature. He has a sense of right and wrong, and the conscious power of choosing one course of action in preference to another for himself. He says of the acts of his neighbor that they are right or wrong, that he is a good or a bad man. He has also feelings of merit or demerit in reference to his own character, thoughts, and actions.

We are linked to our fellow-men by ties of interest or affection, and we have a social nature; but it is in the moral nature that we find the only real distinction in kind between man and the lower animals. His intellect, emotions, and social nature are simply conditional for this higher moral nature; and they in turn are so modified by it that the social nature at least is what it is, because man is a moral being.

Let us turn now to this higher nature. And as its central power and guide, so far as man can be a guide to himself, we recognize conscience, the arbiter of right and wrong. We leave to the moralist the analysis and mutual relations of this and other moral and intellectual powers, and deal with their acknowledged action and results. Whenever our relations to other beings are understood by us, conscience demands that we act according to those relations. It is a moral instinct to secure uniform results in moral relations, as natural instinct works among the lower orders of sentient beings. We may mistake in our judgment right from wrong, and as free moral agents we have power to do violence to our conscience ; but conscience never fails to demand what the judgment pronounces to be right. We thus infer that we were made to do right, because all in us that tends to wrong-doing is antagonistic to conscience, and we have the power to obey conscience. If, then, we have implanted within us a principle that ever demands the right, and condemns the wrong act, and we have given to us the power to obey that monitor, we have the highest proof that we were created by a moral Being, by one who preferred right to wrong, and preferred it to such a degree that He gave us in our constitution the strongest tendency possible towards the right that could be given without taking away our free agency or accountability. But because we have in us this conscience, and at the same time the ability to choose in reference to ends and with a knowledge of results, we have strong grounds for inferring that we are accountable beings. We infer so, because accountability seems needed to complete our relations to moral acts. If there were no accountability or retribution, the forebodings of conscience would be to man what instinct would be to the animal if there were nothing in nature to meet the demands of instinct.

Conscience is the moral monitor and ruler of man, and there is no peace for him but in following its commands. It not only brings punishment for wrong-doing by its own action, but it does this chiefly by a foreboding of other punishment to come. The idea of futurity seems ever linked with it. It is common to man in all places and in all ages. By no other characteristic is the race so completely one. It is the voice within all men that not only demands the right and forbids the wrong, but suggests relations to some Being from whom we cannot escape, that can give rewards and inflict punishment. It becomes, therefore, the cornerstone on which rests our belief in God as our moral Governor, and of the immortality of the soul. As we infer the being of God from design, and then judge of His natural attributes by the variety and nature of His works ; as we recognize His power to provide, in the constitution of matter and in its collocation, for the satisfaction of our intellectual and emotional nature ; as we see that He has made us with powers and faculties capable of improvement, and has laid in the constitution of things a foundation for that unlimited improvement by giving us power over nature, the faculty of speech and the ability to transmit knowledge from one generation to another—as in all this we recognize a God having like attributes with ourselves, but infinite in degree, so in the nature of conscience implanted in man, we find proof that He regards right and wrong. We cannot help referring to our Creator as high attributes as He has conferred upon us. Not to do so, would be to ignore the accepted axiom in moral reasoning, that the cause must be equal to the effect. If He merely provided for us as intellectual and moral beings, He must be of the same nature to comprehend our wants, and when we accept the truth that we were created by Him, the argument certainly is not weakened. From our own constitution we can find no fitter language in regard to His character than the words of Holy Writ: " He that planted the ear, shall not he hear, he that formed the eye, shall not he see, * * * he that teacheth man knowledge, shall not he know?"

Every man has within him constant evidence of the existence of a moral nature. It simply remains to consider the power of this nature in the individual, and its relations to others. And it is first to be observed that the approval of conscience is the highest source of enjoyment to man, and the upbraidings of conscience are the severest torment Sustained by an approving conscience, men have endured every suffering and submitted to death itself. Under the upbraidings of conscience, men have become filled with remorse for the past and forebodings of the future, till life became a burden, and escape from torment has been sought for in death itself. The very moral constitution of man, then, is such that happiness comes to him from doing right, and suffering from doing wrong. What doubt, then, of the character of Him who gave that moral constitution?

It is not only true that we have this faculty which impels us to the right for its own sake, without any reference to the acts or the judgment of others, but we are in addition to this affected by the opinion of others. We know that they have the same moral constitution that we have, by which they decide moral questions, and we know that the estimation in which we are held by men depends upon their opinion of our moral character. We desire to stand well with them. There is great support in their approval of any course of action, especially if conscience justifies the course. And there is a sense of shame and baseness, when we receive the censure of others and are conscious that their condemnation is just. Thus it is that public opinion has such great power; a power that few men can long withstand unless sustained by an approving conscience. The fact that this opinion may be misled by prejudice, and in some cases be absolutely wrong, does not alter the argument. Men demand what they think is right as a general thing, and if they demand what they know to be wrong, they may hate and even destroy the one who will not yield, but they never can despise him; and when the frenzy of passion has passed away, they honor him. We thus find the moral constitution such, that our common relationship to others impels us to right action.

We are also linked to a portion of the race by peculiar ties. There is the relation of parent and child, brother and sister, husband and wife. The nature of man is such, that the disgrace of any wrong act done by us, attaches itself not to us alone, as reason would seem to dictate that it ought, but also to those most nearly allied to us, for whom we naturally have the strongest affection. And our virtues are the richest reward we can make to parents, and the best legacy we can bequeathe to those who come after us. We are impelled, then, by the deepest love we have for earthly friends, to pursue a right and virtuous course.

It seems wrong that the innocent should suffer in any degree for the sins of others; but the fact that they do suffer, and that those are affected most for whom we have the deepest love, shows the strong influences that have been brought to bear upon us through our most intimate relationships, in favor of virtue; and the certainty that the Being who established these relations, desired virtue in us even more than the happiness growing out of these relations.

No man ever enjoyed himself under the influence of hate, jealousy, anger, or any passion that counsels evil to his fellow-men. Such passions are in themselves torments, while every sentiment of good-will towards men brings happiness by its very exercise. Nothing can be plainer than that He who established this relation, desired us to seek the happiness of our fellow-men.

We find in ourselves certain appetites and passions. They are needful for us, administering to our enjoyment and the good of society when indulged in with moderation, but bringing disease of body, decay of mind, and the degradation of the whole man when indulged in to excess. The common observation of men has convinced them that avarice, gluttony, drunkenness, and licentiousness, are sources of degradation and suffering. They plainly have not the approval of Him who made man.

There is among men a vast amount of physical suffering ; the misery of want, the pains of disease, and Death itself, the King of Terrors. The great amount of this suffering can be traced directly to vice. It not only brings anguish of mind, but it often sows the seeds of disease in us, to be transmitted to our children, to bear in us and in them its legitimate fruits—pain and early death. How much of the suffering around us from poverty and disease can thus be accounted for, and how much more might be thus connected with vicious courses of life, by going back and searching the history of past generations !

So far we have considered man's moral, physical, and social nature as directly demanding a virtuous life of him. They all three work in the same direction. But the physical world is also adapted to secure this. The common wants of life, and the desires created by civilization, are constantly demanding more labor. Labor is painful, or at least it has such an effect upon the system as restrains the man from vicious action. It gives health and vigor to the body, and yet has a tendency to moderate those appetites and passions that are so apt to injure and destroy men by their over-indulgence. When men are so situated that they never know what it is to labor with mind or body, they are generally found walking in that broad road that leads to misery and death. An Eden would be fitted for a race that had no tendency to over-indulgence and sin. But this world as it is, with its thorns and thistles, its blight and mildew, its frosts and tempests, its whole machinery demanding labor, that man should eat his bread by the sweat of his face, is the best possible world for us as we are now constituted. A world demanding no fatiguing labor is only fitted for perfect beings.

But it may be asked: Why should man be so constituted, that all these relations producing so much suffering should be needed to induce him to choose virtue instead of vice? The object we have in view does not demand of us an answer to this question, nor does the place I occupy allow me to enter the contested field of theology to give my opinion of the origin of sin and suffering in the world. They are here. We accept the fact, and simply inquire if the constitution of man and of this physical universe are such as to encourage men in vicious courses or to check them. On this point we think nothing can be plainer than that the path of virtue is the path of peace. And if we accept all these relations as established by a personal Being, we can infer nothing with greater certainty than that He is actuated by love to man and hatred of sin; that He has so constituted us and the world as to bring strong inducements to bear upon us to live virtuous lives. If we choose vice, His love will not save us from suffering, but manifests itself rather by scourging us back into paths of rectitude and virtue.

But when we have seen how little man can accomplish in this world, even when bending all his energies of body and mind in the direction of virtue and truth, we are struck with the small results reached by him compared with his abilities and desires. He evidently has the capacity for unlimited improvement, and the desire for it, but time is wanting. All other orders of beings on this globe complete the cycle of their existence, and rise as high as they are fitted to rise. But man is in this respect a failure, the machinery is out of joint, or rather if this world is his only home, it never was properly adjusted. There is no possibility of his rising so high in this world as to satisfy the conditions of his intellectual being. His life, when longest, is but a summer's day for labor; while broad harvest fields wave before him that he feels conscious of the power of gathering, if life were longer. He can comprehend the possibility of another life. He feels conscious of power to improve it and enjoy it for ever. He longs for it, and shudders at the prospect of oblivion. Shall he, of all created beings, be debarred from using the powers with which he has been endowed? Shall no opportunity be given him for the development of those powers? Shall he alone have desires to which there is nothing to correspond, so that it is impossible that they shall ever be satisfied? Is his whole constitution a cheat? Shall every other part of nature show the Creator's love to man, by the provisions that are made for his wants, but here in his highest aspirations and interests, shall he be mocked with delusions? We cannot believe this. It is contrary to the whole analogy of nature, contrary to every work of the Creator which we have thus far studied. *If there is a Creator of man, who is a lover of truth, then man must be immortal.* There must be a conscious existence for him after this life. Nor can we see how the time ever can come when it will be more in accordance with his nature for consciousness to cease than it is now. Grant a future life, and the great enigma of the present life is solved; man stands complete, the last and noblest work of God.

We have now traced the hand of a Creator in all His works. We have not only seen evidence of power, wisdom, and skill, in the relations of the physical world, but we have seen that all the powers of man are wisely balanced. His intellectual and moral natures have great provisions made for them, and still greater provisions are reasonably inferred to be in store for him. In this whole investigation we have recognized a Being having all the higher attributes of man, but above him in excellence and condition of existence. If this Being were now to throw aside the invisible form of existence and appear as man, as a friend among us, what are some of the questions that we should wish to ask? If He has spoken to man at all, these very questions that we need to ask respecting our higher relations and interests, are the questions He has answered.

We should desire to know more than we can learn from the world itself, of its origin and of the creation of man. We should desire to know in what relation we now stand to the Creator, and what He requires of us in return for the benefits we are receiving at His hand. Above all, we should wish to know something more of the future; something of what lies beyond the grave. All these inquiries are answered in the Bible, which comes to us claiming to be the Word of God. It is not our design to enter into any extended argument to prove the inspiration of this book, but briefly to show that it meets the requirements of man's nature, and thus has a claim founded on the argument from design and adaptation, to be considered the work of God. Although it claims that it was given to man by supernatural power, as the first fruits of the earth were also prepared for him, the Bible is a natural provision for man's moral nature, as the fruits of the earth are a natural provision for his physical wants.

Let us then trace the actual coincidence of the moral instincts and desires of man with the moral law and the teachings of the Bible. God is set forth in the Bible not only as a Creator, but as our constant Preserver, Benefactor, and moral Governor; or as blending all these characters in one, *our Father in Heaven*. We are assured that in His hand our breath is, and His are all our ways; that even the very hairs of our heads are all numbered. This ever-present care is foreshadowed by those all-pervading forces that affect all matter, like gravitation that binds suns and systems in their place, and from which the floating dust in the sunbeam cannot escape. This assurance of constant care meets a want in our nature. It is such care as we should expect from a benevolent Being of infinite power over the helpless beings that He had made in His own image. It therefore commends itself to our reason. We may for a time forget our weakness; but in danger, when the elements are abroad in their fury, or when disease has fastened upon the system, then it is we feel our need; then we desire and ask for the very care, protection, and support, which the Bible promises.

It recognizes the need of the human soul of support from without itself, and it promises the favor and protection of God himself to all who will seek it.

It comes to us not only with a Father's promises which satisfy the longings of our hearts, but it lays His commands upon us. This is reasonable. It is in accordance with the whole analogy of nature and all our relations to our fellow-men, that where benefits are conferred there should be corresponding obligations resting upon those receiving the favors. And we are not to judge of these commands thus laid upon us, that they are or are not adapted to our nature, by our desire or want of desire to obey them, but by their fitness to secure our highest good if obeyed. And experience teaches us that as all malevolent passions are torments, so all benevolent affections are sources of pleasure in their very exercise. Love is not only the foundation of the moral law of the Bible, but it is the fulfilling of the law. There is no malevolent feeling approved of in the Bible. The moral law, then, not only secures the happiness of men by the acts it enjoins in reference to each other, but it brings happiness by the very act of obeying. How impossible to conceive of any more perfect adaptation! What is the adaptation of the air to the lung, of the order and beauty of the world to the intellectual and emotional nature of man, compared with this adaptation of the moral law to his moral nature, in consequence of which the very act of obedience secures to him never-failing enjoyment and ever-increasing strength! What higher evidence of design!

In its special commands we find the same adaptation to the welfare of the race. In the reverence for the aged and to rulers, in obedience to law, in kindness to the unfortunate, we have those principles which would promote the welfare and happiness of individuals and communities.

Civilization is the natural and highest state of society; and it is only by following the precepts of the Bible, in private and public action, that a real civilization can be secured and maintained. There may come to be for a time a high degree of polish and culture without the recognition of these precepts, but it will be only a sudden glare of light. Such a civilization will be cruel, and contain within itself the elements of its own destruction.

Nor does the Bible show its adaptation to the nature of man only in what it demands. It is equally apparent in what it forbids. The Bible lays no prohibition upon man that will diminish his enjoyment. Its word of warning is never heard except as we are ready to enter those paths that are sure to lead to ruin if we follow them to the end. Their entrance may be bordered with flowers and promise every sensual gratification, and the simple may enter in with songs and laughter; but those who have learned the history of the past and have moral power to restrain themselves, never enter them. When they seek their highest good in the light of history and their own constitution, they are found walking according to the precepts of the Bible. In it every evil passion, every debasing desire, is denounced. It stands and utters its warning voice against intemperance, licentiousness, avarice, and injustice. It declares that those who take pleasure in them shall in the end find sorrow. The experience of thousands has been sad evidence of the truth of its declarations. It is venerable with the age of centuries, but it is no more obsolete nor wanting in its adaptations to man now than the light of day is to the eye, or water to the thirsty soul. It goes on filling its place in supplying the wants of man, like all the great provisions that have been made for him in nature.

Thus far we have found in the Bible only what is intimated in nature. The written word speaks, indeed, with an explicitness that we search for in vain among mere contrivances and tendencies. But we should naturally expect that such a book would not only make clearer the revelations of nature, but that it would also give some knowledge that nature does not reveal at all. We should expect it, because man's nature demands an answer to some questions to which no satisfactory answer can be found in nature. As we rise from the natural to the spiritual world, we should expect that there would be some exceptions to the ordinary laws of nature, or more strictly that new laws would be discovered distinct in kind from anything in the physical world, as we find the vital force presenting phenomena very different if not antagonistic to gravitation and other physical forces.

One question of vast importance to the happiness of man is this:—Can sin be forgiven? If left to the light of nature alone, I know not where to look for an affirmative answer. A remedy for the effects of sin may be intimated by the healing leaves and balsams; but that sin can be forgiven through repentance, finds no parallel in any of our relations to nature. We might argue from our own constitution, that our Creator would on some conditions blot out our sins as we forgive others. But we never could be sure of this; and if we accepted it as true, the conditions of His forgiveness no one could with certainty discover. We can find nothing to favor forgiveness of sin in all the physical universe. All its laws answer, No! They are inexorable. The fire burns, and the cold seals up the fountains of life.

He who leaps from the precipice must fall; he who transgresses the laws of health must pay the penalty, and no repentance will change the result. Is this stern law of strict penalty to hold dominion over man as a moral being? When he has sinned, must he carry the burden for ever? Must he be goaded by the stings of conscience, and his relations to his Creator be so changed that he must ever remain a guilty being in his presence? Must he be drawn down by every sin for ever, as gravitation brings bodies towards the centre? If so, the world would be gloomy indeed, and deep despair would settle down upon the most thoughtful of the race. But the Bible plainly proclaims forgiveness on the condition of repentance.

Repentance is not only enjoined as a duty, but forgiveness of sin and acceptance with God are declared to be the result. It is not our province to enter upon any defence of Christianity, nor to present any technical theological explanations as to the nature of this repentance, nor the ground on which free forgiveness is offered in the Bible. We simply accept the declaration that man may be forgiven and the penalty of the broken law escaped. We do not now inquire for methods, but for results. And this great truth of forgiveness of sin through repentance meets one of the deepest wants of man's nature. It puts the key into his own hand to open his prison door, and gives hope and courage instead of settled gloom and despair.

The last great truth in respect to which man

needs light from a written word, is the immortality of the soul. We have already seen from the constitution of man that immortality is needed to make him correspond in completeness to other created beings. But when from the light of nature we are led to admit the fact of immortality, how vague must be all our conclusions respecting a world which the body does not enter! "It is a dread unknown," from which we shrink almost as much as from annihilation. Besides all this, belief in a future life, so essential to the highest well-being of this life, could never exist with any definiteness among the mass of mankind if left to the light of nature. It needed the Bible to bring life and immortality to light. It was needed that the dead should be raised, and that our Saviour himself should rise from the tomb, to make immortality anything more than a grand philosophical speculation. The future life as presented in the Bible, is all that can be desired to satisfy the wants of the whole being. The power of language is exhausted in describing the blessings of that state which all may enjoy.

We have then in the Bible a guide of life which the experience of all past ages has proved to be the best for the progress and happiness of the race. The wisdom of the present can devise nothing better. We have in it a plain statement of our present relations to our Creator. We have not only the assurance of a future life, but its conditions are so fully set forth, that nothing more can be added to influence the present life, or satisfy the highest aspirations of the human soul.

In the Bible the spiritual nature of man finds that perfect adaptation, which the physical nature finds in the world. And if there is found in man anything that rebels against the Bible, it never fails to tend to degradation. So that in every respect, when men follow the Bible and when they reject it, there is proof that it is fitted for man; that there is no substitute for it. With its truths, he is complete; without them, he is an unsolved enigma, a being groping his way in blindness, he knows not whither. He is in a prison of doubt, and there in darkness he must remain; for not even the wisest of men can, without the Bible, solve the questions which his spiritual nature suggests. If there is in the whole range of nature a case of adaptation more varied and complete than the Bible to the wants of man, we know not where to look for it. We accept it as the grand provision, worthy of the being for whom it was made, worthy of the infinite Creator by whom it was bestowed.

LECTURE XII.

THE MOSAIC AND GEOLOGIC RECORDS.

Natural religion not sufficient.—Supposed origin of the Bible.—Correspondence to the works of nature.—Seeming disagreement.—First chapter of Genesis.—Testimony of Humboldt.—Purpose of the Bible demands some account of the creation.—The position taken in the argument.—Chemistry our guide before the sedimentary rocks.—Progress in creation.—First condition of matter.—Gravitation.—Effect of bringing particles together.—Light.—Nott and Gliddon.—Geologic day.—Hugh Miller's view.—Firmament.—Office of the atmosphere.—Dry land.—Introduction of life.—Plants created first.—Sun and Moon.—Water animals and birds.—Land animals.—Man.—Picture of creation as presented to an intelligent being.—Seventh day.—Conclusion.

We have now considered the Bible as a provision made to meet certain wants of man, growing out of desires and capacities implanted in him. In this respect it is such a provision as we might expect, from the whole analogy of nature, would be made. By accepting the Bible, we round out and complete the argument from design, as shown by adaptation of means to ends. Without the Bible, man, in the desires of his highest nature, would be like a being created with the torment of thirst, in a world destitute of water; or with a perfect eye, in a world of eternal darkness; or with the desire to breathe, where no air ever existed.

The defenders of natural religion cannot stop when they reach the Bible. It is only when this keystone is in its place, that the arch of argument will stand. Natural religion can never supersede a written Revelation. Nature simply assures us that there is a God, and that He has established certain relations for us. It then leaves us in doubt in regard to the consequences of our relationship to Him. So far from taking the place of Revelation, Natural Theology, when rightly studied, impels the soul to cry out for the living God; to desire to hear the Word of Him whose handiwork is seen in the heavens, and in the machinery and adorning of our earth. It prepares men to expect Revelation. And as men advance in civilization and science, the Bible becomes more and more necessary.

But it may be said that this Bible is the work of man, and it meets his wants because it has grown out of his wants. These desires and capacities, of which men are conscious, have led them to wander in the field of imagination to find conditions to meet the wants of their spiritual nature. And these conditions are embodied in the God of the Bible, and the future world which it reveals. Men with different desires would have a different Revelation, and thus it happens that the Bible is only one of the Sacred Books that have been accepted by men.

The Bible is thus presented as the work of dreaming enthusiasts, who have given the outgrowth of their own yearnings as the revelation of things that do exist. There are various arguments against this view, which belong strictly to the theologian; but there is one argument against it which fairly belongs to natural religion. It is the actual correspondence of the Bible with the works of nature. In this respect it is peculiar. Written in an early age, by a people little versed in the natural sciences, it challenges criticism in this respect. As morals and politics have never gone beyond the principles laid down in the Bible, so science has found nothing here contrary to its teachings. All seeming collision, and all fear of collision, have arisen from an ignorance of nature, or that narrow view of Bible exegesis which is constantly transferring something of the reverence which is natural for the Bible, to the old commentators, who have explained the Bible. To show the actual correspondence of the Bible with the works of nature, no better portion can be selected than the first chapter of Genesis; for there alone are the operations of nature made the object of special revelation. If any portion of the Bible presents claims to be inspired, it is certainly this portion; for it claims to record events that transpired before man was created.

In other places, nature is referred to only for illustration, and hence the common usage of speaking of things simply as they appear must be expected. But when the Bible proposes to give a history of the creation, it must ultimately stand or fall by that record. It will survive all the mistakes made in exegesis ; but if ever the time comes when it is plainly convicted of error here, its infallibility is gone. But it is not enough for the sceptic to overturn any attempted harmony of nature with the Bible ; he must show that there is an actual contradiction between them. And we are not disposed to take refuge in pictorial representations and allegories, to escape the danger of his criticism. If the first chapter of Genesis can be explained away into an airy nothing, the same may be true of the rest of the Bible. If the Bible is what it claims to be, we believe that a real correspondence will be found between its description of creation and the structure of the earth—as perfect a correspondence as the laws of language and the object in view would allow. It is not important here to discuss the date of the Hebrew Scriptures. We have no doubt Moses was the author of the Pentateuch ; but if it were written at a later day, even as some self-confident critics affirm as late as the time of David, there would be no explanation given how such a Book could have been written by the men of that time. We look in vain, among the surrounding nations, for evidence of the exalted notions of God and the creation which are found in every portion of the Bible.

We are to remember that this Book is not the product of one man, nor of one school of philosophers. It is the collected writings of ages—of men in the highest and lowest stations of life—of those versed in the sciences of their times, and those among the unlearned and ignorant. But in not a single book of the Bible can be found any expression that can be reasonably tortured into antagonism to that high and pure Monotheism which the highest philosophy must accept, nor against the revelations of science in the physical world. References to science are never introduced in the Bible for their own sake; but whenever introduced, if fairly tested by the laws of language, they meet the requirements of every science as fully as any book written at the present time for the same purpose would meet the requirements of any science.

If we take the books not strictly scientific, written by the most learned men within the last ten years, by men conversant with the sciences, their illustrations and references to nature are no more in accordance with science than the Hebrew Scriptures. The grand and clear conceptions of the universe which they present, have been acknowledged even by Humboldt, who was certainly as competent as any man that ever lived to appreciate the accuracy and significance of the language in describing the physical creation. Nor can he be charged with any undue desire to magnify the Bible, or to substantiate its claims. "It is," says he, "a characteristic of the poetry of the Hebrews, that as a reflex of Monotheism, it always embraces the universe in its unity, comprising both terrestrial life and the luminous realms of space; it dwells but rarely on the individuality of phenomena, preferring the contemplation of great masses. The Hebrew poet does not depict nature as a self-dependent object, glorious in its individual beauty, but always as in relation or subjection to a higher spiritual power. Nature is to him a work of creation, and order the living expression of the omnipresence of the Divinity in the visible world."

And in reference to the one hundred and fourth Psalm, he holds this remarkable language: "We are astonished to find in a lyrical poem of such limited compass, the whole universe—the heavens and the earth—sketched with a few bold touches." This is the testimony of him who had seen more of nature than any other man that ever lived; had looked upon the heavens and the earth with a scientific eye, gathering those grand principles which he has woven into his great work, the COSMOS. And with all his knowledge gathered by travel, from books and with converse with the *savans* of his age, he acknowledges his inability to equal the Hebrew poet in delineating the universe. He is astonished at the accuracy with which the whole subject is set forth by the Hebrew bard in the dark ages of the world's scientific history. After such testimony, it is no unfair claim to make, that those, who flippantly talk of the Bible as being in whole or in part obsolete and contradictory to the modern revelations of science, shall show us some tangible proof of their assertions that shall at least offset the testimony of the author of the Cosmos.

The whole Bible being written confessedly for the moral instruction of the race, we expect to find in it only so much of nature as its purpose demands. That purpose certainly demands some account of the present order of things. All that could be required of such an account would be that it should be sufficiently explicit to answer its purpose of assuring the race that the world was created by God, who still continues to rule it, and that its bold touches should be so truthful that the revelations of science should in the end harmonize with them. No such account can be held responsible for the opinions or mistakes of those who have attempted to explain it. Most of the Christian world believe that the coming of the Messiah was foretold by the prophets, and that his character was perfectly sketched by them; but the whole Jewish nation, to this day, while accepting the Old Testament, regard Jesus of Nazareth as an impostor, and are still looking for a Messiah whose character shall harmonize with the Scriptures. While there is such a diversity of opinion in regard to the character of Christ compared with the prophecies respecting the Messiah, it is not strange that there should be difference of belief in regard to the correspondence of the Bible and the structure of the earth. We doubt very much whether any man has science enough to trace out the correspondence fully, even to the satisfaction of his own mind. But on the other hand, we are quite as sure of the statement which we tried to substantiate in the early part of this course, that the account of the creation of organic beings given in Genesis, is as probable, viewed from a scientific stand-point, as any theory of creation that has ever been broached. Now, as to the second question, whether that whole account really accords with the revelations of geology, we answer that we believe its correspondence is such that if we cannot in every instance be sure we are right, we can challenge opposers to show a want of agreement. On this point, in the present state of science, we choose to take the position assumed by Butler in his Analogy, respecting the immortality of the soul; that the contrary cannot be shown. Having made these explanations, and wishing to be distinctly understood as disclaiming all pretence of absolute certainty, we proceed to show what seems to be a reasonable correspondence of the Bible account of creation with the revelations of science. The ground has been traversed by able men, and in such investigations we gladly borrow from them all the light they can shed upon our pathway. *

There was a long history to our globe before any permanent records were left in the sedimentary rocks. When we have gone back to the first forms of life that appeared upon the globe, and to the deep rocks below them, we look off into what has been regarded by Hugh Miller and some other geologists as a dark unknown. It is by the light of chemistry alone that we can thread our way back beyond the positive record of geologic formations. And we be-

* It is proper to state that this lecture was prepared twelve years ago, essentially as it now stands. It is impossible in a single lecture to give a full discussion of the subject or to quote from authors. Those who would fully understand the present state of the discussion, should read Hugh Miller, Dana, Lewis, and Dawson.

lieve, that a knowledge of chemistry and the physical forces of matter will guide us as safely here, as the remains of animals and plants do in unfolding the later history of the globe.

"*In the beginning God created the heavens and the earth;*"—a grand, sublime announcement—which is borne out by the evidence of wisdom and skill in all organic beings, in the structure of the globe and the constitution of matter itself. It is the very sentence we should select to embody the results of all the investigations presented in this series of lectures.

But the writer does not leave the account here. The omnipotent God of the Jews might well be represented as speaking the world into existence in a moment. But instead of this, the lapse of time, the succession of days and progress in creation from lower to higher forms of life, are all asserted. Changes are described as occurring before life was introduced, and then life rises to higher and higher forms till man appears. And to this all science agrees. It is not to this grand outline that objection is made, but to specific things, which we will notice in their proper place.

The second verse describes the earliest condition of the earth.

"*And the earth was without form and void, and darkness was upon the face of the deep.*"

It seems as though every chemist must believe that there was a time when the materials of our earth, and probably of the solar system, floated in space in a gaseous form. If so, no language could better describe the condition:

"*Emptiness and desolation*"—"*Without form and void.*"

And the Spirit of God moved upon the face of the waters, or fluids, which would represent all the materials of which the globe would ultimately be formed. God is represented as acting directly, because the forces are only his method of action. Now every scientific man knows, that if the materials existed in a gaseous form according to the theory of Laplace, the first force called into action would be gravitation—that force that binds planets in their orbits, and from which the invisible atom cannot escape. The rushing together of these elements under the action of this force, which gives the earth its form, might well be called the moving of the Spirit of God. If God is the Creator of the earth and the controller of all its changes, no language could be better chosen to represent movements produced by this force, which must necessarily have been the first called into action to bring the particles together. For it is gravitation alone that acts upon all matter and at all distances.

Now when this force was brought into action, we look into the nature of matter by the light of chemistry to see what results would follow. And when we have transcribed the words of Moses, we have the exact result which the latest revelations of science show must have followed.

"*And God said, Let there be light; and there was*

light." Light is not spoken of as something created, but as a result.

When the materials of which this globe is composed were brought together by gravitation, the simple condensation and chemical action both combined to produce light and heat. The rocks and waters of the globe are the result of combustion. We have seen the compound blow-pipe in which iron burns like straw, and platinum vanishes in vapor. That flame is simply the union of oxygen with hydrogen when only enough combines to form a few drops of water. Who can conceive of the heat produced when the waters that fill the ocean were formed? We have seen the light when the fine wire of iron or steel or magnesium is burned; how must the very heavens have been filled with light when the materials of which all our rocks were formed were burning! We think of the waters and rocks as incombustible, but we must constantly remember that they are the products of combustion; and all we have to do is to decompose them and bring the elements together again, to have that intense combustion on a small scale which lighted up primeval darkness, when the mighty mass of elements that compose this globe was brought into action. For ages the earth must have remained a blazing gaseous globe. It may be said this is theory; but it is a theory that rests upon a most substantial basis, the chemical nature of the water and the rocks of the earth. We only state what we believe to be the necessary result of bringing the materials of the globe together. It is what we should believe if the Bible had never been written.

And here we notice the criticism of that once famous book, Nott and Gliddon's "TYPES OF MANKIND," that Moses made a sad blunder when he represented light as being created three whole days before the sun and moon were ordained to give light upon the earth. The very thing which they refer to as a blunder, will stand while chemical science remains, showing either that Moses was inspired, or that he was in science far in advance of the authors of the "TYPES OF MANKIND."

If the earth were thus formed, it must have been ages before any essential change occurred, or at least a change so great as to be reckoned a new order of things.

And this period we regard as a geologic day. No better language could have been used to describe the beginning and close of such a period. It was in the great movements of God's work, what the day is in the work of man, and therefore "*yōm*," was the best word that could be used ; and no modern critic that I know of, even of the most orthodox school, now contends that "*yōm*" means simply twenty-four hours. It may mean that, and it may stand for any length of time. We have only to pass to the second chapter to see that Moses uses the same word to embrace the entire time which he had before described as constituting six *yōms*. "*These are the generations of the heavens and the earth when they were created, in the* DAY *that the Lord God made the earth and the heavens."* There are also other meanings of the word day.

In the fifth verse of the first chapter it is also said: "God called the light, day."

Here it is simply a name, as God named all the works as they were finished.

Since then we find Moses using the word *yōm* in the second chapter in such a way that all must agree it means a long period; and since the best critics on both sides of the question acknowledge that *yōm* is not necessarily a period of twenty-four hours, we cannot see that we do any violence to the principles of sound exegesis when we adopt that meaning which harmonizes with the revelations of the earth.

In addition to this, we may say that Hugh Miller's view seems sound in his whole treatment of the three days which he has attempted to account for. We think a legitimate use of the word day is in reference to the time when any order of things so took the lead as to constitute a distinct epoch. We use it now in the same way. Washington's day was when he was exerting his influence in the armies and councils of the nation. And so in the changes in the earth's geologic history. They may have been going on together, but the *day* of each creation was when its activity rose above that of all others, having, as it were, possession of the globe. And these great epochs are properly spoken of by Moses as days. They began and they closed, and he applies the usual Jewish method of describing the beginning and close of the natural day, "*evening*" and "*morning;*" and these terms do not seem in any respect to limit or explain the word "day."

But it is to be borne in mind that Moses speaks of three days, before he represents the sun as taking his place in the heavens to divide the day from the night. From which it seems almost self-evident that an ordinary day could not possibly be meant by him.

It is plain that chemistry is the only science that can possibly guide us in unravelling the first day's work of creation, the production of light; and it is by the same science mainly that we are to trace the changes still further, until we find in the sedimentary rocks evidence of the mechanical action of water. And what would be the changes which must have occurred after the mingling and union of the elements which we have described as the first epoch or day of creation?

We know well what changes must have occurred, if the laws of matter were the same then as now. As heat was radiated from the glowing earth into space, the whole mass was gradually cooled, until the materials of which the rocks are composed became simply a melted ball; the air, the waters of the earth, and all volatile substances, still forming a dense cloud around its whole surface. Still later a crust was formed upon this globe by cooling, and waters were condensed upon it, covering the entire globe. For continents and mountains were impossible till the crust in after ages became thick enough to hold its place when thrown up. For countless ages that crust must have thickened beneath the waters that grew deeper and deeper as the lower temperature of the globe allowed more and more to be condensed from the air, until the atmosphere, with a perfect ocean beneath and dense clouds above, took its place as a divider of the waters which it holds to-day. Thus by the natural change of the globe was produced the condensation and separation of the mingled elements, until the two permanent gases which were prepared to constitute the atmosphere were left mainly free, and had gained their proper place, and had commenced one of their great offices in the machinery of creation.

How now do the words of the Bible correspond with this description which we have made, guided by the known laws of nature?

"*And God said, Let there be a firmament in the midst of the waters, and let it divide the waters from the waters.*"

The word translated firmament means simply expanse, anything that is spread out. And the criticism that has been made that Moses taught that there was a solid sphere above us, has no foundation in the Holy Scriptures. That doctrine belongs to a later day, if not to a heathen philosophy.

The great office of this firmament is to-day what it was when first separated from the condensing elements. It is the great water-bearer. From the waters beneath go up the unseen streams, till in the colder upper regions they condense in clouds and pour down their treasures upon the earth. All the springs and rivers are pouring back into the ocean the mighty tide which this firmament has separated from the waters beneath, and poured down as from open windows in the heavens. Were it not for this office of the atmosphere the earth would be a desert. And all the vast accumulations of sedimentary rocks over the whole globe are evidence of the work it has done in dividing and transporting the waters, through all geologic ages. This was its first appointed work, to divide the waters from the waters, and thus to prepare the globe for man. And we have in the lowest stratified rocks evidence of its work before any life appeared upon the earth.

And when now the swift thunder-cloud pours down its deluge, or the wide-spread storm-cloud pours down, day after day, its torrents, until the swollen rivers cannot contain the abundance, it is the firmament established of old, that divides the waters beneath from the waters above.

When ages have rolled away, the earth covered with the ocean, and far above with a thick canopy of cloud, the crust becomes thick enough to keep its place, when lifted by forces beneath, or by the contraction of the cooling mass within. Now it is possible for dry land to appear; not only possible, but the necessary result of the continued cooling of the earth.

"*And God said, Let the waters under the heaven be gathered together into one place, and let the dry land appear, and it was so.*"

We need not add a single word. It seems impossible that any chemist and geologist can be found, who fails to see the grand simplicity and accuracy of this record, as corresponding with those ages in the history of our earth that pass before him as his sciences unravel the mystery of the rocks. He sees, indeed, the result produced by what are called the forces of matter, while the Hebrew law-giver keeps ever before us the personal Creator.

The globe is now prepared for life. Its temperature is reduced, and the pillars of the earth have been set. No lofty mountains are yet possible, but land just above the waters.

Up to this point, all changes could be produced by the known forces of matter; but for the introduction of life upon the globe, we have no possible account to give, except that it was done by creative power. A new principle was joined to matter. Let us inquire what can be learned from Geology of the introduction of life. First, we infer that plants were created before animals, because all animals depend upon them directly or indirectly for food. We judge that many existed of which we have no direct knowledge, the evidence of their existence having been blotted out, unless it be found in veins of plumbago in the early rocks. But it is well settled that the earliest plants of which we find any remains were of the lowest type—the flowerless plants, algæ, ferns, and the like. The most abundant vegetation was in the coal period, when those vast accumulations were stored away for our use.

After that, higher types of plant life appear, those with flowers and seeds; and at last, at the time or near the time of the introduction of man, those plants most useful to him, the fruits and cereals, were introduced. Now, if we look upon the introduction of plant life, as one great epoch, how perfectly it corresponds with the Bible account. "*And God said, Let the earth bring forth grass, the herb yielding seed, and the fruit-tree yielding fruit after his kind, whose seed is in itself upon the earth, and it was so.*"

The word rendered grass, should be rendered the tender plant or the budding plant springing up. That it was not ordinary grass is apparent, because that belongs with seed-bearing plants. The description applies well to the early plants that produced no proper seeds, the flowerless plants that flourished so abundantly till after the coal period. We have, then, the creation of plants first. In this both records agree. We have the tender plants, the seed-bearing plants, and the fruits whose seed is in themselves. In this account both records agree. We have plants coming to their greatest luxuriance in the early age; so that altogether the great epoch which in geology naturally attracts our attention, after the raising of the land, is the introduction of plant life, and here the two records agree.

If any say that in the early rocks we have more animal than plant fossils, we admit it; but every man who knows anything of geology knows why. The early plants were more easily decomposed than the corals and shells that remain. But the more animal life we find, the more plant life there must have been to sustain it.

We come next to the creation of the sun and moon. "*And God said, Let there be lights in the firmament of heaven, to divide the day from the night; and let them be for signs and for seasons, and for days, and years. And let them be for light in the firmament of heaven to give light upon the earth: and it was so.*"

It must strike every one as remarkable that Moses should give an account of light and the introduction of plants upon the globe, before describing the creation of the sun, moon, and stars, from which the earth now receives its light and heat. No impostor would have done that. Now, if we examine the coal plants in all parts of the world, we find them plants of low type, such as grow luxuriantly only in the tropics; a hot, damp atmosphere being their best locality. These coal plants are found in nearly all parts of the earth. There are beds of coal in Greenland, where now only a few Arctic plants can grow. It is plain that in the coal period there was a very high and uniform temperature all over the globe; the heat of the tropics, where the Greenland glaciers now rest. This heat so distributed could not come from the sun alone, but from the earth not yet cool. It was one great hot-house; and consequently the air was constantly filled with dense clouds in its upper regions. For ages there could have been no clear sky as we now have. The sun existed in some form all the time, but it had not taken its place to mark the seasons. Its heat was not needed as it is now, if it affected the earth at all. Of the necessity of its light, there is not the same certainty. The earth still has its own sources of light, in the aurora, and in its shooting stars which give it scattered sparks of the same light as gives the sun its glow. It is reasonable to infer that, from the intense action of its forces, the earth in its early history had light enough for its low type of vegetation. But if not, so far as there was light from the sun, it was dim and diffused light struggling through the dense vapors ; the sun itself probably never appearing.

But at the close of the coal period, the earth had so far cooled, that condensation had probably, in a measure, cleared the air ; and now was the time when the sun could appear in the heavens ; and the cooling earth began to be dependent upon him for heat as well as light. And the moon began to give borrowed light, and the stars to glitter in the heavens, where they had been for ages, but not for the earth. They all now had their relations established and their work appointed for this earth, simply by the changes in the earth itself. And when they were thus ordained, this was their day. And the evidence we have that they were thus brought into action, at this time, is found in the nature of the changes that then occurred, and the higher type of life that then appeared.

" *And God said, Let the waters bring forth abund-*

antly the moving creature that hath life, and fowl that may fly above the earth in the open firmament of heaven."

We now have brought before us the work of the fifth day. It was the day of animals in the waters, *their day*, because now in their abundance and magnitude they have possession of the earth. It is said that God created great whales. The word used in the Hebrew is "tanninim," which undoubtedly means huge, devouring monsters, like the crocodile, the animal (tannin) being used as an emblem of the destroying kings. (Jer. li. 34.)

It is a fitting word to denote those saurian monsters that were the tyrants of the earth in the Mesozoic time. They filled the waters, while huge birds and flying reptiles congregated on the shores.

This day, like the day of the plants, has a mighty sweep of time; but it was after the coal period that the huge saurians left their remains in the rocks, and reptiles and bird-like monsters left their tracks on the sandstone of the Connecticut valley.

"*And God said, Let the earth bring forth the living creature after his kind, cattle and creeping thing and beast of the earth after his kind; and it was so.*"

Here we have the work of the sixth day. The dry land is to have its share of life, which up to this time has been confined mainly to the waters. And corresponding to this account, we find the sixth great epoch of the earth's geologic history to be that characterized by the abundance and the size

Creation of Man.   317

of the land animals, when the earth fairly trembled beneath the tread of the mammoths, the mastodons, and the megatheriums. We gather their bones in almost all parts of the earth. Look at the huge monsters that have been dug up in our own country, and in South America. In the far north, their tusks supply ivory for exportation. This Tertiary and post-Tertiary period, perfectly corresponds to the picture of the sixth day's work. It was the day of land animals.

But, before the close of the sixth day, the record is: *"And God said, Let us make man in our image after our likeness."* The appearance of man, then, according to the Bible, was the closing scene in the great drama of creation.

Now, without entering into the disputed question of chronology as to the number of years man has been upon the earth, or of the unity of the race, we know of no scientific man who does not consider that man was the last term in the series, whether he believes in development or direct creation. Man is not only the last term that has appeared, but he is the last term possible, according to the plan of structure sketched in the first fish of the Silurian waters. We have then the six great epochs completed. If there had been in the universe some intelligent being like man, before whose eyes the whole scene of creation could have passed, the grand pictures that would have attracted his attention would have been in the order we have described.

First. The gathering of the elements by the mighty,

all-pervading force of gravitation, giving a world of light.

Second. The condensation of the globe and the waters upon it, so that the atmosphere should take its place as the divider of waters.

Third. The forming of dry land and the appearance of plants, increasing in quantity till they culminated in that abundant vegetation that covered the land in the coal period, stretching, as it must have stretched, from pole to pole, wherever land appeared.

Fourth. The appearance in the heavens of the sun and moon and stars, to do their appointed work while the world should stand.

Fifth. The abundance of animal life filling the waters.

Sixth. The sudden increase of life upon the land, in animals huge in size and higher in organization than any that had before appeared ; and finally, the appearance of man, with such powers that he was the lord and master of all.

If, now, that being had been called upon to give an account of the whole scene in the limits of a single chapter, could he have exceeded in accuracy and fulness the description given by Moses? We have seen a part of the changes produced through the operations of natural forces. Moses carries us one step further back to Him who holds the forces in His hand.

We feel justified in applying to this grand epic of the creation, the substance of the language which Humboldt applied to the hundred and fourth Psalm.

We are astonished to find, in a description of such limited extent, the whole geological history of the earth so accurately sketched by a few bold touches,

The Mosaic record goes further still, and speaks of the day of rest. We have no evidence of new creations since man appeared upon the globe. We are not told in the Bible that the evening and the morning were the seventh day. God rested from the works of creation on the seventh day, and we have no evidence that that day is completed yet. All of the moral relations of this rest and the establishment of the Sabbath are foreign to our present purpose, which is simply to compare the two records so far as they both extend. But when the Bible passes on to the moral history of the race, we have no positive revelations of nature that enable us to continue the comparison. And this work has been done so fully by Hugh Miller, whose works are known to almost every reader, that nothing would be gained by a lengthy discussion. But certainly nothing is more natural than that six days should stand as representatives of the six great epochs in creation, when God appeared only as a Controller of matter and the Builder of the universe, and that the seventh should stand emblematic of that epoch when, creation having ceased, the great manifestations of His character were those of the Sustainer and moral Governor of the universe.

We have now completed the work which we proposed to do at the commencement of these lectures. We might have given our whole time to a single department in nature. But we have chosen rather to tread various paths, and from all these short excursions we have returned with the same result. Every organic being has been found to be provided for. The elements are mingled by weight and measure. There is order and harmony everywhere. Man finds the world answering to his intellectual and emotional nature, and in all its constitution encouraging him in virtue and frowning on his vice. What the world does not provide for his moral nature, is found in the Bible, which thus takes its place as one of the natural provisions for his wants. The moral law of the Bible, and the constitution of nature, demand from him the same course of action. The two revelations are one in their teaching, so that we close as we commenced, by adopting the sentiment of him who founded this Institute; that

"*The most certain and most important part of Philosophy (is) that which shows the connection between God's revelations and the knowledge of good and evil implanted by Him in our nature—and that there is a conformity between Natural Religion and that of our Saviour.*"

THE END.

A List of the Publications

OF

G. P. PUTNAM & SON,

661 Broadway, New York.

OLTE (Amely). MADAME de STAEL; A Historical Novel: translated from the German by Theo. Johnson. 16mo, cloth ext., $1.50.

[*Putnam's European Library.*]

"One of the best historical novels which has appeared for a long time."—*Illust. Zeitung.* "Worthy of its great subject."—*Familien-Journal.* "Every chapter brings the reader in contact with eminent personages, and entertains him in the most agreeable and profitable manner."—*Europa.*

LACKWELL. STUDIES IN GENERAL SCIENCE. By Antoinette Brown Blackwell. 12mo (uniform with Child's "Benedicite"). Cloth extra, $2.25.

BLINDPITS—A NOVEL. [Reprinted by special arrangement with the Edinburgh publishers.] 1 vol. 12mo, $1.75.

⁎ A delightful story, which everybody will like.

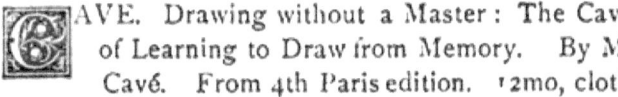AVE. Drawing without a Master: The Cavé Method of Learning to Draw from Memory. By Madame E. Cavé. From 4th Paris edition. 12mo, cloth, $1.

⁎ "This is the *only method of drawing which really teaches anything.* In publishing the remarkable treatise in which she unfolds, with surpassing interest, the result of her observations upon the teaching of drawing, and the ingenious methods she applies, Madame Cavé * * * renders invaluable service to all who have marked out for themselves a career of Art."—Extract from a long review in the *Revue des Deux Mondes*, written by Delacroix.

"It is interesting and valuable."—D. HUNTINGTON, *Prest. Nat. Acad.*

"Should be used by every teacher of Drawing in America."—*City Item, Phila.*

CHADBOURNE. Natural Theology; or, Nature and the Bible from the same Author. Lectures delivered before the Lowell Institute, Boston. By P. A. Chadbourne, A.M., M.D., President of University of Wisconsin. 12mo, cloth, $2.00. Student's edition, $1.75.

"This is a valuable contribution to current literature, and will be found adapted to the use of the class-room in college, and to the investigations of private students."—*Richmond Christian Adv.*

"The warm, fresh breath of pure and fervent religion pervades these eloquent pages."—*Am. Baptist.*

"Prof. Chadbourne's book is among the few metaphysical ones now published which, once taken up, cannot be laid aside unread. It is written in a perspicuous, animated style, combining depth of thought and grace of diction, with a total absence of ambitious display."—*Washington National Republic.* "In diction, method, and spirit, the volume is attractive and distinctive to a rare degree."—*Boston Traveller.*

CHILD'S BENEDICITE; or, Illustration of the Power, Wisdom, and Goodness of God, as manifested in his Works. By G. Chaplin Child, M.D. From the London edition of John Murray. With an Introductory Note by Henry G. Weston, D.D., of New York. 1 vol. 12mo. Elegantly printed on tinted paper, cloth extra, bevelled, $2.00; mor. ext., $4.50.

CHIEF CONTENTS.

Introduction.	Winter and Summer.	Wells.
The Heavens.	Nights and Days.	Seas and Floods.
The Sun and Moon.	Light and Darkness.	The Winds.
The Planets.	Lightning and Clouds.	Fire and Heat.
The Stars.	Showers and Dew.	Frost and Snow, etc.

"The most admirable popular treatise of natural theology. It is no extravagance to say that we have never read a more charming book, or one which we can recommend more confidently to our readers with the assurance that it will aid them, as none that we know of can do, to

'Look through Nature up to Nature's God.'

Every clergyman would do well particularly to study this book. For the rest, the handsome volume is delightful in appearance, and is one of the most creditable specimens of American book-making that has come from the Riverside Press."—*Round Table, N. Y.*, June 1.

CLARKE. PORTIA, and other Tales of Shakespeare's Heroines. By Mrs. Cowden Clarke, author of the Concordance to Shakspeare. With engravings. 12mo, cloth extra, $2.50. Gilt edges, $3.

⁎ An attractive book, especially for girls.

COOPER. Rural Hours. By a Lady. (Miss Susan Fenimore Cooper.) New Edition, with a new Introductory Chapter. 1 vol. 12mo, $2.50.

"One of the most interesting volumes of the day, displaying powers of mind of a high order."—Mrs. HALE's *Woman's Record.*

"An admirable portraiture of American out-door life, just as it is."—*Prof. Hart.*

"A very pleasant book—the result of the combined effort of good sense and good feeling, an observant mind, and a real, honest, unaffected appreciation of the countless minor beauties that Nature exhibits to her assiduous lovers."—*N. Y. Albion.*

CRAVEN (Mme. Aug.). ANNE SEVERIN: A Story translated from the French. 16mo.

[*Putnam's European Library.*]

*** "The Sister's Story," by the same author, has been warmly and generally eulogized as a book of remarkably pure and elevated character.

DICKINSON'S Life, Letters, and Speeches. The Life and Writings of the late Hon. Daniel S. Dickinson, of New York; including Speeches in the Senate, and on various public occasions, Private Correspondence, etc. Edited by his brother, Hon. J. R. Dickinson. 2 vols. large 8vo. Published for subscribers. Cloth, $10.00; half calf, $15.

"A valuable contribution to our political literature, * * belonging to the most striking events of our times."—*N. Y. Times.*

DINGELSTEDT (Franz). THE AMAZON. Translated from the German by J. M. Hart. 16mo, cloth extra, $1.50.

"Full of scintillations of wit, * * sparkles throughout with vivacity and fanciful humor."—*Leipsic Blatter.*

"Unquestionably the most charming novel that has appeared for some time."—"*Ueber Land und Meer,*" *Stuttgart.*

EGGLESTON (Geo. W.). THE SEARCH AFTER TRUTH. 16mo, cloth.

FAY. A new System of Astronomy. By Hon. Theo. S. Fay. Richly illustrated. For Families and for Students. 12mo, with Atlas, quarto. *(In press.)*

FAY. A new System of GEOGRAPHY. By Hon. Theo. S. Fay. With finely executed Maps. For Families and for Students. 12mo, with Atlas, quarto. Cloth extra, $4.25. School edition, $3.75. [See Separate Circular.]

₊ These volumes have been prepared with the greatest care, and have cost several years of labor under the suggestions and supervisions of Humboldt, Ritter, and the most eminent Geographers and Astronomers of Europe. They are on a new plan, and the maps and illustrations are admirably executed, at large expense.

GODWIN. The Cyclopædia of BIOGRAPHY: A Record of the Lives of Eminent Persons. By Parke Godwin. New edition, with a Supplement brought down to the present time. By George Sheppard. In one volume, crown 8vo, cloth, $3.50; half-calf, $6.

" We can speak from long experience in the use of this book, as a well-thumbed copy of the first edition has lain for years on our library table, for almost daily reference. A concise, compact biographical dictionary is one of the most necessary and convenient of manuals, and we seldom failed to find what we looked for in this excellent compendium."—*Home Journal.*

GENERAL GREENE'S Life. The Life of Nathaniel Greene, Major-General in the Army of the Revolution. By George Washington Greene, author of Historical View of the American Revolution. 3 vols. 8vo. University press. The first volume is now ready. Price to subscribers, $4 per volume.

The history of our life as a nation loses both its philosophical and its practical importance if separated from the history of the Revolution. A careful study of the War of Independence would have saved us thousands of lives and millions of money in the War of the Rebellion. Next to the life of Washington, it is in the life of Greene that this history is to be sought: nor can it be fully understood without reading both. It is in the hope of contributing to the materials for this study, and in the conviction that to preserve the memory of great and good men is one of the highest offices of patriotism, that these volumes are offered to the student of American history.

" The book is most valuable and most interesting, and ought to be in every library in the Union."—*Round Table.*

" Let every father give this book to his son, that the young generation, instead of receiving distorted impressions from the perusal of such trash as that of the Headley, Spencer, and Abbott school, may see in their true light the glory and shortcomings, the success and the failures of that glorious period of American history, and that they may learn to emulate the example set by Greene and his compeers."—*N. Y. Evening Post.*

www.ingramcontent.com/pod-product-compliance
Lightning Source LLC
Chambersburg PA
CBHW030747230426
43667CB00007B/873